CONTRACT STRATEGIES FOR **MAJOR PROJECTS**

CONTRACT STRATEGIES FOR **MAJOR PROJECTS**

MASTERING THE MOST DIFFICULT ELEMENT OF **PROJECT MANAGEMENT**

EDWARD W. MERROW

WILEY

Published by John Wiley & Sons, Inc., Hoboken, New Jersey.
Published simultaneously in Canada.

For general information on our other products and services or for technical support, please contact our Customer Care Department within the United States at (800) 762-2974, outside the United States at (317) 572-3993 or fax (317) 572-4002.

Wiley also publishes its books in a variety of electronic formats. Some content that appears in print may not be available in electronic formats. For more information about Wiley products, visit our web site at www.wiley.com.

Library of Congress Cataloging-in-Publication Data is Available:

ISBN: 9781119902096 (Hardback)
ISBN: 9781119902119 (ePDF)
ISBN: 9781119902102 (ePub)

Cover Design: Wiley
Cover Images: Top: © RistoArnaudov/Getty Images
              Bottom: © AvigatorPhotographer/Getty Images
Author photo: © Stephanie Dupuis Photography

Printed and bound by CPI Group (UK) Ltd, Croydon, CR0 4YY

C004462_221022

I dedicate this book to the memory of Iain A.R. Smith.
The world was a better place with you in it.

Contents

Acknowledgments

The IPA staff of dedicated professionals around the world made this book possible. Without the data garnered from their careful evaluations of nearly 1,200 capital projects, there would have been nothing to write about. The thing that unites my IPA colleagues above all else is our love of projects and commitment to seeing them done better.

My reviewers for this work were extraordinary. In alphabetical order because their contributions were uniformly excellent:

Bill Cherne was formerly chief executive officer of Cherne Contracting Corporation. With Bill as its hands-on leader, Cherne was a leading industrial constructor in terms of overall quality in the United States. An all-union shop, Cherne professionals understood construction and construction management at a level that was the best. Bill brought that knowledge to his review.

Michael Loulakis is a construction lawyer of the first rank. Mike was trained as an engineer before turning to law. He combines deep knowledge of construction law with an engineer's feel for projects. He has been awarded all sorts of honors, is a member of the National Academy of Construction, and is a fellow of the American College of Construction Lawyers. Mike continues an active practice of bringing sound advice to owners and contractors.

Jason Walker is one of the finest researchers I have known in my career—and I have known a good many fine researchers at Rand and IPA. Jason was until very recently the principal deputy director of IPA's Research Division and was responsible for client-funded research. Jason contributed to this effort in two ways: he executed some of the research on which I relied, and he provided excellent review and comment as I wrote.

Graham Winch is a professor at the University of Manchester Alliance Business School. Graham's work has moved the understanding of projects forward in both public and private sectors. He is respected by academics and practitioners alike. He is one of the few academics I have met who understands projects to be a serious field of study in addition to being about project management.

I am really lucky to have these four distinguished members of the community willing to carefully review and critique my work. I am even luckier to be able to call all four of them dear friends. If there are mistakes in my conclusions, they belong to me and me alone. These gentlemen may well have tried unsuccessfully to fix them.

My hearty thanks to Kelli Ratliff and Jeanine Clough for turning my scribbles into understandable graphics. This is a complex subject, and graphical representations are often essential to comprehension. If you find the graphics sometimes opaque, you have no idea how difficult they were before Kelli and Jeanine applied their magic.

Thanks to my Wiley editor, Richard Narramore, and the entire Wiley crew that worked to make the book a reality.

Finally, my thanks to everyone at home and work who put up with me writing this book while trying to keep up my day job.

Introduction: What This Book Is About

When a manufacturer or resource development company wants to build a new facility or refurbish an old one, the owner personnel put together the business case for the new project, develop a scope for the project, and assemble the preliminary design. If the facilities require a good deal of exacting engineering, an engineering contractor usually performs the final stage of preparation on the engineering side, while owner personnel put together the execution plan. Few companies in the process industries[1] maintain the people resources needed to engineer the final stage of preparation on their own. After owner authorization, a contractor will be required to execute the detailed engineering, and that contractor will also usually procure all of the major equipment and the engineered materials for the project. The owner will require a construction contractor to build the facility. Contractors may or may not be involved in the commissioning and startup of the facilities depending on the skills and preferences of the owner.

The process of figuring out how the contractors will be selected, how they will be paid, how much work any one contractor will do on the project, and the legal framework under which the work will be done (the contract terms and conditions) is what we call *contracting strategy*. For reasons that will become obvious, the owner must form the contracting strategy for a project early in project development or the contracting decisions will be entirely tactical and expedient rather than strategic and thoughtful.

---

[1]By the process industries, I mean the sets of firms around the world that produce oil and gas, minerals and metals, commodity and specialty chemicals, pharmaceutical products, and food and other consumer products. One of the characteristics of process industry projects is that they usually require substantial amounts of engineering.

For some, contracting strategy is a matter of strongly held beliefs that sometimes resist any appeal to facts. This point was underscored for me recently when I asked a project system director of a large, publicly owned airport if he wanted to join a study of contracting strategies for airport projects we were proposing. His answer "No! I know integrated project delivery[2] is the best contracting approach, and I don't want anybody trying to prove otherwise!" For many others, the contracting strategy followed on any particular project is more accident than design. By the time contracting strategy is broached as an issue with an owner project team, it is often too late in project development to make any changes: "Well, we are just doing what we always do." Or my favorite response: "We are just doing what the FEED[3] contractor suggested."

Employing engineering and construction contractors to execute a project may not seem like an inherently difficult task. As individuals, we hire professional service firms all the time—doctors, lawyers, dentists, and so forth. Hiring engineering and construction contractors is much more difficult for a number of reasons. Projects are *joint products* of an owner and the contractors. It is not a simple matter to parse out who is responsible for what, even in retrospect. As projects get larger and more complex, control of the project and the contractors' performance becomes progressively more difficult. The lack of transparency gives rise to endless variations on the "principal-agent" problem, which, as we will later discuss fully, is the problem that sits at the heart of contracting. Finally, the contracting entity for projects is not a person but an organization—a corporation—and exactly who makes the decision about the contracting strategy and process within that corporation often materially affects how well the decisions

---

[2] Integrated project delivery (IPD) is a particular type of contracting strategy that will be discussed in Chapter 6.
[3] FEED is an acronym for "front-end engineering design," which is part of the work that should be completed just prior to the final investment decision (FID).

are made. Decision-making responsibility is often assigned to the wrong entity within owner organizations or is assigned ambiguously.

My first goal for this book is to bring facts to the discussion of which contracting strategies work best and in what circumstances. Contracting strategy is the most difficult problem for most project managers. Contracting for engineering and construction services is always a combination of hoped for collaboration and feared conflict. For that reason, contracting strategy is less about the legalities of contracts and much more about human behavior. Some facts about what works should be the start of any contracting discussion, but owing to lack of reliable data, anecdote and opinion often have had to suffice as poor substitutes.

My second goal is to provide insight into *why* different contracting strategies produce different outcomes. That goal requires that we discuss the underlying principles that shape the effects of contracting strategy, for example, the principal-agent problem, the principles of risk pricing and risk assignment, and the principles of sound project preparation by owners. A focus on the principles that underpin contracting is essential because the principles provide the basis against which we must test any particular contracting strategy. When a contracting strategy flouts a core principle, that contracting strategy will lead to grief.

My third and ultimate goal is that an accounting of the facts of what works and what does not in contracting for industrial projects might facilitate reform of the sorry state of owner/contractor relationships. It is an understatement to say things have not been going well. Many contractors are just barely profitable. Many owners are frustrated and unhappy with contractor performance. The problems are deeper than the current state of contractor demographics. My hope is that some focus on the facts will help start positive change.

Point of View: What Constitutes Success?

To have a coherent discussion of contracting, it is necessary to define what successful contracting means. Success, of course, is defined differently depending on who is defining it. Throughout this discussion, I will be considering the various dimensions of success and failure from the viewpoint of those investing in the asset that the project will create. Contractors may object that defining success in this manner leaves their welfare out of the picture. But upon reflection, I believe that contractors would have to agree that if a contracting strategy routinely produces poor-quality, high-cost assets in which contractors are the only ones making money, the model is not sustainable. Conversely, if an approach produces good results for owners, that approach is ultimately sustainable only if contractors are successful as well. The problem is mostly one of finding a *stable* mutually beneficial model.

I find that many owners as well as contractors wonder if the current engineering and construction market is a sustainable business model. I share that concern, which is one of the reasons I felt compelled to write this book. My position, which is supported by data throughout, is that the key weaknesses in the current market start with weaknesses in owner project organizations. Owner project organizations are too weak to create a stable, self-enforcing business relationship between owners and contractors. Those driving the relationships on the owner side are frequently too transactional in their approach to foster a stable market. It is my hope that this book may help move the discussion toward more sustainable and robust relationships in the future. Just to be clear, however, I do not believe that gimmicky contracting approaches will accomplish that goal. The focus on project fundamentals must remain strong.

The Context

Contracting for a project must start with the project. How big is it? How many distinct elements of scope does it contain? Where is it going to be geographically? Geography is the single most important element in understanding the contractor market for most projects. How technically difficult is the project? Does the project use routine technology or require something new to the owner or even new to the industry? We will discuss all of these issues later as we explore how the project and the contracting strategy interact.

Next, we need to consider the competence of the owner projects organization to undertake this particular project. Does the owner have the personnel needed to front-end load—fully define—this project? Does the owner have estimating, planning, and scheduling capability? Can the owner field a strong controls team? Does the owner have the capability to do quality control and inspection of engineering and construction? Has the owner built this sort of facility recently, and are those who remember that project still around? Owners with weak project organizations struggle with all forms of contracting, but some forms are poison for them. Blithely assuming that one can do anything by simply buying consultants, agency personnel, or individual contractors from the market suffers from the defect of not actually being true.

Defining the Elements of Contracting Strategy

Like any other aspect of project management, contracting requires a series of activities and decisions, which need to be supported by work processes that guide how things are done at a given owner company. I see seven major elements of contracting strategy, each of which needs to be navigated successfully. Often discussions of contracting strategy begin and end with the compensation scheme that will be used: fixed price (lump-sum) or reimbursable. Although compensation scheme is important, it is but a single element in the mix, and compensation scheme is often dictated more by the market than by owner strategy.

> **Structure:** By phase and activity, how much work should any one contractor do? I consider structure to be considerably more important than the compensation scheme in understanding contracting. In many projects, a single contractor is asked to do all of the work from front-end engineering right through startup. We dub this structure an "FEPC."[4] Alternatively, the owner could, in principle, select different contractors for every phase of the work: a FEED contractor, a detailed engineering contractor, a procurement contractor, a construction contractor, and lastly a commissioning and startup contractor. This is rarely done, but that doesn't mean it hasn't happened. Engineering and procurement of equipment and engineered materials are so intimately integrated that engineering and procurement are almost always structured together. However, separation of FEED, detailed engineering and procurement, and construction is quite common. Structure is important to project outcomes in ways that may be surprising. It is certainly more important than any other single feature of contracting. Structure is the primary topic in Chapters 3 through 6 and is an important consideration as we discuss incentives in Chapter 8.

> **Compensation:** For any given work, will the contractor be paid a fixed amount, or will the compensation be based on hours expended or "units" of work performed? Compensation

---

[4] FEPC means "FEED, (detailed) engineering, procurement, and construction."
FEED is an acronym for "front-end engineering design," which is a major element of the final preparation of a project prior to execution.

scheme is often the feature that owners think about first, but it probably should be down the list of concerns. We come back to compensation in virtually every chapter of the book.

Supplemental incentives: Closely related to the basic compensation model is the decision to use additional incentives or not. Years of research into the application of incentives in contracts has taught us that incentives rarely work the way owners think they will. We explore the use of supplemental incentives with data in Chapter 8.

Contractor selection: By what process will contractors be selected? Contractor selection processes vary considerably from owner to owner and project to project. Some owners use rigorous prequalification processes, while others select primarily based on prior experience with the contractor. Some owners have formal competitions for all major projects, while others select with an unstructured process. The selection process should start with an effective prequalification process, which we discuss in Chapter 7.

Packaging: How will different physical work scopes be bundled? Smaller projects tends to have only a single scope package or possibly two. Very large projects have little choice but to have multiple scope packages, also called the *vertical splits of work*, because there is too much work for a single contractor to take on or because different parts of the work require very different skill sets. Packaging is discussed in Chapter 11 when we discuss how contracting effectiveness is affected by project scale.

Risk assignment: How do the terms and conditions in the contract allocate responsibilities between the owner and a contractor? This really comes down to the owner philosophy toward risk and negotiation with the contractor about which risks belong to whom. In risk assignment, the compensation scheme and the terms and conditions are both important contributors.

Control of the contracting process: The contracting process within owner companies often suffers from the problem of too many cooks in the kitchen, all of whom think they are the chef. A number of owner functions need to be involved, but only one can be in charge. I will argue in Chapter 10 that it is often the wrong one.

The Organization of the Book

When planning the writing of this book, one of the things I learned very quickly is that contracting does not lend itself to a neat chronological narrative. Instead of moving along in a line, the story tends to spread out rather like Bruce Springsteen's "river that don't know where it's goin'." While hoping to keep the subject within some banks, here is how it is laid out:

Chapter 1 discusses what I see as the 10 key principles of contracting. Contracting strategies that violate a key principle are likely to be unsuccessful. Sometimes owners and contractors are violating a key principle without even being aware of it. When thinking about a contracting strategy, test it against the 10 principles.

Chapter 2 presents the database and methodology. My editor always wants this data stuff in an appendix, but I argue it is too central to relegate to a place no one will go. The data help tell the story of contracting and do so in a way that is unique. The methodology is straightforward enough, and especially so for readers familiar with Independent Project Analysis, Inc. (IPA).[5] I will do my best to explain for those who are not.

---

[5] All of the data for this book were gathered as part of IPA's normal project evaluation process. More about IPA and its role in the process industries is discussed in the appendix.

Chapter 3 starts by defining the six most common contractual forms for industrial projects. It also introduces what many readers may find a peculiar way of thinking about different forms; I argue that how we structure the amount of work given to a contractor is considerably more important than how we pay the contractor. In Chapter 3 we get to the heart of the matter: how do the most common contracting strategies affect project outcomes? The outcome that most project, C-suite, and business[6] professionals care about most is cost, and the story there is really quite interesting. We look at schedule as well and then look at projects with different drivers—schedule-driven projects and compliance-driven projects.

Chapter 4 explores *why* different contract forms behave the way they do. And Chapter 4 addresses what I consider one of the great paradoxes of contracting: why do owners so often choose contracting strategies that contribute materially to poor results?

Chapter 5 is devoted to unusual EPC contracting strategies: functional (duty) specification contracting, design competitions, convert-to-EPC-LS, and Guaranteed Maximum Price (GMP). As we will see, some of the strategies are not used often for good reasons, but others are good performers that are overlooked and underappreciated.

Chapter 6 discusses three more unusual strategies for industrial projects: integrated project delivery (IPD)/alliancing, partnering alliances, and repeat supply chain contracting. IPD seeks to use contractual arrangements and language to foster improved collaboration between owners and contractors on a one-off basis. Partnering alliances use both the contractual arrangements and active relationship management

---

[6] Often business sponsors profess to care more about schedule than cost, but as we will see in Chapter 3, that is often not really the case.

to support collaboration over multiple projects. Repeat supply chain effectiveness is supported, not by additional contract language and agreements, but by careful relationship development and maintenance over time and multiple projects.

In Chapter 7 we take up contractor selection and in particular contractor prequalification. Failures in prequal often start our contracting headaches for a project. If we can fix prequal, then contractor selection will go better and be a bit less perilous.

Chapter 8 is about trying to deal with the core problem in contracting: the principal-agent conundrum and the silver bullet that some owners believe they have in their guns: the use of various incentive schemes to supplement the incentives of the basic contract. We will discuss such schemes at some length and explore whether and how they work.

Chapter 9 is about risk allocation and risk pricing. Every contract assigns responsibilities to the parties. If the contract is well crafted, those responsibilities are accompanied with downside risks for nonperformance. But projects are intrinsically joint products of owners, contractors, and other vendors and suppliers. The joint product nature of projects often makes the risk assignment messy, imprecise, and downright confusing. Further complicating the problem is that owners often want to shift as much risk as possible onto the contractors and often believe that doing so is smart business. Contractors in turn want to avoid as much risk as possible; they *know* that is smart business! Further complicating risk allocation is the fact that owners and contractors are usually very different in their abilities to carry financial risk. Industrial owners are highly capitalized firms; contractors are very thinly capitalized.

Chapter 10 addresses one of the thorniest questions within owner organizations—who should control project contracting? My answers will ensure that some readers will hate me; my modest ambition is that everyone won't.

In Chapter 11, we discuss how the effectiveness of various contracting strategies changes with the scale of the project and the role of packaging the scopes of work and the complications that multiple scope packages create. Many of our worst contracting problems are with large projects. Finding strategies that do not degrade seriously with project size is an important consideration.

We conclude in Chapter 12 with a review of what I believe are the most important conclusions. I offer my recommendations to owners on the development and articulation of their contracting strategies. There will be no silver bullet, and the implementation of changes in contracting approach may be quite difficult for some organization as it may require building people infrastructure before changes can take hold. But the potential payoff is huge—over the long term getting project contracting strategies right may be the difference between company success and failure.

I have never met a project manager who thought that the process of hiring the right contractors for a project was fun. One told me, "Contracting is like second marriages: a triumph of hope over experience." I have found many project professionals and owner purchasing folks who believed passionately in some particular form of contracting but rarely the *same* form of contracting. And as one PM said wryly, "The worst contractor ever was the one on the last project, and the best contractor ever will be the one on the next project." He dubbed his position "realistic optimism."

I don't think the contractors like the process any better. They spend a great deal of time and emotional energy putting together bids or proposals for projects, often knowing that their chances of winning are low. They often feel they must say things that are borderline implausible about the owner's capabilities and shoddy front-end work and their ability to work around it so they will not be kicked out of the competition. And all that for a "hand-to-mouth" existence.

Everybody agrees, it isn't easy! Regrettably, this book cannot promise to make contracting easy, but we can at least bring systematic facts to the discussion and hope to clear away some of the dense fog surrounding the subject. If you, the reader, agree that end is accomplished, I will consider it a success.

The Applicability of This Book

As I will discuss in the next chapter, the data that underpin my discussion are all drawn from industrial projects, that is, projects that produce products to be sold in hope of making an economic profit. I believe, however, that the results of our analysis and the conclusions drawn apply to all projects, but with some caveats.

A good deal of our discussion deals with the cost effectiveness of different contracting strategies. To the extent that cost is not a concern for a class of projects, the conclusions regarding cost effectiveness are simply not relevant. However, adherence to cost budgets is relevant for virtually all projects everywhere, so conclusions about cost predictability of different strategies still apply.

Broadly speaking, I believe the conclusions in this book apply to public-sector infrastructure projects as fully as to industrial projects. However, public projects tend to have what in the industrial sector we would call *weak owners*. A weak owner is one in which the owner does not maintain a sufficient number of experienced project staff and lacks the work processes that are characteristic of successful project systems.

CHAPTER 1

Ten Key Principles of Contracting

Writing a book about contracting strategy is a good deal harder than it might seem. Contracting is a subject that is full of exceptions. There are relatively few conclusions that appear to hold universally. Contracting is sensitive to the locale, the state of the market, the capabilities of the owner, the pool of available contractors, and, of course, the nature of the project under consideration. But over many years of studying contracting strategies and practices for industrial projects, I have arrived at a set of conclusions to which there seem to be few, if any, exceptions. These conclusions are what I call the 10 *principles of contracting*. As I explore the ins and outs of contracting strategies for industrial projects over the next 11 chapters, I will return to these principles again and again. If one pursues a contracting strategy that flouts one or more of these principles, it is very likely that trouble is ahead. If circumstance forces one to adopt a strategy that runs afoul of a principle, it is vitally important to understand that and mitigate the damage. The 10 principles of contracting are

1. There is no free lunch; the principal-agent problem is ever-present.
2. Contractors do good projects well and bad projects poorly.
3. Complex projects require simple contractual approaches.

4. Owners are from Mars; contractors are from Venus.

5. Risk transfer from owners to contractors is often an illusion; the big risks stay at home.

6. Contractors have shareholders, but they are not *your* shareholders.

7. Contractors normally win contracting games, not owners.

8. If you assign a risk to a party who cannot manage it, the risk will go unmanaged.

9. All contracts are incentivized; the question is always, how?

10. Economize on the need for trust.

Principle 1: There Is No Free Lunch

Economists like to remind us that no matter how little we personally pay for lunch, somebody somewhere paid for it fully. In contracting, I like to use the "free lunch" lesson to remind everyone that no contracting strategy is without problems. What is a good strategy in a down market may be a mess in an up market. What works for a smaller project may not work for a larger project. What works for a standardized project may well not work for a bespoke project. In contracting, there is no formulaic approach that is bound to succeed. All attempts to find a silver bullet will be disappointing. There are no successful gimmicks.

Over the years, IPA has worked with many companies who thought—for a while—that they had found the perfect contracting strategy. For one, it was incentivized reimbursable contracts; for another it was integrated project delivery (IPD), which is also called *alliancing*; for another it, was LSTK;[1] and so forth. Any strategy that is one-size-fits-all-for-all-time is bound

---

[1]Lump-sum turnkey is a form of engineering, procurement, and construction (EPC) contract that has the contractor turn over a fully commissioned, started-up, and operating facility to an owner often with a performance guarantee.

to fail sometimes. Often when failure comes, it is in spectacular fashion.

By far the most damaging contracting strategies are those that appear to be working while they are actually disastrous. Let me offer an example. A major chemical company was in a long-term "partnering alliance" with a prominent engineering, procurement, and construction (EPC) contractor. The contractor did all of the chemical company's major projects on a sole-source reimbursable basis. It was a seeming miracle that every project came in on budget and on time, and the owner was very pleased. When the company finally benchmarked and discovered that the projects were nearly 30 percent more expensive and 20 percent slower than their competition, it was too late to save the company.

This regrettably true story brings us to the core problem that prevents any free lunch in contracting: the principal-agent problem. When we contract, an owner (the principal) hires someone (the agent) to act on their behalf. Even in the best of circumstances, the behavior of the agent is unlikely to be exactly what the principal wants. The agent's understanding of the objectives is unlikely to be identical to the principal's understanding, and, of course, the agent probably has goals that are not perfectly consonant with the principal's. The principal-agent problem sits right at the heart of what makes contracting so difficult. We will come back to it repeatedly.

The key antidote to the principal-agent problem is transparency. The more transparent a contractor's performance is to the owner, the less room there is for the contractor's performance to wander away from the owner's objectives. The more transparent the owner's behavior is, the less anxiety the contractor will have about being taken advantage of. We will return to the theme of transparency as well a number of times. It is very important.

An old friend and U.S. federal judge, T. Rawles Jones, used to remind me: "Contracts should always say what they mean and mean what they say."

Say What They Mean

Part of the process of generating transparency is the use of straightforward and simply stated contracts. The clearer the contract, the clearer everyone's understanding of their obligations. Complex and arcane language works directly against one of the most important elements of a good project contract: risk assignment. An owner needs to know how a contractor will make money on the project. The smart owner always welcomes the contractor making a profit. But the owner needs to foreclose any nonobvious and unintended ways that money can be made. Simplicity and transparency help generate that outcome.

Mean What They Say

Contracts place obligations on both parties. Those obligations need to be taken seriously. So if the contract provides audit rights for the owner, then it behooves the owner to audit from the start. If the owner doesn't bother, those rights will soon be gone. Any later claim of unexercised rights is often dismissed by the contractor and later by the arbitrator or court. If the contract stipulates no "reservation of rights," then get a monthly release of rights to make claims later.[2] If the contract establishes a change process, then it behooves the owner to get that change process in place immediately, not down the road when change orders have started to accumulate on the PM's desk.

---

[2]*Reservation of rights* is a term in American law in which party A announces to party B that notwithstanding some partial remedy, all rights to other or additional remedies remain in place. For example, even though party B did not inform party A in real time about the development of a claim, party B has reserved the right to perfect that claim at a later time. Reservation of rights complicates the liability structure for a contract. If the contractor has reserved its rights, the owner needs a very strong controls organization with excellent record keeping and exercised audit rights. If the owner has reserved rights, the contractor is more likely to assume a defensive posture early in the project. Releases are a mechanism to limit reservation of rights and avoid big late surprises in terms of claims.

Principle 2: Contractors Do Good Projects Well and Bad Projects Poorly

At first glance, this principle may seem to be a tautology. It is not. Owner behavior shapes contractor performance. This is a reality that IPA research has demonstrated over and over again. When the owner has clear objectives for the project, has a competent, fully staffed, cross-functional team, and completes the front end of the project with excellence, the contractor's performance is systematically splendid. When the owner has hazy or conflicting objectives, the project fails. If owner operations and maintenance people have been left out of decision-making, late major changes will occur or fundamental errors may have been made in scope development. If the cost or schedule targets are not achievable by humans, the project will fail. If the front-end engineering and project execution planning are deficient, the project will fail. After years of hammering away at these issues with the data, the project management community around the world accepts these things as true. Any of these deficiencies, none of which are controlled by a contractor, will nonetheless leave the contractors looking stupid and incompetent. Owners have the most leverage in projects. Owners set direction and set the table for the projects. Therefore, it is inevitable that owners will make the big mistakes—poor business case, wrong scope, disgruntled stakeholders, and so forth. Contractors will inevitably make lots of little mistakes, but very few projects bleed to death from a thousand paper cuts.

Contractors may make convenient scapegoats, but they are rarely to blame for bad projects. A little reflection will make clear why this must be true. The situation in which a deeply incompetent contractor could survive would be outside a market system. Markets ruthlessly weed out incompetent contractors. In most places in the world, engineering and construction contracting is very competitive.[3] Owners award very few projects without competition of some sort.

When one appreciates that owners shape project outcomes and not contractors, it is immediately apparent that contracting is a second-order issue for projects, not a dominant one. Being a second-order issue, however, does not mean that contracting is unimportant.

Principle 3: Complex Projects Need Simple Contracting Strategies

Complexity is the enemy of transparency. Complexity exists in projects in a number of dimensions.

- Scope complexity increases with the number of distinct scope elements. A project with a lot of infrastructure development, for example, will always be a complex project.
- Shaping complexity increases as the stakeholder set becomes larger and more diverse. Problems with host governments and regulators and local communities all add to project complexity.
- Basic Data complexity occurs when the basic technical data for the project are in development during the front end rather than fully available and confirmed. This is almost always the case for new resource extraction projects and occurs in other sectors whenever new technology is involved.
- The three dimensions of complexity mentioned will almost always generate organizational complexity for the project. More subteams will be required with more functions involved, many of which do not speak the same professional language.

---

[3]I recognize that for very large projects and for technically very difficult projects, markets are typically not nearly as robust as for smaller and simpler projects. But competition is the norm even for megaprojects.

Higher complexity should encourage those generating the contracting strategy to keep things as simple as humanly possible. Contracting with complex incentivization schemes should be avoided because the situation will make it harder to separate out who was responsible for what. Clear risk assignment should be the order of the day. Generally project complexity means there will be more interfaces to manage with more contractors and third parties working side by side. When possible, it is best to have all contractors working on the same basic contract form in such situations.

Principle 4: Owners Are from Mars and Contractors Are from Venus

To borrow from the wonderful book title, owners and contractors could not be more different sorts of economic entities. Owners earn from assets. Projects are a cost center that creates the assets. Markets measure owner success and failure by the returns and cash flows that their assets produce. Industrial owners tend to be heavily capitalized with big balance sheets, and most assets are fixed. Once an asset is in place, it can produce large amounts of free cash if prices are good.

Contractors are almost exactly the opposite. Rather than earning from assets, contractors earn via a markup on staff hours sold and markups on transactions, such as procuring equipment and material. Contractor balance sheets are asset light. The amounts of money that move through a contractor may be huge, but the margins tend to be very thin on that volume, and free cash flow is modest at best.

The economic differences between industrial owners and contractors have profound implications for contracting because they shape perceptions and reality of project-related risk. The biggest project risk for an owner is that the prices for the product the project makes will fall or the volumes that can be sold will not approach capacity. Project overruns and schedule slips, while very unwelcome, are rarely catastrophic. For the contractor working on a fixed price contract, even a small overrun means no profit, and a large overrun can ruin the year (or worse).

A simple mind experiment shows the difference. If a capital project overruns by 25 percent and the owner absorbs all the overrun, that extra 25 percent is *added* to the corporate balance sheet as an asset, and the business now has to earn against a larger asset than they had hoped. But, if the contractor absorbs that 25 percent overrun, the amount is *subtracted* from the corporate balance sheet, and the contractor has no asset to show for it. And recall, those balance sheets were asset light at the outset. When we discuss the pricing of risk later, these economic differences become front and center. The economic differences between owners and contractors also show up in disagreements about contract terms. Because the contractor is typically short of free cash flow, timely payment is extremely important. Many owners find those concerns overblown and posturing. They shouldn't.

Principle 5: Large Risk Transfers from Owners to Contractors Are More Illusion Than Reality

When I work with some owner lawyers on contracting for projects, I am struck by their belief that contracts change reality. For example, if we assign risk for the timely delivery of critical equipment to the contractor, we will no longer have to worry about the equipment arriving late. Although it is true that transferring the risk may cost the contractor money, at the end of the day the project is still late, which means that our cash flow is late, and the customers who were promised product are still unhappy with us, not the contractor. The consequences of risks in projects will eventually come back to the owner whenever the risks are not effectively managed regardless of risk assignment.

There are examples in which contractors have in effect subsidized the asset balance sheets of owners. Sometimes contractors significantly underbid a lump-sum project and proceed to deliver that project with excellence. But, there are not very many such examples. Most of the time, contractor losses on projects do not translate into owner gains. Lump-sum contractors in large loss positions search for ways to shift those losses back to the owner. Sometimes it shows up in claims; sometimes it shows up in poor quality; sometimes it shows up in an unwillingness to bid on the next project.

There are not many examples of wealth transfer from contractors to owners for the simple reason that contractors do not have much wealth to transfer! If losses on projects were routine, there would be no contractors, or at least there would be no lump-sum projects. All of the big downside risk has to end up in the owner's lap. If the project is the wrong asset for the business—a huge risk—that is purely an owner risk, although it probably also results in a badly developed and executed project. If the project has operability problems, that ends up as the owner's risk even if the contractor is hit with big performance penalties. Penalties do not operate plants. Contractors live with a project for a short while; owners live with the resulting asset for a generation.

Principle 6: Contractors Have Shareholders and They Are Not *Your* Shareholders!

This principle may sound obvious, and it should be. However, it is easily forgotten and is not trivial. One can be sure that contractor managements will try to behave in ways that will generate profits. If they decline or fail to do so, they will be replaced. Contractor managements have an ethical obligation to their shareholders to generate profits. What that means in principle and in practice is that there will always be some degree of tension between owner project managers and contractor management. Pretending that the tension isn't there is just that: pretense.

At the contractor working level, however, contractor staff are driven by the same things that drive professionals generally: the need to provide for themselves and their families while trying to do meaningful work well. This means in practice that generating collaboration at the working level should never be difficult.

The owner should seek to *control* the drive of contractor managements to make profits. That is not the same as seeking to *minimize* contractor profits. Owners have an important long-term interest in the contractors working on their projects making a profit. When an owner does everything in its power to minimize contractor profits, they gain a reputation that forces contractors into defensive postures if they are going to take on work from the owner at all. The strongest contractors will simply be unwilling to work for such owners.

Controlling contractor profits requires owners to understand what avenues the contract creates for profits. It also requires specific owner capabilities to control those avenues of profit-making. Owners get themselves into trouble when they adopt a contracting strategy for which they lack the practices, personnel, and skills to control. We will return to this issue often in the chapters ahead.

Principle 7: Contracting Games Are Rough Sport

Both owners and contractors sometimes want to play contracting games. A contracting game is a tactic to make more money (if the contractor) or pay less (if the owner) by setting up claims, by gaming incentive formulae, by using the schedule for advantage, and by using damages and penalties for leverage. These are games in the sense that every device has a countering strategy that seeks to nullify the device. Incentive games are widely practiced and will be discussed at length in Chapter 8. Claims games are less common in industrial projects but can be very disruptive and time-consuming.[4]

In my experience, *contractors are almost always more skilled at playing contracting games than owners.* This is not surprising; contractors generally have more to lose than owners and get a lot more playing time than the average owner project manager. When owners use incentive devices, for example, they often do not even realize they are playing a game, which facilitates their losing repeatedly.

The biggest problem with contracting games is that they obscure the fundamentals of what is driving contractor and owner behavior regarding the contract. For example, in a fixed-price contract, the dominant incentive for the contractor is cost minimization. Adding another incentive, such as for schedule, probably does not change the contractor's calculus, but it does change the owner's expectations—otherwise they would not have inserted it. The more devices that are added to the mix, the more confusing the incentive structure becomes. And games often beget more games. For example, a schedule incentive in an EPC lump-sum encourages the contractor to play schedule games that will ensure the schedule incentive whether or not any schedule acceleration is achieved.

---

[4]See James G. Zack, "Claimsmanship: A Current Discussion," *Transactions of the AACE*, 1992.

Principle 8: Assigning a Risk to Someone Who Cannot Control It Is a Fool's Errand

One of the most important elements of contracting is the assignment of risks among the parties to the contract. But risk *assignment* is not risk *management*. Owners routinely assign risks in contracts to contractors who actually have little or no ability to manage and thereby control the risk assigned. Sometimes owners keep risks when they lack the expertise necessary to manage it. For example, owners should rarely keep field labor productivity risks. They almost always lack the skills to manage field productivity. I have seen owners keep responsibility for laydown management in the hope of saving a little money only to completely bungle the laydown yards and subject themselves to unnecessary claims.

When a contractor is assigned a risk that it cannot manage, what happens? Sometimes, the contractor raises his bid price in hopes of covering the risk. That will certainly occur when it is a sellers' market for engineering and construction services. In other cases, the contractor will immediately start working on ways to shift the risk back to the owner through a claims development process or muddying the water around who is responsible for what.

Sometimes the magnitude of a problem is inherently not knowable. That should make the item a potential carve out for a contingent change. For example, sometimes soil conditions cannot be fully known until extensive excavation has occurred. In those cases, the owner needs to create a contingent reserve rather than follow the usual passing of that risk to an EPC contractor on a fixed-price contract.

Sometimes known or suspected risks are simply unmanageable. That should be a candidate for force majeure, but owners generally want to limit force majeure to the narrowest possible definition and seek to offer the most limited relief possible when force majeure is triggered.

The worst situation is the passing of a risk from the party that can substantially control it to the party that has no substantial control. That not only means the risk will not be managed effectively; it also creates a significant moral hazard.[5] The moral hazard is that the party who actually controls the risk now feels free to disregard it. Owners commonly face this problem on reimbursable construction that leaves them responsible for field labor productivity. This occurs repeatedly in the other direction when an owner passes risk associated with poor front-end definition work, an owner responsibility, to a fixed-price contractor.

Principle 9: All Contracts Are Incentivized

Every contract contains within its reimbursement scheme and terms and conditions a set of behavioral incentives for the owner and the contractor. The compensation scheme incentives and terms and conditions usually dominate and control behavior to a much greater extent than any incentives added in other ways. For example, a fixed-price contract to execute a given scope of work is a perfectly cost-incentivized compensation scheme. One hundred percent of all savings the contractor generates is kept by the contractor as additional profit. Any and all other incentives contained in the agreement are likely dwarfed by the cost incentive.

---

[5]*Moral hazard* is a term borrowed from insurance and economics. A moral hazard is created whenever a party who controls a risk bears no negative consequences for the risk materializing (or could even gain if the risk materializes). The problem on running up excessive hours on reimbursable contracts is an example of gaining from a moral hazard.

The incentive structure in reimbursable contracts is often quite complex and often not properly understood by owners. Owners often believe that the (usually fixed) fee contained in the contract is the dominant incentive for the contractor. However, reimbursable contractors can have other, often more important, income streams from a project. There may be profit contained in the overhead rates ("the multiplier"). There may be hidden profits in the equipment transactions. There may be profits associated with subcontracts or labor brokers and so forth. Some of these hidden streams are not entirely ethical and may be illegal in some cases, but that does not mean they do not exist.

We will discuss the effectiveness of using incentive schemes for cost, schedule, operability, and safety in Chapter 8. But oftentimes owners do not even fully comprehend the incentive structure that the basic contract creates prior to adding additional incentives. That means they will have absolutely no idea how the incentives they add will actually play out. That is why we see so many dysfunctional and unintended consequences of incentive schemes.

Principle 10: Economize on the Need for Trust

Industry associations such as the Construction Industry Institute in the United States or the Major Projects Association in the United Kingdom often extol the virtues of owners and contractors developing mutual trust. I certainly agree that trust is a valuable commodity. But like all valuable things, one should economize on how much trust is required to make things work out. I am not suggesting that owners and contractor should mistrust, but rather that the contracting strategy should economize on how much trust it requires to be successful. Some readers will no doubt interpret this principle as an expression of cynicism. It is not. It is, however, a rejection of wishful thinking as a contracting strategy.

Generally, trust is appropriate only when the trusted party sees being trustworthy as valuable for themselves. This is the way things work in most business relationships and most especially in the relationships between a professional services firm (such as a contractor) and their clients. Lawyers seek to do their best for clients as a matter of professional ethics and because they want to keep clients. Physicians do their best to keep their patients healthy as a matter of professional ethics and because they want to keep their patients. Most business contracts are self-enforcing because they are executed in the context of an ongoing business relationship that both parties see gains in continuing. One can trust the other party whenever being untrustworthy would be stupid behavior by that party.

The problem for contracting in the context of engineering and construction services for projects is that the situation does not always foster self-enforcing contracts. Many projects are contracted on a "one-off" basis. The contractor can expect no follow-up work. On large projects the gains or losses associated with the contract are so large that any potential follow-up work becomes irrelevant. Over the last 30 years in North America and Western Europe, owner-contractor relationships have becoming increasingly transactional in nature as owner engineering organizations have been downsized and more project decisions on contracting have been controlled by purchasing organizations or business professionals rather than by project organizations. Whenever the context does not foster self-enforcing contracts, economizing on the need for trust is the wise course.

Trust is not a contracting strategy, yet some contractual approaches depend heavily on trust in situations in which trust does not have much value to the trusted party. In those situations, trust becomes very expensive.

Summary

The 10 principles of contracting are not normative principles; they are not intended as guides to morally correct behavior. They are *empirical* and *logical* principles. The principles are sometimes violated due to ignorance. Sometimes they are violated due to wishful thinking that the conflict and tension in contracting can be washed away with good intention. Perhaps most often, however, they are violated due to greed and in hope of gaining an unfair advantage.

When I am evaluating a proposed contracting strategy for an owner client, I do so with repeated reference back to the 10 principles. A contracting strategy that disregards the principles, or is premised on overriding them, will almost always fail. It is also important to understand that a well-written contract will not supersede a strategy that violates the principles of contracting. Poor contracting strategy can debilitate the best written contract.

CHAPTER 2

Data, Methods, and Nomenclature

For almost all industrial firms, the process of creating a capital project proceeds in phases, also known as *stages*. Owners organize the stages to facilitate decision-making about whether to proceed. These decision points (or *gates*) are intended to make it easy to withdraw from an unpromising project before a great deal of money is spent. The staged process illustrated in Figure 2.1 is quite typical throughout the industrial world. We dub the stages prior to authorization *front-end loading* (FEL). The process starts with the articulation of a business need for a capital project and the development of a tentative business case around that need. If the decision-makers deem the business requirement compelling, the project passes through the first gate.

FEL-2 focuses on the development of a project scope that achieves the business requirements in terms of product produced, quantity needed, quality of product, and so forth. Most

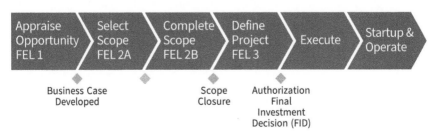

FIGURE 2.1 Standard stage-gated project development process.

industrial firms have their own engineering personnel do scope development without the assistance of an engineering contractor. There are exceptions, of course, and one contracting strategy that we will discuss later, functional specification contracting, leaves some or all of the scope definition up to a contractor to perform. When the scope is fully identified, the owner project team can produce a meaningful cost estimate and schedule for the project.

Most companies now have installed a "check gate" in the middle of FEL-2 to ensure that the basic scope is coming together fast enough that there will still be time to complete the FEL-2 work before the second gate decision is scheduled.[1] If the benefits defined in the business case still look good against the cost and schedule forecasts, the decision-maker passes the project on to stage 3. The second gate, which corresponds with the closing of the scope, is almost always the real decision point to proceed with the project. The next phase will involve spending a good deal of money that cannot be recovered if the project is abandoned.

In the vast majority of industrial firms, an engineering contractor is hired to execute most of the work in stage 3 with the owner's supervision.[2] The stage 3 work consists of progressing the engineering design and planning the execution of the project. That is the so-called FEED portion of FEL-3. IPA rates FEED as *complete* when the heat material balances are closed and all piping and instrumentation diagrams are complete, reviewed, approved, and issued for (detailed) design. FEED is preliminary when P&IDs are not complete, reviewed, approved, and IFD, and is grossly deficient when less than 50 percent of P&IDs are completed or when the heat and material balances have not been closed, which has the effect of potentially undermining the P&ID

---

[1]The calendar always plays a role in the front-end process, as it must and should. If the scope development team cannot arrive at a workable scope pretty quickly, it is quite likely that they never will, in which case the project should be abandoned.
[2]The exceptions are the few firms that maintain extensive engineering capability in-house.

work. The issue of whether FEED and the other elements of FEL-3 are complete will recur many times in this book. The completeness of FEL substantially governs the risk profile of a project. The risk profile is intimately connected to the contracting strategy.

The fact that an engineering contractor is required to accomplish the stage 3 work makes it vitally important to start the development of the project's contracting strategy early in stage 2 so the stage 3 work can proceed without delay if the project is passed through the second gate. The contracting strategy will often shape the decision about which contractors to consider for stage 3 work. The selection of the stage 3 contractor is important because in most industrial projects, the stage 3 contractor will be awarded at least the engineering and procurement for stage 4, execution. Frequently, the stage 3 contractor will execute the entire project.[3]

The chronological context for contracting then is that strategy development must occur in stage 2 for most projects and even earlier for functional specification contracting. In most cases, after setting the contracting approach, the owner begins prequalification of the contractors who might be employed to do stage 3 and execution work. We will discuss the prequalification process and its many pitfalls in Chapter 7.

Description of the Database[4]

Throughout this book I will refer to a database of 1,148 major[5] projects that have been completed by industrial firms around the

---

[3]Only one contract strategy routinely changes contractors between stages 3 and 4—EPC lump-sum.

[4]IPA has studied contracting by site organizations extensively; perhaps one of my colleagues will choose to write a separate book on the subject.

[5]The term *major* here does not mean "very large." The smallest project in the dataset is about $15 million. In this context, *major* means a project that is normally executed by a central projects organization rather than a site organization or business unit.

world. This database is the result of the work of IPA project and research analysts as they have evaluated these projects at various stage-gates during the projects development. Referring to Figure 2.1, IPA routinely evaluates projects for our clients at gates 2 and 3 and then again after plant startup is complete. We also collect operational performance data after 12 to 18 months of operation.

Each evaluation combines the completion of a structured data collection instrument and a face-to-face interview with members of the owner project team, often with the lead contractor personnel present. We hold separate interviews with the owner's project business sponsor. Thousands of pieces of information are collected via the structured interview protocol. In addition, the project team provides all of the key documentation for the project including the basis of design documents and the project execution plan. At each interview there is a discussion around the contracting strategy and plans, and the relevant documentation is also obtained. What results from this process is a holistic picture accompanied by detailed data of each project. At each evaluation, we provide a detailed report to the owner on the status, risks, and uncertainties surrounding the project.

The data that support our analysis include projects from more than 100 industrial firms around the world. Table 2.1 summarizes

TABLE 2.1   Contracting Database

Project Characteristics	
Number	1,148
Average project cost (2022 USD)	$460 million
Range of project costs (2011 USD)	$15.5 million to $15.8 billion
Average execution duration	27 months
Average cycle time duration	46 months
Number of owners represented	109
Mean authorization year	2Q 2009
Projects with any new technology	7.5%

some key characteristics of the database employed here. I excluded small projects normally executed by site organizations because the contracting approaches employed by sites are distinctly different in many cases from the contracting approaches taken for larger projects. I included only about 100 projects with total costs over $1 billion USD (in today's dollar terms). I could have included many more of the larger projects, but I did not want the discussion skewed by megaprojects, which tend to have more challenges than the typical project. However, essentially all conclusions in this book apply equally well to projects of all sizes. The effects of project scale are discussed at a number of points. The median project in our database was authorized in 2010 and the most recent in early 2019. Later authorizations are truncated by my desire to use only completed projects so the links between contracting and outcomes could be fully explored. About 7 percent of the sample employed technology was new in commercial use. The use of new technology does influence contracting decisions as well as add risk with respect to project outcomes.

Figure 2.2 shows the location of the projects in our sample. More than 40 percent of the sample comes from North America, but there is good representation from Europe and Asia, including

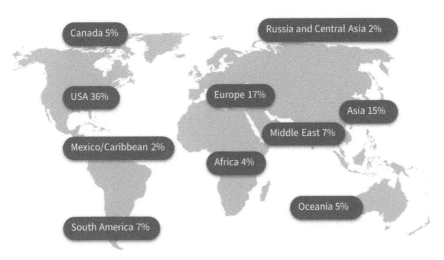

FIGURE 2.2   Project sample geographical distribution.

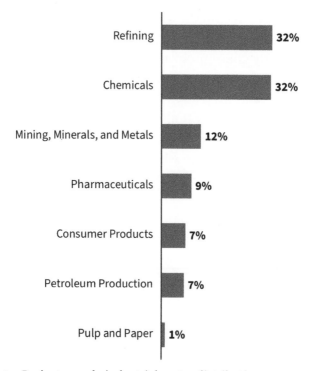

FIGURE 2.3   Project sample industrial sector distribution.

China, Southeast Asia, and the Indian subcontinent. About 7 percent of the sample comes from the Middle East, where EPC lump-sum remains the most common contracting form. The only substantially underrepresented regions are Russia and Central Asia.

Also, Figure 2.3 shows the breakdown of industrial sectors in the database. Petroleum refining and chemicals each constitute 30 percent of the sample. Within chemicals, about two-thirds are commodities, and the other third specialties not including pharmaceuticals, which are a separate sector. Mining and metals processing constitute about 12 percent of the sample. The selection of contracting strategies is affected by the industrial sector, and there are some differences in project performance by sector as well. Different contractual strategies behave in much the same way regardless of industrial sector.

I elected to exclude certain sectors because I was concerned they would distort the results. I excluded projects that were subject to rate-based regulation in the power and pipelines sectors because those projects are subject to what economists call the Averch-Johnson effect.[6] Rate-based regulation creates a systematic incentive to over-capitalize facilities, which distorts their cost competitiveness. For that and other reasons, I also excluded nuclear power plants and nuclear materials processing. I also excluded hazardous and nuclear materials waste cleanup projects because governments are usually heavily involved in those projects, and government involvement tends to inflate cost and time.

Project Types

We define types of projects with the typology shown in Figure 2.4.

Greenfield projects are entirely new projects at a site with no existing company facilities. Greenfield projects usually require significant infrastructure investment and are therefore on average larger than other project types. Almost one project in five in our sample is at a greenfield site. Over a quarter of this sample are co-located projects. A co-located facility places a new production plant at an existing industrial site. Usually, the site is owned by the owner of the new plant, but that is not necessary to the placement in this category. Co-located facilities benefit from existing support infrastructure such as access and other transportation, water, and power. An expansion involves the increase of production of an existing product at a site. Expansions are sometimes able to reuse engineering and equipment specifications from

---

[6]See Harvey Averch and Leland L. Johnson, "The Behavior of the Firm Under Regulatory Constraint," *The American Economic Review*, Vol. 52, No. 5 (Dec., 1962), pp. 1052–1069. See also Sherman, R., Gibson Jr., G. E., Merrow, E., Parrish, K, (2021), "Examining the Impact of Rate-of-Return Regulation on Capital Project Planning" (ASCE CO.1943-7862.0002069), *Journal of Construction Engineering and Management*, Volume 147, Issue 8. American Society of Civil Engineers (ASCE).

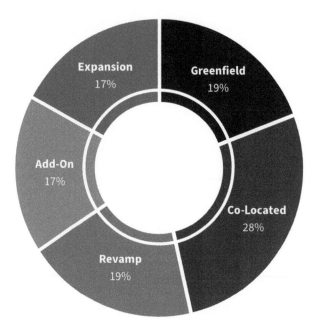

FIGURE 2.4 Project sample project type distribution.

the existing production line. The fourth most common type of project in our sample are "revamps." When most of a project's cost is associated with refurbishing an existing facility, the project is placed in this category. Revamps are widely considered the most difficult projects in the process industries because they must account for the status of the usually old and worn-out facilities as well as working around operations. Construction for revamp projects is frequently shoehorned into scheduled plant shutdowns. Our final project type are "add-ons." Add-ons build a new processing unit at an existing site that must be integrated into existing operations.

Project type influences contracting choices. For example, project teams generally prefer engineering and construction contractors who are familiar with the site for revamp projects. Greenfield and co-located projects are more likely to entertain bids from any qualified contractor, often on a global basis. Add-ons and expansions fall somewhere in between. Project size, rather than project type, tends to govern whether the project seeks a large international contractor rather than a smaller, more regional or even local firm.

The Sample and Potential Sample Biases

I believe that the dataset represents a reasonable cross section of industrial projects executed around the world. The projects represent about $525 billion in capital and span the major industrial sectors outside regulated and government-sponsored industries, such as infrastructure. There are, however, some known biases. First, the companies that work with IPA on a regular basis, and therefore provide much of the data, are better performers than those that do not. We know this from our experience benchmarking capital projects for companies for the first time. Those initial baselines are poorer than later performance more than 90 percent of the time. Because I control for key owner practices as I explore the relationships between contracting and project outcomes, differences in owner sophistication should not affect any conclusions about contract strategy efficacy. However, the bias in owner sophistication will affect contract strategy selection and any conclusions about the overall health of industrial projects around the world.

Second, we know that certain countries are underrepresented, especially Russia and Central Asia. Again, that could (and probably does) affect statements about the health of projects generally as projects in Russia and Central Asia are known to be problematic.

Third, we know there is a slight bias in the projects that our clients allow us to close out. By contract all of our clients are required to provide data on completed projects. But when the projects are particularly dreadful, they sometimes seek to slip out of that requirement, especially if the project is subject to major claims and litigation. They sometimes succeed. Fortunately, most of our clients are really quite courageous in sharing their disappointments.

The Data Normalization Process

When assessing project outcomes, both cost and schedule require careful normalization to render any comparisons between projects valid. If we compare more than 1,000 projects executed all over the world over a 20-year period without normalization, the comparisons made and conclusions reached would not only be suspect, but they could well be downright misleading. The same normalization process was used for all 1,148 projects in our sample. That process proceeds in seven steps:

1. We remove the cost and schedule effects of abnormal weather, low-probability/high-consequence events, and force majeure events. Strange things happen. For example, we have three projects in which a critical piece of major equipment went overboard during ocean transport. We have projects that find themselves in the middle of intense civil conflicts and projects hit by typhoons and tornados. We have project sites shut down by the authorities in the midst of a coronavirus pandemic. Without normalization, these things muddy the analysis without adding any value and insight.

2. Any scope additions must be added to the authorization estimate for the purposes of understanding cost deviation. Scope changes must be distinguished fully from design changes. Scope changes alter the functionality of the project. Design changes are changes necessary or thought desirable to achieve the *original intended functionality* of the project. We never adjust for design changes. Scope additions are often disruptive to the project process; we do not adjust for any of the "ripple effects" of scope changes because those effects resulted from a choice to alter the scope. A good many such changes reflect poor functional integration of the project team during scope development, such as the absence of an active business sponsor or lack of operations involvement in the scope development process. Those are project system flaws, not candidates for normalization.

3. We review all of the cost allocations with the client project estimator to ensure they conform to the IPA common work breakdown structure and code of accounts for the type of facility being constructed.

4. Any scope deletions are removed from the authorization cost estimate to maintain constant scope between estimated and actual costs. Again, no ripple effects are normalized no matter how large because scope changes are a feature of the project and project system, not an external and uncontrollable influence.

5. All future escalation is removed from the FID estimates. We want all effects of market forces to reflect our common indexes rather than be idiosyncratic to the project or the owner company.

6. We normalize for location differences. IPA maintains at-location costs for most countries in the world and many sub-regions within countries.

   a. We generally do not adjust equipment costs as we consider most equipment purchased to be world open market (WOM) in all cases except where local purchase is mandated.

   b. Engineering is generally WOM except in cases where local engineering is required by law and differs from WOM costs.

   c. Construction labor and construction supervision are adjusted based on the location of the labor and construction management that will be employed for the project.

   d. Specialty costs (scaffolding, heavy lift, etc.) are adjusted to local norms.

7. We then translate all costs using our cost indices to a common point in time. For this book, I chose to use January 2022 as my base. All costs must be brought to a single point in time while correctly converting currencies as spent when multiple currencies are involved unless currency values were fixed by hedging. We adjust the line items by applying price change

indices to each of the major elements of cost: equipment, bulk materials such as concrete steel and pipe, engineering, construction labor and construction management, etc. IPA's Data Management Group maintains price indices for all project inputs and location factors for cost and productivity for most locations in the world.

The Knowledge Behind the Data

At the risk of repeating myself, statistics without understanding causation are just numbers. When IPA analysts evaluate a project, we insist that their work is not complete until they understand "the story" of the project. That understanding of the project's story is recorded not only in their reports to the client but in the backup narrative that accompanies every project record when it is finally closed out. The interviews with those who actually developed and executed the project provide the context and nuances that the data collection protocol could never capture by itself. The interviews are guided by the interview protocol that gathers thousands of variables on each project at each engagement, but the knowledge of the project is generated more holistically. Finally, the analysts write a document that captures key learnings and issues from their engagement that is an integral part of the project record for IPA. We regularly have three major engagements with each project: two on the front end and one to close the project after it has completed startup. Finally, a written report to the client concludes each engagement.

In writing this book, I had access to all of the histories of each one of the 1,148 projects in the database. These written histories provide the depth and nuance needed to understand how the contracting strategy chosen for the project played out in practice. The database, rather than being a sterile set of numbers, is actually a deep pool of knowledge about each project. There are discussions of when the construction management organization simply could not keep up with the number of construction inter-faces the strategy had created. There are detailed discussions of how late and inaccurate engineering made the constructors look like idiots instead of skilled professionals. There are lots of instances in which the owners believed they had skills in the area of construction management they simply did not possess. All of these background stories provide the potential for insight that numbers alone can never supply.

Statistics and "Statistical Significance"

Much of this book reports on our search for patterns in the rela-tionships among project practices, contracting strategies and approaches, and project outcomes as measured by cost and time. It is well understood that humans are good at seeing patterns and sometimes too good (i.e., seeing patterns where none actu-ally exist).[7] The statistical analysis in this book helps to mitigate the problem of seeing patterns where none exist. Where I believe a pattern logically should exist based on my conceptual structure of contracting and projects, the statistics help me feel comfort-able with that conclusion or uncomfortable as the case may be.

It is essential to remember that statistics are associational, not causal. When describing a result as "statistically significant," we are saying that the association probably did not occur randomly, and we use the conventional cutoff of 0.05 (5 percent) to report a result as statistically significant. The use of the value-laden word *significant* is unfortunate. *Statistically significant* does not equate to *important*. After all, the correlation between grass and the color green during active growing seasons is highly statistically significant while being of very little import to most. It is essential to understand that statistical significance does not prove causa-tion. For example, it is correct that birth rates are higher in places

---

[7]See, for example, Nate Silver, *The Signal and the Noise*, London: Penguin Books, Limited, 2012.

where the density of nesting storks is higher. That relationship is "statistically significant." But the conclusion "therefore, storks bring babies" is absurd. Storks prefer to nest in rural areas, and birth rates tend to be higher in rural areas. Causation exists only within a conceptual structure and does not derive from the statistics. When we discuss the relationships between contractual approaches and how the principal-agent problem plays out, that is a conceptual argument that leads us to expect certain outcomes. The statistics then help support or cause us to question that conceptual structure.

As we report on statistical results throughout this book, we will use the following convention to report the results:

Pr.|type of statistic|<.0XX

which should be read: the probability of the stated relationship occurring by chance with repeated tries is less than .0XX based on the particular test employed (e.g., a t-test, z-score, a X^2 (chi-square), or whatever).

Often, we will discuss statistical results noting that "factors X and Y have been controlled." For example, contracting approaches often have very different results when a project is well defined than when it is poorly defined at authorization. For example, a poorly defined lump-sum project will be subject to endless changes and will usually shift all of the overrun risk that the contract passed to the contractor back onto the owner. Conversely, a well-defined lump-sum is much more likely to force the contractor to eat any overrun. What this "controlled for" means in practice is that we have included the control variables in our statistical model while looking for the effect of contracting.[8]

---

[8]The reader should not interpret this discussion as the use of step-wise regression. We generally avoid the use of step-wise and prefer least-squares, logit, probit, or nonparametric routines such as robust regression or other nonparametric tests as required.

Summary

Our sample of projects is, we believe, a good cross section of industrial projects. There are projects large and small, simple and complex, with strong representation from six industries—chemicals, petroleum refining, mining, pharmaceuticals, consumer products, and petroleum (oil and gas) production. We also have some representation from pulp and paper. The projects are from around the world with only Russia and Central Asia under-represented. The projects were developed and executed by more than 100 industrial firms, again of all sizes, descriptions, and home locations. We have a good distribution of types of projects from revamps to greenfields, with all in between. The projects were executed by all of the world's largest industrial contractors and a host of regional and local contractors. So, let's proceed to explore the relationship between contracting strategies and project results.

CHAPTER 3

Contracting and Project Outcomes: The Common Strategies

I n this chapter we will define and present the project results for the four most common approaches to contracting engineering and construction services for industrial projects. One of these approaches has three forms, bringing the total number of strategies examined to six. These strategies account for about 80 percent of all industrial projects. Then we will discuss the advantages and disadvantages associated with each form. We will explore the underlying reasons they behave the way they do in Chapter 4.

The Key Performance Indicators and Their Measurement

We will discuss these six measures of project success:

- Construction safety
- Cost competitiveness

- Cost predictability
- Schedule competitiveness
- Schedule predictability
- Cycle time competitiveness

We will also discuss one other outcome that is significant for only one type of contract—startup and operability are poorer for EPC-LS projects than for any other contract type. After controlling for the use of new technology, there are no significant differences in startup and operability among the other contract types.

Construction safety is described by three measures: the recordable incident rate (recordables), the days-away-from-work/restricted work/job transfer rate (DARTs), and fatalities.[1] Safety statistics follow a Poisson distribution in which a good many observations have zero in any category. Therefore, we examined the probability that an accident of a particular type (recordable, DART, or fatality) would occur for a project using a particular type of contracting strategy.

Cost competitiveness measures the capital cost of a given project versus other projects installing equivalent facilities. After normalization of costs, described in Chapter 2, cost competitiveness is measured using a number of statistical models: cost-capacity models compare the cost as a function of output capacity and technical characteristics of a facility. Cost-effectiveness models compare the efficiency of installing a given scope. Different models are used for different types of facilities (e.g., continuous chemical process plants, machine installation projects, batch process facilities, and so forth). Finally, costs are compared against like-for-like facilities in the IPA databases described in Chapter 2. We display cost effectiveness in the form of an index

---

[1]We follow the definitions and reporting format of the U.S. Occupational Safety and Health Administration. Rates are determined per 200,000 construction field hours. If the reader is more familiar with rates per million hours, simply multiply the result by five.

in which 1.0 is equal to industry average. Cost indices below 1.0 are more cost effective, and those above less so.

For facilities producing commodity products, that is, products that are sold primarily based on price rather than unique product characteristics, cost competitiveness is the single most important measure of project success provided that operability is not compromised. Companies that spend more capital to produce a commodity product than their competitors generate an inferior return on capital and are eventually forced out of business, usually through acquisition by a better competitor.

Although cost competitiveness is the single most important factor for commodity companies, it is often not seen as most important for a commodity project by the business sponsor of the project.[2] That business sponsor may be more interested in speed or in avoiding any overrun than in cost effectiveness. Although there are times when a commodity project must be schedule-driven,[3] most schedule-driven commodity projects are schedule-driven for the interests of the particular business or business sponsor, not the corporation and its shareholders.

Cost predictability is simply whether a project overruns or underruns its authorization cost estimate. Perhaps not so simply, the actual cost and the estimated cost have been reconciled for changes of scope,[4] location adjusted, and adjusted for inflation (escalation in project parlance) and for fluctuations in

---

[2]In fairness, cost competitiveness is often difficult to measure. It requires a strong database and substantial expertise to generate a correct measure. By contrast, cost growth is relatively easy to measure.

[3]For example, there are some commodity projects that are timed to a particular customer commitment. Occasionally, a project must be schedule-driven to meet a regulatory compliance requirement.

[4]Scope changes are discretionary changes in functionality. For example, if after authorization the business decides to increase or decrease capacity, add or subtract a product, improve or forego storage, etc., those are all scope changes. Design changes, by contrast, are changes required to meet the original objectives of the project and involve no change to intended functionality. The two terms—*design changes* and *scope changes*—are often used interchangeably but should not be.

currency values. Only then is the ratio of actual-to-estimated costs calculated.

Schedule competitiveness is the time counterpart of cost competitiveness—how long did it take to execute[5] the project relative to other projects of similar scope and size. Except in the most unusual of circumstances, projects should never be executed slowly. Some costs are simply a function of time, such as project management costs. More importantly, economic value is always time-dependent. In certain industry sectors such as pharmaceuticals and consumer products, time can make or break the economic result. When market share is dependent on beating others to market, time and value are almost synonymous.

Schedule predictability is the measure of the time required for execution relative to the amount of time promised at authorization expressed as a percentage of promised time. The only adjustments made are for unusually bad weather striking the site during construction, force majeure events, or pandemic, such as COVID-19. The priority attached to schedule during the front-end development of a project (which is the period that matters most) differs by industrial sector, but in ways that are not entirely intuitive. Figure 3.1 shows the percentage of capital projects by sector for which schedule is the most sought after result as determined by the business sponsoring the project.

It makes sense that the sector with the most interest in schedule is pharmaceuticals because getting a drug to market in a timely way and ahead of the competition is often key to profitability. What is less obvious is why the minerals mining sector is almost the equal of pharma in putting schedule first. From an economic perspective, such schedule emphasis by minerals makes no sense. When one considers that the mining sector is the industry most characterized by internal competition for

---

[5]Execution time is measured from the mobilization of detailed design through to the mechanical completion of facilities, that is, ready in principle to operate.

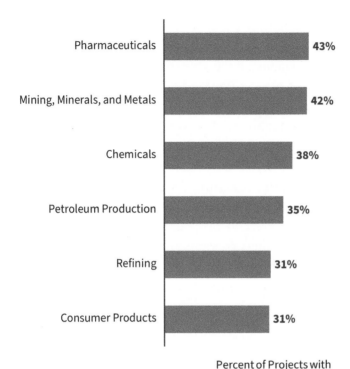

FIGURE 3.1 What industries prioritize schedule during FEL?

capital and poor project governance, the importance of schedule is more understandable, but not commendable. The other surprise is that consumer products lags all other sectors in schedule prioritization. Oil and gas projects put schedule first in just over one-third of projects—about the same percentage as petroleum refining. The average is somewhat misleading for petroleum production because the percentage of schedule-driven projects is very sensitive to the oil price at the time of authorization. Note as a matter of logic, by the way, that schedules should not be sensitive to market prices because the price cycle is usually shorter than the project execution and startup time. The same is true for major projects in refining and chemicals, but that reality does not often change behavior.

I raise the issue of schedule because schedule is one of the factors that guides decision-making around contracting approach. Some contracting approaches have a degree of schedule flexibility, while others do not. We will come back to the issues of cost and schedule priorities throughout the book.

Cycle-time competitiveness is our last measure of project outcomes. The cycle-time clock starts when the business charters a team to start scope development for a new capital project and stops when the resulting facility is in steady-state running (i.e., at the end of startup). Cycle time measures how long it takes a business idea to be translated into a business asset. Holding all driving factors, such as project size and complexity constant, cycle time has much more variance from project to project than execution time. The variation comes from the front-end loading time. As Figure 3.2 shows, the front-end loading time is driven by priority given to schedule by the

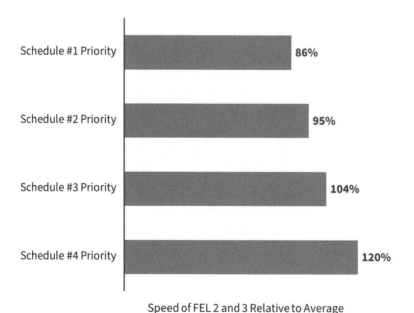

Speed of FEL 2 and 3 Relative to Average

FIGURE 3.2 Front-end time responds to schedule priority.

business sponsor. When schedule pressure is highest, front-end loading is accomplished in about 86 percent of industry average time. As schedule priority declines, the front-end loading duration increases significantly. Unfortunately, the quality of front-end loading tends to decline as schedule priority increases (Pr.|t|<.03), and the probability that the owner team was fully staffed during FEL declines even more significantly (Pr.|z|<.002).

Most of those who write about contracting strategy tend to emphasize the payment scheme over everything else—is it lump-sum or some form of reimbursable? When one says, "It is an EPC contract," many project folks assume that means EPC lump-sum. When I say EPC, I mean the particular contractor did engineering, procurement, and construction management and construction. After I understood whether the project is EPC, I would want to know whether the EPC contractor also undertook FEED as part of stage 3. The compensation scheme would be my next concern, not my first. For reasons that will become more obvious as we work through outcomes, I tend to think that *structure* is more important than compensation in a number of ways. By structure, I mean how many phases of the work are given to a particular contractor, not how they are paid.

We now define the six most commonly practiced contracting strategies for industrial projects. The first three are the EPC strategies. They involve a single contractor leading the execution of a project from the start of execution (or before if the same contractor performed FEL-3) through to the end of the project. That EPC contractor may be responsible for the entire project or may be one of a number of contractors working on the project, each executing their particular scope assignments. The second three contract strategies are the split forms. The split forms transition from a contractor who performs engineering and procurement (EP) to a different contractor or set of contractors who manage and perform construction. That EP contractor usually performs FEL-3 (FEED) as well.[6]

The Primary EPC Options

The three primary EPC options—EPC lump-sum, EPC reimbursable, and EPCM—are defined and described in the following sections. Together they constitute 55 percent of our sample and probably make up a larger percentage of industrial project contracting approaches generally.[7]

Traditional Engineer-Procure-Construct-Lump-Sum (EPC-LS) aka Design Build

The traditional and most common form of EPC-LS entails hiring an engineering contractor to execute front-end engineering design that carries the engineering through the development of piping and instrumentation diagrams that are ready for detailed design to start. Of course, all plot plans and equipment arrangements are complete, and the electrical single-lines are complete. In a thorough FEED, all of the engineering for the "outside battery limits" (i.e., outside the main processing areas) is brought

---

[6]For large projects with multiple distinct scopes and different contractors executing those scopes, I classified the project in terms of contracting strategy by the form that accounted for most of the work. This rarely presents a problem because owners generally prefer to use a single contract approach for all the scope packages. The exceptions tend to be small packages on a larger job. For example, if the project is being executed on an EPCM, it might have an EPC-LS for waste water treatment. I would still classify it as EPCM. The only difficult-to-classify cases are EPC-LS on the main plant, the so-called "inside battery limits," with reimbursable forms for the utilities and supporting infrastructure (outside battery limits). I chose to go with the ISBL strategy for classification purposes.

[7]We have deliberately over-sampled unusual contracting approaches so as to have a sufficient number for analysis. By doing so, we depress the percentage of the primary approaches.

to the same level of detail as the inside battery limits portion. The FEED contractor generally performs under a reimbursable contract, although lump-sum payment schemes for FEED are not unknown.[8] When the FEED work is complete, it is combined with the project planning work to form the technical basis for an invitation to bid (ITB) that is sent to a set of prequalified EPC contractors who have already agreed that they are interested in bidding on the project scope. It is customary *not* to invite the FEED contractor to bid for fear that doing so would discourage other bidders who may believe that the FEED contractor has an insider's advantage.

The owner's issuance of the ITB is generally followed by rounds of questions and requests for clarifications from potential bidders. The size and complexity of the project and the quality of the FEED package drive the number of question rounds required.[9] The contractors who elect to bid submit their bids, which are then evaluated by the owner team. Owners often use a two-step process in which the technical submissions are opened, evaluated, and ranked first, and then the commercial (price) bids are opened. The owner selects a winner and a second-place contractor and then negotiates those terms and conditions to which the winner took exception, as well as other elements of the technical submission or commercial bid. This process can take anywhere from a few months for a simple project to as many as 18 months for a megaproject. On large projects, the scope is often

---

[8]Executing FEED under a lump-sum payment scheme makes sense only when the FEED deliverables can be described completely, which means it is probably a project the owner has done before in a similar configuration. When FEED was lump-sum, the FEEDs were often incomplete with a good deal of arguing between owner and contractor about what "complete" means.

[9]In some bidding contests, the number of question rounds is contained in the ITB and is often constrained to one or two. While it is understandable that the owner wants to move things along, it is better practice to allow some flexibility in the number of question rounds. Obtaining clarity and full understanding of the scope by the bidders results in better-quality bids that are more easily compared.

divided into packages that are subject to separate EPC-LS competitions. We call this EPC-LS multi-prime.[10]

Projects employed traditional EP-LS as their primary contracting strategy in 19 percent of the projects in our sample. More than half of the EPC-LS projects were in the Middle East or Asia, where two-thirds and one-third of our samples, respectively, were EPC-LS. It is a less common form elsewhere in the world, but the form is used for some industrial projects in every geography in our sample. Australia and Canada are the only locations where EPC-LS is uncommon, although still employed occasionally. The fact that EPC-LS is so uncommon in Canada and Australia is instructive. Both are large, thinly populated countries with more industrial projects than their size would suggest. Neither country welcomes imported labor. As a result, both countries are easily over-heated construction markets. That makes EPC-LS a disadvantaged form because EPC-LS in a hot market environment draws a substantial risk premium from lump-sum bidders.

EPC-LS contracts are what I call the perfectly cost-incentivized contract. One hundred percent of all savings on the project, no matter how they are generated, accrue to the EPC contractor rather than the owner. All of any overspend, unless it is generated by owner changes or force majeure, also accrue to the contractor. Every owner knows this, but they often behave as though it is not true. We will discuss this in Chapter 8.

EPC Reimbursable (EPC-R)

This form is actually almost always FEED EPC-R where the FEED contactor continues on into execution and does all of the

---

[10]In multi-prime EPC-LS arrangements on megaprojects, the question arises whether the owner will manage the contractors and their interfaces or if a project managing contractor (PMC) will be hired to take on those roles. The hiring of a PMC is clearly associated with poorer outcomes for megaprojects. See Merrow, *Industrial Megaprojects*, op. cit. p. 299.

work on some form of reimbursable compensation. The most common compensation scheme is payment for hours plus overheads and fringes for engineering and construction and procurement at cost with a small procurement fee. Generally, profit is in the form of a fixed fee, and the fee is sometimes adjusted upward or down by various incentive schemes. On occasion, some parts of construction may be contracted to disciplinary subcontractors. For example, it is not uncommon for site preparation and other civil work to be done by a sub. But the basic form remains. Typically, the EPC contractor will execute construction with directly hired labor, and the EPC will undertake all aspects of construction management down to and including the gang foreperson.

The EPC-R form is less popular today than it was 20 years ago. I suspect that the EPC contractors have actually driven the change as they have come to prefer EPCM, which imposes fewer construction management burdens on them. EPC-R comprises less than 7 percent of our sample, and almost half of those projects are located in the United States and Canada. The remainder are scattered lightly around the word. And EPC-R is not even particularly popular in the United States—only 9 percent of industrial projects use the form. But it is very unpopular elsewhere.

Engineer-Procure-Construction Management (EPCM)

EPCM is now the world's most common form of contracting for industrial projects. It has become dominant in Western Europe as in-house engineering and procurement have waned over the past two decades. It is the preferred form in much of South America and completely dominates industrial contracting in on-shore Australia. It is marginally the most popular form in the United States, which tends to be more eclectic in contracting than other regions. Perhaps most surprising, EPCM has become the "go-to" form in much of Asia, whereas EPC-LS used to be the norm just 20 years ago.

Like EPC-R, EPCM avoids any transition of contractor responsibilities from the start of FEED all the way through to the completion of facilities. If the FEED contractor is not selected to continue on into detailed engineering, it is all but certain that the reason is that the owner and the contractor are not getting along. Unlike EPC-R, construction is executed by a different contractor or contractors but under the supervision of the EPCM. Most common is the use of disciplinary construction contractors rather than a general contractor for construction. The great majority of EPCM contracts are reimbursable for the EPCM's activities.[11] The compensation scheme for constructors may be lump-sum, time and materials or reimbursable hours, or unit rates.

Split Form Contracting (aka Design-Bid-Build)

Split form contracting entails the contractual and organizational separation of construction activities from engineering and procurement with the use of different firms. The only construction activities of the F-EP firm are to answer questions about its design; they have no role whatsoever in construction management. In split forms, the procurement activities of the EP firm are generally confined to major equipment and engineered materials. Nonengineered materials are typically procured by the constructor(s). Like EPC-R and EPCM, split forms are almost always feed-engineer-procure contracts. It is rare to "change horses" at the FEED to execution point in split forms. Split forms share that advantage with F-EPC-R and F-EPCM.

---

[11]About 10 percent of EPCMs in our sample were lump-sum. The differences in outcomes were not substantial enough to justify separating them out as a group. They were marginally less expensive but marginally longer in schedule. They experienced a little less cost growth but more slip in execution schedule than the reimbursable EPCMs. On a net basis, there is little difference.

Split forms come in four varieties in terms of compensation, only the first three of which are well enough populated to justify discussion.[12]

Reimbursable FEP followed by lump-sum construction (Re/LS)

Reimbursable FEP followed by reimbursable construction (Re/Re)

Lump-sum EP following by lump-sum construction (LS/LS)

The outcomes of these three forms are sufficiently different that they merit some individual treatment. The last form (LS/LS) is usually preceded by reimbursable FEED, but sometimes the FEED is also lump-sum. In either case, the contractor that will ultimately do execution EP performs FEED. Also included in these groups are instances in which the owner did FEED and detailed engineering in-house. In some of these cases, the owner also did construction management. Strictly speaking, that should be classified as EPCM. However, the projects do not behave like EPCMs but like split forms. The reasons for this are discussed at some length in Chapter 4.

Contracting Strategies and Project Results

Contracting strategy is not the most important factor driving project outcomes. The contracting strategy is clearly less important than a strong rationale for the project, a strong and functionally representative owner team, and thorough project preparation.

---

[12]The final alternative (lump-sum engineering and procurement followed by reimbursable construction) is too unusual to permit systematic analysis and often was not the originally intended strategy at all.

Also, there is no contracting strategy that does not result in some great projects and some miserable ones. But it is not usually the contracting strategy that determined that result. Nonetheless, contracting strategy is important for some project results and most especially for the cost competitiveness of a project.

Part of the decision process for selecting a contracting strategy is how the strategy fits with the priorities of the project. The conventional wisdom is that one should not select EPC-LS if schedule is very important; one should opt for EPC-R or EPCM instead. The conventional wisdom says that one should avoid EPC-LS for projects that involve new technology and again opt for EPC-R or EPCM forms.

When we actually look at the data, it appears that project characteristics play a minor role at best in the selection of contract strategies. When schedule is the top priority for the project, the use of EPC-LS drops from 19 percent to 17 percent. The lack of EPC-LS sensitivity to project characteristics is expected because EPC-LS is the mandated form in a number of countries and therefore cannot be sensitive to project characteristics. There is, however, a significant change in the use of EPCM when schedule is top priority—from 28 percent of the time to 34, but the added EPCMs come mainly from Re/LS, not from EPC-LS.

When we introduce any level of new technology in projects—even simple things such as new integrations of fully commercial technology—the use of EPC-LS declines very substantially, from 20 percent in the case of purely off-the-shelf technology to 11 percent when anything new is being done. We can see this change in the data because almost none of our new technology projects were executed in mandatory EPC-LS countries. The beneficiary of the drop in lump-sums was EPCM, which makes up 36 percent of projects with any degree of new technology. While the movement away from EPC-LS is altogether understandable, the move to EPCM may be less so. EPCMs with new technology perform markedly worse than some split forms in every outcome.

Contract Type and Safety Performance

For project managers, owner and contractor alike, the greatest burden that most feel is their responsibility is that everyone who works on the project will return home safely every evening. Safety is driven by the quality of the safety program operating on the project and a high degree of collaboration on safety between the owner and the contractors. Unless both owner and contractor "walk the talk," safety suffers. When safety incidents occur, the owner must be willing to inconvenience the project to make the point that safety matters.

When looking at the relationship between contracting approach and safety, it appears that EPC-LS is the safest form of contracting with respect to recordable injuries and DART cases, but is strangely 50 percent more prone to fatalities. When looking at very large numbers of field construction hours, the relationships among recordables, DARTs, and fatalities are quite regular. This is because if projects experience lots of recordables, DARTs and eventually fatalities will result. This is why many companies with strong safety programs often focus their attention on first-aid cases—the level below recordables—as the precursors to recordables and beyond. Therefore, to find a large group of projects with fewer recordables and DARTs but many more fatalities would seem to be an aberration.

Unfortunately, it is not. Rather, it reflects the strength and enforcement of the reporting requirements. Figure 3.3 shows the reported accident rates for our three safety statistics when dividing the world into strong reporting regions—Western Europe, the United States, and Canada—and weak reporting regions—Asia, the Middle East, Russia, and Central Asia.[13]

[13]A reader can quarrel with my use of the simple per project accidents rates here as potentially misleading. Because safety data have a distinct Poisson distribution, negative binominal regression is a better technique for modeling. However, 99 percent of my readers would find the reporting of those results opaque, and it turns out that the simple injury rates are a reasonably good representation of the pattern regardless of modeling technique. I also controlled for project size when looking at the distribution by industrial sector, and the pattern does not change in any appreciable way.

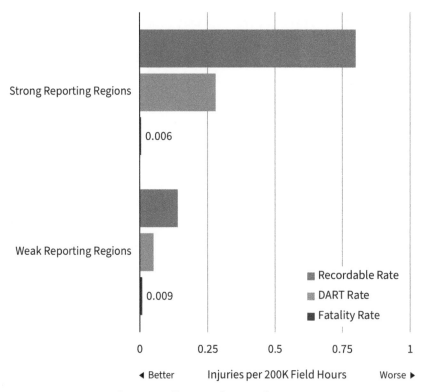

FIGURE 3.3 Reporting rates distort safety results.

Remarkably, it appears that the strong reporting regions, which also are regions of higher average craft skill level and productivity, are many times *more dangerous* than the weak reporting regions. Obviously, that is nonsense. EPC-LS appears safer because it is much more common in the weak reporting regions. The matter of the 50 percent higher fatality rate is explained by the fact that fatalities are the one type of accident that is very hard to hide.

Construction safety is quite different in the various industrial sectors represented in our database. The pattern of safety shown in Figure 3.4 from our data corresponds to what IPA has seen in overall safety performance of the industrial sectors for many years: mining, pharmaceuticals, and consumer products experience many more safety incidents per 200,000 hours worked than

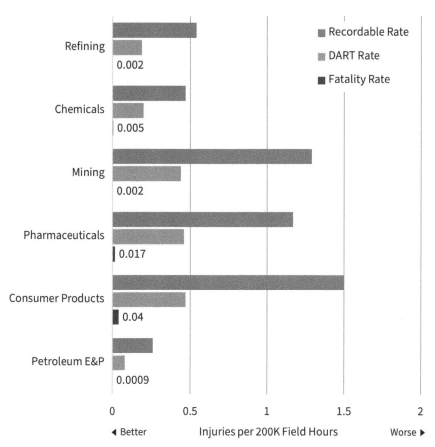

FIGURE 3.4 The industrial sector drives safety outcomes.

petroleum refining or chemicals.[14] The higher rates in the mining industry perhaps reflect inherently less safe working conditions. Pharma and consumer products, however, have no such excuse. Pharma and consumer products firms tend to have less corporate focus on capital projects than their counterparts in chemicals and petroleum, which are much more capital-intensive sectors. Those weaker project organizations play out as less able to mount and implement effective safety programs.

---

[14]Note that I did not include petroleum production projects in this discussion. Too many of the petroleum production projects in our sample were fabricated in Asia, a low-reporting region. The remaining sample would be too small to be reliable.

The upshot is that when we control for industrial sector and regional reporting standards, there is no relationship between contracting approach and the safety of the workers constructing the facilities. The only surprise is that EPC-LS is not clearly less safe than other forms, because owner involvement in execution may be less in the EPC-LS projects.

Cost Competitiveness and Cost Predictability

Most industrial projects (76 percent of our sample here) make commodity products, that is, products that are successful in the marketplace mostly or completely on the basis of price rather than unique characteristics. In other words, these products have to compete with more or less identical products made by others. Consequently, in commodities the most important outcome of a capital project is cost, subject only to good operability. Of the controllable factors that drive returns on investment, cost is far more important than schedule in commodity products.[15] In smaller projects that can be executed quickly (e.g., in 18 months or less), schedule may be important in grabbing a customer or catching an upcycle in prices. But in larger projects, market timing is a fool's game because our ability to accurately forecast ups and downs in market prices in all but the shortest time period is very limited.

In a commodity company, the beneficiaries of low cost are the shareholders and the corporate cadre that directly represents them. But that enthusiasm for low capital cost is not necessarily shared by others in the organization. Operations, for example,

---

[15]Of course, sales price and sales volumes are far more important to returns than capital cost. However, in commodity products, price and volumes are not controllable by a company.

may prefer a facility that is easy and convenient to operate over a lower-cost facility that would produce better returns but less easy operation.

But the most important group in commodity companies that often lacks interest in low capital cost are the businesspeople actually sponsoring the project. For many businesspeople, the most important aspect of the project process is securing the money needed for their project and then seeing to it that the project does not overrun. In other words, they prefer predictability to competitiveness. The evidence for this is quite compelling.

Good cost predictability is a highly prized project outcome. When a project manager and business sponsor deliver a project at or below the promised cost, both look smart even if the project cost more than it should have. Conversely, project managers will often be viewed negatively if a project overruns, even a small amount, *even if the project is actually highly cost effective.* This is because cost overruns are easily measured and highly visible. In many project systems, overruns are not even adjusted for things outside the project team's control, such as the emergence of escalation during execution or currency fluctuation.

In a study conducted by my colleague, Paul Barshop, he demonstrated that the best single predictor of business sponsor satisfaction with a project was a cost underrun.[16] Table 3.1 summarizes his key findings here. The projects are divided into five groups based on the competitiveness of the projects' authorization estimate. Each group is a column in the table. The most competitive group is the first column that promised capital costs of less the 85 cents on the average dollar. These projects finished with an average overrun of about 4 percent but remained the most competitive group at completion. The last column contains

---

[16]Paul H. Barshop, "Using Target Setting to Improve Cost Competitiveness: The Proceedings of the Annual Conference of the Industry Benchmarking Consortium," 2011, Independent Project Analysis, Inc.

TABLE 3.1	**For the Businesses, Success Is Determined by Underruns, Not Competitiveness**

	Cost Index for Authorization Estimate				
	Less Than 0.85	0.85 to 0.95	0.95 to 1.05	1.05 to 1.15	Greater Than 1.15
	◀◀ More Competitive				Less Competitive ▶▶
Did the project meet all business objectives?*	67%	63%	68%	63%	**78%** Pr<0.04
Safety recordable rate	0.86	0.79	0.80	0.94	0.91
Operability index**	1.01	1.02	1.01	1.02	1.03
Execution schedule	1.02	1.00	1.09	1.02	1.07
Cost deviation	3.7%	2.7%	2.1%	1.9%	**−3.1%** Pr<0.01

*Question posed to business sponsor within six months post-startup. Percentages are the frequency the business sponsor answered "yes."
**Operability Index allows direct comparison of operability performance across project and industry types. Lower index values are worse performance, and higher index values are better performance.

the projects with the most noncompetitive estimates at FID— all in excess of 115 percent of industry average for the scope being built.

Across the groups, there is no difference in safety, operability of facilities, or execution schedule.[17] But the final column's projects were highly noncompetitive; their median cost index at authorization was 1.28 and at completion was 1.25. But those projects, because they were so substantially overestimated, underran by 3 percent and were celebrated as the most successful group of

---

[17]There were also no differences by the cost categories in terms of key practices such as front-end loading and team integration.

projects by the business sponsors. They were no safer; they were no faster; they did not operate better. The only positive attribute of those very expensive projects is that they underran their authorization estimates—at the expense of the shareholders.

The fact that many business sponsors of projects do not care about cost effectiveness poses real problems for contracting strategy. A preference for cost predictability above all else pushes the contracting decision-maker toward EPC-LS contracting with terms and conditions that are onerous for the contractor. But in many markets that sort of strategy will produce astronomically high costs or no bids at all. In the cases where EPC-LS is not available, EPCM appears to be the beneficiary. EPCM is more predictable than EPC-R but is so because the estimates are inflated. The results in Table 3.1 manifest a basic problem in a great many industrial project delivery systems: a lack of effective governance.

Figure 3.5 shows the cost competitiveness and cost growth results for each of the primary contract strategies used in industrial projects. The first three strategies are the "EPC approaches": EPC-LS, EPC-R, and EPCM. The EPC-LS projects end up just at the average for the 1,148 projects in our sample in terms of

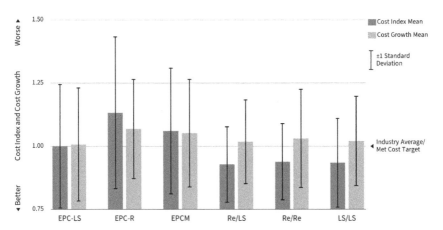

FIGURE 3.5 Cost competitiveness and cost growth by contract approach.

cost competitiveness and with cost growth of less than 1 percent. What is noteworthy, however, is that there is quite a lot of variance in both cost effectiveness and cost deviation. The variation in cost effectiveness is not at all surprising; when project markets are hot, EPC-LS pays a premium of about 10 percent; when markets cool off, the premium disappears, and when markets are down, the contractors make less than no money, and the projects are inexpensive. The variation in cost growth for EPC-LS is generated by changes on the plus side and by overestimated contingencies in the estimates on the low side. The average contingency in EPC-LS owner estimates was about 8 percent. The amount typically required was about 5 percent, leaving a median underrun of about 3 percent of the owner's FID estimate. Of course, the contractors included contingency in their bids, but that amount is almost never visible.

The most expensive contract form is EPC-R. Owners pay an average premium of 13 percent (Pr.|t|<.0001) more than overall industry average for those projects. More telling, the premium paid for EPC-R compared to the split form contracts is 21 percent (Pr.|t|<.0001), and controlling for the completeness of front-end loading does not change that result at all. EPC-R also carries the highest real[18] cost growth of any contractual form.

The EPCM form carries a 6 percent cost penalty relative to the sample average (Pr.|t|<.0001) and a penalty of over 12 percent relative to all projects excluding EPC-R (Pr.|t|<.0001). Controlling for FEL does not move the result. To some readers, 6 percent may seem like a smallish price to pay. However, for a typical project, spending 6 percent more will decrease the return on investment almost 1 percent. Spread that across the portfolio, and it is the difference between a successful and unsuccessful

---

[18]Recall that cost deviation has been normalized to remove the effects (plus and minus) of scope changes, foreign currency fluctuation, and project-specific inflation (escalation). Nominal cost growth is generally higher, and often considerably higher, than real.

industrial commodity company. EPCM projects averaged 5 percent in cost growth with a lot of variation.

Looking now to the three split form approaches, there are two surprises. First, all three forms are significantly (Pr.|t|<.0001) less costly than all other mainline contract forms. Second, all three forms produce remarkably similar results—less than 2 percent in cost performance and cost deviation. The Re/LS form and the LS/LS form do have less variation in cost competitiveness and cost deviation than other contractual approaches. The Re/Re form is more variable in both cost competitiveness and deviation *except when construction was done with unit rate construction contracts* rather than simple reimbursable or time and material forms. When unit rates were used, the cost performance is 89 percent of industry average, and the cost growth is negative 5 percent with a standard error of 15 percent and 11 percent, respectively. Unit rate construction contracts effectively shift labor productivity risks from the owner to the constructor, while other reimbursable forms do not. Unit rate construction is popular in Western Europe and has become popular in much of Southeast Asia. Unit rate construction contracts are unusual in Canada and the United States, which lack a substantial quantity surveyor cadre.

Schedule Competitiveness and Schedule Deviation

Some contractual approaches are faster than others. As Figure 3.6 shows, EPC-LS, Re/LS, and LS/LS are about 4 to 8 percent slower in execution than EPC-R and EPCM. Note, however, the Re/Re yields no speed to the EPC-R and EPCM forms at all. For the EPC-LS form, the schedule is in the control of the EPC contractor. That contractor will tend to float the schedule to whatever point will generate the lowest cost project but never any slower than that lowest-cost point. EPC-LS contractors will never want

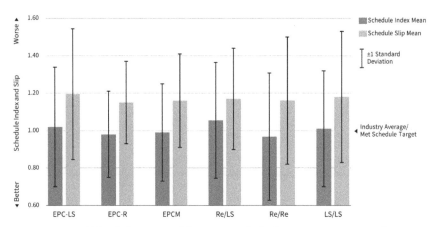

FIGURE 3.6 Schedule competitiveness and slip by contract approach.

to be slower than the low-cost point because they want to complete the project, pick up the 5 to 10 percent retainage that the owner is holding, and move on to the next project.

For the Re/LS and LS/LS forms, the slower schedule performance is the natural result of choosing the easiest way to manage lump-sum construction contractors, which is to have them work the job in a sequential fashion. First the civil contractor prepares the site and pours foundations, then the mechanical contractor sets equipment and erects structural steel and installs all the process pipe, and finally the E&I contractor completes the job. Although all of the interfaces with specialty contractors must be managed, the big sources of interference claims and complaints are removed from the process. Note that it is not the EP contractor-to-construction contractor(s) transition that slows things down as much as the sequential construction. The Re/Re projects, which have the same issues of transition, are actually a little faster than EPC-R and EPCM, neither of which has a contractor transition.

Cycle time is summation of front-end loading starting with the start of scope development, execution, and startup time (i.e., the time needed to achieve steady-state production). As shown in Figure 3.7, the only real cycle-time difference is for traditional EPC-LS contracts. The time added by the bidding

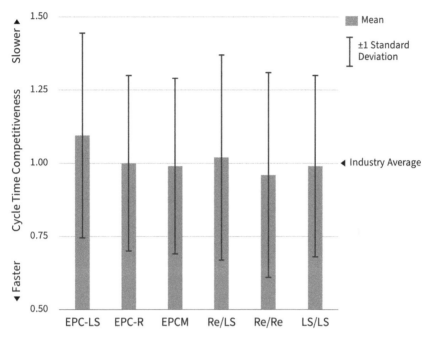

FIGURE 3.7 Cycle-time competitiveness by contract approach.

process after the end of FEED cannot be made up via time savings anywhere else. It is a well-known downside of the EPC-LS strategy.

When Speed Is King

The results shown in the two previous figures are the averages in terms of schedule for the different primary contracting forms. But how do these contract forms behave when the owner decides that speed is of the essence, which is the case in more than a quarter of major industrial projects? Do we get the speed? What does it cost? As shown in Figure 3.8, every contract form save one is materially faster when the owner deems speed to be critical to success.

The three EPC forms all end up at about 12 percent faster than the industry average when the project is schedule-driven. But there

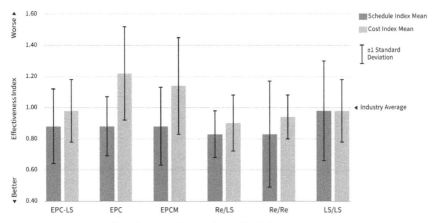

FIGURE 3.8 Speed and cost when schedule-driven.

is a degree of self-sorting going on here. The frequency of EPC-LS contracts goes down when projects put speed first, and only when the needed speed is thought possible is the form used. Not only does speed improve for these projects, but the EPC-LS projects displayed only 11 percent slip versus 20 percent overall for EPC-LS.

Also of note, the cost effectiveness of EPC-LS did not change when schedule-driven. When projects are considered by the owner to be schedule-driven and EPC-LS is the chosen strategy, the owner includes a hard end date, usually reinforced by liquidated damages for late delivery. When contractors approach the bidding on such projects if they believe the schedule is achievable but not comfortable, they add a cost premium. That cost premium often forces a change of contracting strategy or even abandonment of the project by the owner. If contractors believe they can achieve the schedule easily, they do not add a cost premium because to do so would jeopardize a successful bid.

EPC-R and EPCM achieved the same schedule performance—about 88 percent of industry average, but their cost performance deteriorated substantially. A 10 percent improvement in schedule costs owners a 10 percent increase in cost for both these contract forms. Both groups also slipped their schedules badly—12 percent for EPC-R and 17 percent for EPCM. In other words, EPCM projects over-promised more their ability to produce speedy projects. However, in the EPC-R and EPCM forms, there is usually no penalty for late delivery of the project.

The big, pleasant surprise in this analysis is the performance of the Re/LS group under time pressure. Those projects went from being rather slow in normal circumstances to being the fastest group when under pressure, averaging 83 percent of industry average execution time. When schedule-driven, they abandoned the sequential construction strategy.[19] In the process, they achieved superb cost results at 90 percent of industry average. As expected, the Re/Re group were very fast while maintaining their cost advantage over the EPC forms.

The split form contracting strategy that did not perform at all well under time pressure were the LS/LS projects. They gained only 3 percent in execution speed while ballooning their slip to 25 percent and adding 5 percent to cost. There are too many observations for the results to be accepted as a fluke. I strongly suspect the problem for this group was the lump-sum engineering contract. Preparing bid packages for lump-sum engineering contractors, even using the strategy of bidding unit rates that will be converted to lump-sum, requires that work be done out of normal order if speed is to be gained. Any engineering contractor working on a lump-sum compensation scheme would be very reluctant to agree to do their work out of the normal fashion. When reviewing these schedule-driven LS/LS projects, I found that they did attempt to use incentives for schedule but did not seek to employ liquidated damages. I would venture that attempts to impose LDs would have resulted in no contractor willing to take on the work.

So when speed is deemed essential, EPC-LS is OK if it is really available and if the bidding cycle is acceptable. Generally,

---

[19]This should not lead those using the Re/LS contracting strategy to abandon their sequential approach on non-schedule-driven projects. The sequential approach significantly reduces the strain on construction management by eliminating interfaces, making laydown easier, and reducing logistics problems. Construction management is a scarce and valuable resource these days, and savings on CM skills and resource requirements is important.

however, EPC-LS is not available for time-pressured projects because contractors do not want to take on the risk. EPC-R and EPCM will get you the speed but with a severe cost penalty. Re/LS and Re/Re appear the best way to go. I would also note that there are some big projects in the schedule-driven split form group—up to $1.7 billion—and no tendency for costs to degrade with larger sizes. LS/LS will not work to generate speed, period.

Contracting for Regulatory Compliance Projects

About one industrial project in six is done solely or primarily for the purpose of complying with changes in environmental, health, or safety regulations. These are not modest projects; the median cost is more than $100 million. Because these projects generate no direct revenue, logic would suggest that they should be overwhelmingly cost-driven projects.

Almost none of the compliance projects we have benchmarked over the years have resulted from a sudden or unanticipated change in regulations. Most regulators provide many years of advance notice to industrial firms that changes are coming. Nonetheless, almost 30 percent of compliance projects end up being schedule-driven in execution because they were postponed until they became urgent. Occasionally, the procrastination results from a hope that the regulator will have a change of heart. In reality, that rarely happens. More often, compliance projects are postponed because they lack a sponsor. From a sponsorship perspective, compliance projects are usually orphans. No one seems to be interested in spending sponsorship time on a project that generates no glory, that is, money. But the fact is these projects are necessary to staying in business and end up costing a lot more money than they should.

Contracting for compliance projects can be tricky and is subject to a good many contracting games. EPC-LS is rarely employed on compliance projects. There is really no good reason for this. Only about 20 percent of compliance projects are messy brownfield projects, what we call revamps. Revamps naturally discourage EPC-LS because of the logistical problems associated with working in what is usually an operating plant and because revamps are subject to late surprises. But the great majority of compliance projects are the sorts of projects in which EPC-LS is feasible. For whatever reason EPC-LS is avoided even when the project is not schedule-driven.

The most common contracting form for compliance projects is EPCM. For the schedule-driven compliance projects, more than half are EPCM or EPC-R—the least cost-effective contracting strategies as shown in Figure 3.9.

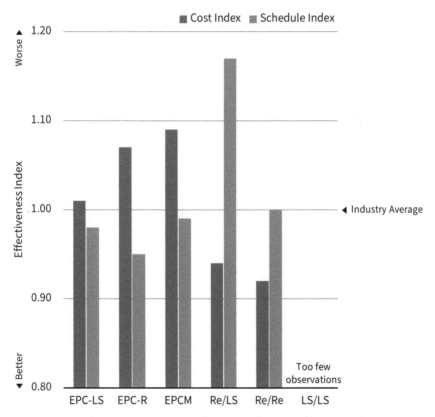

FIGURE 3.9 Contract strategy performance for compliance projects.

The performance pattern we have seen is maintained for compliance projects; the split options offer dramatically lower cost on what should be entirely cost-driven projects. But what happens when we wait long enough that the compliance deadline is looming and the project becomes schedule-driven? As shown in Figure 3.10, the EPC-LS projects disappear, and the EPC-R and EPCM projects become obscenely expensive. The split options maintain their cost effectiveness and achieve fast schedules as well.

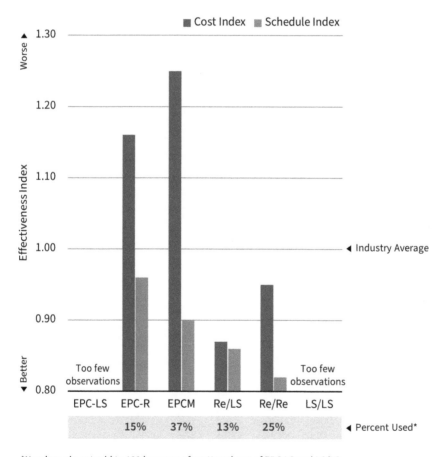

*Numbers do not add to 100 because of scattered use of EPC LS and LS/LS

FIGURE 3.10 Contract strategy performance for schedule-driven compliance projects.

Compliance projects employing EPC-R and EPCM have been subjected to some of the most ruthless contracting games we have seen in capital projects. The most common game was for the FEED-EPCM contractor to slow down their FEED work to push the project into schedule-driven execution where they would have more leverage. We have seen even very sophisticated owners get caught in such schedule games for compliance projects. We have not seen these games work successfully in split form contracting approaches.

Summary

A majority of industrial projects—just over 50 percent—are executed using some form of EPC contract. The reimbursable forms—EPC-R and EPCM—are also almost always preceded by the same contractor doing the FEED work in final preparation for execution. Only the traditional EPC-LS approach usually changes contractors at the FEED-to-execution point. The split forms account almost 30 percent of industrial projects with the remainder being executed under other forms that will be discussed in Chapters 5 and 6.

What our analysis shows quite starkly is that popularity is not determined by effectiveness. The split options are systematically superior to the EPC options. This is true not only in general but also when we confine ourselves to speed-driven projects or to regulatory compliance-driven projects. When speed is required, two of the split form approaches—Re/LS and Re/Re—produce better speed than EPC forms at much lower cost. On compliance projects, which should be cost-driven, split forms are markedly superior. This poses what is perhaps the contracting question of our time: why are owners so often satisfied to select contracting approaches that routinely deliver inferior performance? That issue is explored in Chapter 4.

CHAPTER 4

Exploring Why They Work the Way They Do

I n this chapter, we will explore why the various primary contracting strategies perform in characteristically different ways. We will ask if there are ways to mitigate some of the problems we see in certain important contracting approaches, EPC-LS and EPCM in particular. Given the popularity of EPCM around the world, any approaches to improving the outcomes of that particular contract form would be very useful. We will also discuss one of the great paradoxes in contracting strategy: why the best contracting strategies (for owners at least) are less popular than strategies that are more damaging to owner interests in cost and schedule effective projects.

Traditional EPC-LS (Design-Build Fixed Price)

EPC-LS is the contracting strategy that minimizes the joint product nature of capital project delivery. The goal is to divide the project into three clearly delimited phases: owner-led project preparation, contractor execution, and owner operation. Sometimes, contractor execution extends to starting up the facilities, in which case the contract form is "turnkey." (We will address whether that is a good idea later.) The clear demarcation of responsibilities is one of the key features of EPC-LS. It simplifies the management of the approach while creating important limitations as well.

The EPC-LS form is used in some regions as the primary contracting strategy because government rules make other forms impossible or impractical. Government-owned industrial companies (so called national companies) are most likely to follow EPC-LS contracting because it is required or preferred by their government owner. It is the dominant form in the Gulf Cooperation Council countries in the Middle East for national companies and is common for national companies elsewhere in the world as well. Government preference for EPC-LS is usually ascribed to the desire to make corruption in capital projects more difficult, although I am unaware of any evidence that it does so.[1] Sometimes governments make EPC-LS the only feasible contractual form by requiring government review of contracting decisions down to a very low level—in one case every spending decision over $10,000 USD has to be reviewed. That forces a minimum of contracting decisions and, therefore, EPC-LS.

When projects are externally funded by financial institutions, the lending syndicate often mandates EPC-LS. Many lenders go further and prefer a "wrap contract" with a single EPC-LS turnkey contractor with operational performance guarantees and liquidated damages for late completion. As it is indelicately put, "It is good to have one throat to choke!" In reality, EPC-LS offers

---

[1]Corruption is possible under any contract form. The issue is not really one of compensation scheme but whether a fair competition was held in which all qualified contractors are given an opportunity. In jurisdictions in which EPC-LS is required, it is also common to allow selection only on the basis of price offered. That creates another constraint on EPC-LS bidding competitions and may be even more important than the strategy itself.

little protection against overruns. The variation in actual-to-estimated cost is almost exactly the same for EPC-LS and other contract strategies. The belief that the contract price is a ceiling on what the project will cost is a form of magical thinking or perhaps just confused vertical orientation. The EPC-LS contract price is the *floor* on what the project will cost but certainly not the ceiling! The efficacy of liquidated damages and other penalties will be discussed in Chapter 8. Of course, a lending syndicate's desire to have a single contractor execute a project is not feasible if the project is too large for a single contractor to handle. In fact, about 40 percent of EPC-LS projects overrun the contractor's bid, and when they do, the average overrun is 17 percent of total project cost with the largest overrun being 150 percent.

When EPC-LS projects overrun, changes are the culprit (Pr.|t|<.001). The changes are in turn driven by the defects in the front-end loading (Pr.|t|<.001), especially the FEED quality and the completeness of the project execution planning. In traditional EPC-LS projects, the first task of the winning contractor is to thoroughly review every aspect of the FEED package. Usually, the contract will require the new contractor to identify and request change orders for all of the deficiencies in the FEED package within 60 to 90 days of contract award. After that point, FEED deficiencies will not generally be accepted as legitimate change order items.[2] Of course, what is a "deficiency" is to some extent in the eye of the beholder. The two- to three-month review period is an inevitable feature of the traditional EPC-LS structure. It is thoroughly disliked by most owners as it is often quite contentious, delays the full start of execution, and pushes up the price if FEED errors and omissions are uncovered.

---

[2]Depending on the way the contract is written and the choice of jurisdiction, important but deeply hidden FEED defects may come back to the owner despite the limitation period. Fundamental technology and Basic Data errors, for example, are difficult to transfer to the EPC if the technology decisions were all made by the owner.

Many of the alternative EPC-LS forms, such as design competitions, functional specification contracts, and covert-to-lump-sum contracts, are attempts to avoid the "hard hand-off" between the FEED contractor and the execution contractor while still maintaining the EPC-LS format, at least in part. Occasionally, the owner seeks to avoid the hand-over problem by allowing the FEED contractor to bid and surreptitiously giving that contractor an advantage in the bidding competition. This practice is quite unethical and often deters the best EPCs from entering the competition as they fear they are wasting their time and money.[3]

When projects are well defined, EPC-LS does provide more protection against overruns than any other contractual form, but with some important caveats. If the project was too large for the contractor's balance sheet to absorb anything but a smallish overrun, the EPC-LS form provides little protection to the owner. EPC-LS projects are a major source of contractor bankruptcies, and in my experience that never works out well for the owner. Also, when a lump-sum contractor is struggling with the job, quality will suffer unless the owner has a very strong inspection organization.

The Advantages of EPC-LS

The traditional EPC-LS offers a simple contractual structure with clear risk allocation if the terms and conditions are carefully drafted. Simple contractual approaches are particularly

---

[3]Even if the owner does not "steer" the contract to the FEED EPC, that contractor has significant advantages anyway. If FEED contractors even suspect that they will be permitted to bid, they will look to hide cost in scope that is actually unnecessary and can be removed later. Sometimes soils information will be presented in ways that suggest the soil conditions are less favorable than they actually are. There are a large number of ways to at least modestly inflate scope, and a modest inflation is all that may be necessary to win the competition unfairly. When FEED contractors are allowed to bid in an EPC-LS competition, they actually win more than 50 percent of the time—far more often than we would expect by chance.

good when the project itself is large and complex. Remember, contracts are more about risk assignment than anything else.

The approach is less taxing on the owner project organization for certain skill sets. EPC-LS minimizes owner interface management responsibility, but owners need to be careful not to overdo transfer of interface management. Interfaces with government entities, regulators, etc., should normally be managed by the owner rather than turned over to the contractor. Whether the owner or the contractor will take responsibility for the management of third-party projects being done in conjunction with the effort should be carefully defined in the terms and conditions and the liability for third-party performance carefully assigned. If the contractor cannot actually manage that third-party liability, then remember the principle that risks will go unmanaged if assigned to a party that cannot control them.

The EPC-LS all but eliminates the need for owner cost control in execution. The owner does not need to deeply understand or practice construction management in this form. But the notion that the owner's team can be very small with EPC-LS is a misconception. The EPC-LS form is a fully cost-incentivized approach to contracting. Every dollar saved is a dollar in the EPC contractor's pocket. Every savvy owner using EPC-LS knows this and counters the temptation to cut corners with very robust inspection of more or less everything: design standards, procurement of equipment and materials, and field construction. The owner inspectors need to be skilled and willing to confront the contractor on every cut corner they can find. If the contractor is in a loss position on the project, there will still be some things not found, but they will be small. EPC-LS is a "low-trust" form of contracting whenever the project is viewed as "one-off" by the parties and the project is overrunning.

When available, EPC-LS is perhaps the ideal contract form for highly standardized scopes. When supplier/contractors offer standard package solutions (e.g., for air separation), an EPC-LS approach plays to the strengths of the suppliers provided that the owner does not require something tailored or unique. A related advantage of EPC-LS is that the approach can help to control those within the owner organization that love to change things right up to the last minute. When going EPC-LS, those late changes by the business or operations come with a clear price tag; that in itself is often enough to minimize change.

The fact that EPC-LS can be very cost competitive in a down-market environment is a decidedly mixed blessing. It is true that in a down market the low bid is likely to be at or below the "should cost" of the project. It is also true that if the owner has done everything right on the front end and the contractor has a strong balance sheet or a financially strong parent company, the owner may come out ahead. But every owner thinking of taking advantage of this situation needs to understand that there are a lot of caveats and the contractor will be looking for ways to shed risk, increase the price, and decrease his costs from day one. There is no free lunch.

Factors Militating Against Use of EPC-LS

A number of factors make the use of EPC-LS difficult or even impossible. The most important limitation by far is the state of the contractor market when a project is coming up for a contracting strategy decision. Busy sellers' markets make EPC-LS either much more expensive or simply impracticable. When the market is busy, a contractor's need to win any particular bid declines. That enables contractors to more fully price any risk they see in the work.

The problem for owners is that contractors will price risk at a higher level than most owners would. This conclusion simply accords with the first principle of risk pricing: the pricing of the risk is a function of one's wealth position relative to the downside of the bet. Richer people can afford to be less risk-averse than poorer people. In the industrial world, owners are almost always wealthier than contractors. The financial implications of absorbing a large overrun on a project are profoundly different for a contractor and an owner. On a lump-sum contract, every dollar of overrun that cannot be avoided is deducted from the contractor's balance sheet. By contrast, every dollar of overrun on a reimbursable project is *added* to the owner's balance sheet as an asset. The owner is not happy about having to earn against an asset that is larger than expected, but even a large overrun is very unlikely to do serious financial damage to an owner company. A large overrun on even a medium-sized project could be debilitating for a contractor.

The other factor that becomes important in hot markets is that one may not be able to generate a bid list of three to five genuinely interested contractors. Without at least three bidders, the competition is likely to end up with a high-cost project, and three bidders is far from optimal.[4]

The present market is instructive about the differences between owners and contractors. The current market is not overheated in most areas of the world. Even so, contractors are highly risk-averse. Many major EPC firms are declining to entertain any industrial EPC-LS work because their financial condition is weak and they feel insecure with fixed-price work. Many contractors are declining EPC-LS for infrastructure work as well.

Too Much Time-Pressure. A second consideration that must be weighed carefully is whether the time required for the EPC-LS cycle time is going to be palatable to the business

---

[4]Four bidders is optimal for EPC-LS competitions as it results in the lowest cost project. More than four competitors is actually associated with higher cost rather than lower. That may seem counterintuitive, but it actually makes sense. As the number of bidders goes above four, the chances increase of receiving an exceptionally low bid, a bid separated from all others by 15 percent or more. In those cases, that low bid is often accepted even though it is implausible. Those projects usually go quite poorly. When too many contractors are invited to bid, the interest of the best contractors often declines because they are aware of the incompetent low bid problem. Unfortunately, owners are much more likely to invite three contractors to bid rather than four for EPC-LS work. See Arkadii Lebedinskii, *Bidding Duration Study*, Independent Project Analysis, 2020.

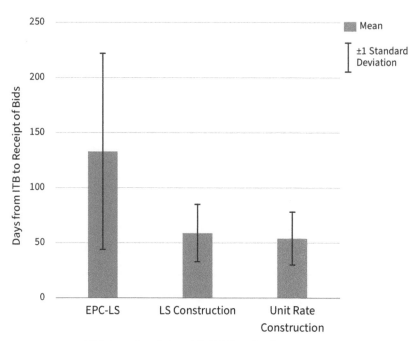

FIGURE 4.1 Bid duration drives EPC-LS cycle time.

sponsors of the project. As shown in Figure 4.1 EPC-LS projects average more than 130 days from issuance of the invitations to bid (ITB) to bid receipt.[5] Larger (more than $500 million) green-field projects require 215 days on average with a P25 to P75 range from 135 to 267 days. Complex process technology adds to the cycle as well. The bidding cycle is only part of the process. After a winner is selected, the contract terms must be negotiated, and the FEED review process delays true project start even more. If the business case cannot stand the added time, EPC-LS may be a nonstarter.

Note that the bidding cycles for construction only competitions are much shorter and that there is no difference between lump-sum construction and unit rate contracts. This becomes important as we discuss other contracting forms.

---

[5]Lebedinskii, op. cit.

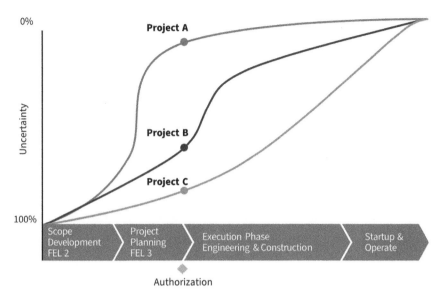

FIGURE 4.2   The timing of uncertainty reduction is key.

Too Much Residual Uncertainty After FEL. Another significant issue in the EPC-LS decision is whether uncertainties in the particular project can be reduced very substantially before we need to issue the ITB. The timing of uncertainty reduction should look like the pattern shown in Project A in Figure 4.2. The owner's goal should always be to present a low-risk project to the contractor community—a project that can be executed quickly and without significant upsets. Smart contractors do not like to enter EPC-LS bidding competitions for messy projects.

If uncertainty is high at the end of FEL 3 (FEED and execution planning), such as in projects B and C, contractors will not bid, or will bid high, or the resulting contract will not be sustainable as an EPC-LS.

There are a number of factors that can drive high levels of uncertainty into execution.

- Project unfriendly locations are places in which regulatory approvals are problematic and government interventions in projects during execution are likely and politics are unstable.

- Remote sites and other sites with inherently difficult logistics are probably poor candidates for EPC-LS.
- Projects using substantially new technology in which significant design changes are likely through much of detailed engineering are not conducive to EPC-LS.[6]
- Projects with significant shaping problems such as unhappy partners and other stakeholders, where disruption of execution is likely, should not be attempted EPC-LS.[7]
- Finally, projects with poor quality or very incomplete FEED are going to be a disaster in the unlikely case that an EPC-LS contract can even be had.

Lack of the Proper Skills. EPC-LS requires the skill to select and manage FEED contractors. That requires a substantial amount of engineering skill. The ability to write a solid ITB and solicit a good number of bids is an under-appreciated skill set. Finally, as mentioned, a strong inspector cadre is essential to mitigating the quality concerns that always accompany EPC-LS contracts.

Insufficient Internal Discipline. Some companies should not attempt EPC-LS simply because they lack the internal disciple essential to keeping EPC-LS projects under control. By this I do not mean the controls function, but the willingness of all owner functions to get their project scope items addressed in FEL-2 and not revisit the scope throughout the project execution process. As the old expression goes, the EPC lump-sum with lots of owner changes is the contract from hell for the owner and the contract from heaven for the contractor.

---

[6]See Edward Merrow, Kenneth Phillips, and Christopher Myers, *Understanding Cost Growth and Performance Shortfalls in Pioneer Process Plants*, The RAND Corporation, 1981.

[7]For a discussion of shaping issues and their effects on projects, see Edward Merrow, *Industrial Megaprojects*, 2011, John Wiley & Sons, Chapters 4 and 5, pp. 53–122.

The contract form depends on allowing the contractor to execute the project without repeated owner intervention. Owners who cannot stomach that should find another contracting strategy. Often changes and interventions lead to conflict with the contractor as well as unending cost growth and schedule slip. We even had one project in which the very reputable Japanese contractor quit the project in the middle of execution, arguing that the endlessly dabbling owner was "not an honorable owner!"

The Operability Penalty. The EPC-LS form carries a small but consistent operability penalty of about 4 percent of nameplate capacity when compared to equivalent projects executed on different contract strategies. This penalty is based on the second six months production after startup, after startup upsets have been resolved. The hit to operability is not surprising as it is known that cutting corners is an ever-present danger with the EPC-LS forms. This result underscores the importance of quality inspectors on the owner team during execution.

Making EPC-LS Work

EPC-LS is a perfectly serviceable contract approach with the right owner personnel, the right mindset, and the right situation. The cost-competitiveness of the form depends on using it in the right circumstances and doing a very good job on the front end. Front-end loading quality is the primary driver of poor cost competitiveness in EPC-LS projects ($Pr.|t| < .009$). And that is not just the FEED portion of FEL-3 but good project execution planning as well.

EPC-LS is often considered a very desirable contract approach by owners because they believe it passes risk materially to the contractor. But if the circumstances are not right for EPC-LS, it often transfers little or no risk to the contractor. It is important to do a sober assessment of the situation before plunging ahead trying to use EPC-LS when it is not the right strategy. When owners do that, they often end up having to change the contracting strategy at the last minute and end up with a strategy for which they and their project were not prepared.

A well-chosen and well-designed EPC-LS does in fact transfer significant risk to the EPC contractor. But sometimes owners try to take advantage of the situation to transfer *all* risk of every sort to the contractor. The terms and conditions in an EPC-LS contract should be designed to clarify risk ownership and management responsibilities but should not be designed to bankrupt the contractor. Sometimes owners will grab a very low bid from a desperate contractor and use their leverage to transfer unreasonable amounts of risk to contractor and then bleed the contractor during execution. In the process, that owner gains a reputation that will make that approach much less likely to generate good bids and more expensive to him in the future. A reputation for being tough *but fair* is a real advantage for owners in EPC-LS contracting because over time such owners will attract more and better EPCs to their lump-sum competitions.

One of the most useful exercises when negotiating an EPC-LS with the winning contractor is to conduct a risk identification and assignment workshop. One of the most unfortunate practices for owner and contractors is to shy away from frank discussions about who is taking what risk during the negotiation of the terms and conditions. When a risk is not thoroughly discussed, it is easy for both parties to believe it is assigned to the other party. Agree to a set of rules to be followed during these negotiations, especially that whoever has greater control of a risk should be assigned the risk. Projects with clear risk assignment, which is then reflected in the contract language, end up with fewer disputes during execution and fewer claims later.

As owners negotiate with risk-averse and wary EPCs, remember there are some key provisions that may make the difference between a successful and unsuccessful result. Chief among these are using waivers of consequential damages; setting limitations of liability, especially capping liability at the value of insurance; and providing a clear and fair change order process. Limiting the downside for the contractor in the ITB will entice better contracting firms to bid. Limiting the downside in negotiations make it more likely that the project will actually get under way.

Owners: finish FEED! Only about half of traditional EPC-LS competitions were preceded by what IPA rated as a complete FEED. The projects that completed FEED were 11 percent less expensive than those that did not (Pr.|t|<.0001). Incomplete FEEDs generate higher low bids. Incomplete FEEDs result in a bid package that looks riskier to the contractors, and they bid accordingly. Incomplete FEED is a purely self-inflicted wound by the owner; it is utterly unnecessary.

I was recently talking with a student of industrial contracting who said that her objection to EPC-LS is that it is "anti-collaborative or at best noncollaborative." I have heard similar comments from other observers in the past. After watching owner-contractor relationships over the course of thousands of capital projects in all corners of the world, I do not find EPC-LS any more or less collaborative than any other contractual form. EPC-LS does establish some clear boundaries for owner behavior—the owner cannot tell the EPC-LS contractor how to do their work. But my experience is that owners should *never* tell contractors how to do their work. Contractors are professionals and should be treated as such. (Do you tell your doctor how your surgery should be performed?) My colleagues and I have seen many EPC-LS projects in which the owner and contractor worked together seamlessly to solve problems and keep the project moving forward to success. We have also seen "collaborative" contracting strategies such as integrated project delivery descend into acrimonious in-fighting on the way to failure. Collaboration is much more about competence and mutual respect than the contractual format for the project.

Understanding EPC-Reimbursable

Reimbursable EPC is a relatively rare contracting form these days for major projects. It is sometimes an owner's contracting strategy of last resort. When no contractor will bid lump-sum on a project or when EPC-LS bids come in unacceptably high, EPC-R is sometimes the fallback strategy. It is often used when high levels of uncertainty persist in a project into execution and an EPCM approach is not feasible. During the hot market periods in the U.S. Gulf Coast and Western Canada regions, EPC-R was used when other forms, including lump-sum construction, were simply not available in the market. EPC-R is used more often when new technology is in play—about 10 percent of EPC-R projects had some technology that was new in commercial use versus about 6 percent of other projects.[8]

If EPC-LS typically has the highest of risk transfer to contractors, EPC-R surely has the lowest. EPC-R places more burden on owners to control the project than any other form. Most owners fear the possibility of the contractor "cranking hours" endlessly on EPC-R projects. Unlike other contractual forms, there is seemingly no built-in stop to the contractor spending more hours due to low productivity in both engineering and the field. The other EPC reimbursable form, EPCM, at least has the change of contractors for construction even if not for any other activity.

Is the owner fear of "cranking hours" a justified fear? We find it is only to a very limited degree. Most of the time when hours are seemingly being "cranked," it is because the front end was not completed. EPC-R projects have more increase in material quantities than any other contract form from authorization to completion. It is true that the EPC-R contractor almost always executed FEED as well as execution. But one of the major downsides of not having a break between contractors at the end of FEED is

---

[8]New technology was actually most prevalent in the Re/Re form at 11 percent of projects.

that owners are tempted (often with contractor encouragement) to "slide" into execution, blurring the line between FEED activities and execution activities. That tendency is no doubt exacerbated by EPC-R projects being schedule-driven more often than any other contractual form except guaranteed maximum price.[9]

In recent years, even EPCs appear to have shied away from EPC-R in preference of EPCM. EPC-R usually involves direct-hire construction by the EPC. EPC contractors have experienced a good deal of difficulty with direct-hire projects because the deep level of construction management that is required is now beyond what many can comfortably deliver. Depending on the terms of the contract, EPC-R often involves significantly more liability for the contractor than an EPCM assignment does. This is especially true if the EPCM has the constructors prime to the owner rather than subcontractors of the EPCM. The EPC-R contractor may be liable for operational performance problems as well, whereas the EPCM contractor rarely is.

Downsides of EPC-R for Owners

EPC-R does not offer many advantages to owners except flexibility.

- It is the most expensive contractual form by a substantial margin. Leaving aside EPCM projects, EPC-R is 19 percent more costly than all other contractual forms on average (Pr.|t|<.0001).

- It is thought by many to offer significant schedule advantages, but the data do not support that conclusion. It provides no schedule advantage when projects are schedule-driven or when they are not. When they are schedule-driven, however,

---

[9]The frequency of schedule-driven projects in GMPs is a result of the popularity of the form among pharmaceutical companies. Pharma companies often have "schedule-driven" as their default project strategy, while other industrial-sector companies rarely do. GMP will be discussed in Chapter 6.

the cost penalty rises to 26 percent (Pr.|t|<.0001). So, one is paying a hefty fine for a schedule advantage that is nil.

- EPC-R projects also take significantly longer to start up and bring to steady-state operation (Pr.|t|<.001).

- EPC-R does not scale well as a contractual form. Larger EPC-R and EPCM projects are progressively more expensive (more on this later in the chapter).

All in all, this is not a contractual approach I would recommend to any client for a major project except in the most dire of circumstances.

A Deeper Dive into EPCM

As industrial landscape changes go, the development of EPCM as the dominant contracting form has been quite dramatic. That begs the question of why this form has become so popular so quickly. A number of forces are at work.

First, a reminder: the form is actually FEED-EPCM where FEED stands for "front-end engineering design." FEED is the engineering side of the final stage of the front-end loading process. When FEED is complete, the project moves to full-funds authorization, aka final investment decision (FID). For a typical project in the process industries, FEED is relatively expensive, typically accounting for 2 to 4 percent of total capital cost. When the EPCM form is selected, the FEED contractor is the EPCM contractor almost all the time (>95 percent). When the FEED contractor is not selected for the EPCM work, it is usually because the FEED contractor and the owner are not getting along.

The cases in which the owner is so unhappy with the FEED contractor as to end the relationship at FEED tend to be highly problematic projects. The core problem is that as soon as the FEED contractor knows it is not going forward into execution, the already problematic FEED process slows down, and the contractor often withdraws his best people. Often the actual contract is of almost no help at all here because the contract did not lay out with enough specificity what all the FEED deliverables were required to be and did not include any consequences for failing to get the work done in a timely way with quality. Every FEED contract should be written so that it is enforceable as a stand-alone contract. "Off-ramps" are difficult to write well but are important for a number of contract types.

Because it is an FEED to EPC form, EPCM avoids one of the most difficult transitions for capital projects: changing contractors at the FEED-to-execution point. Although FEED is considered part of the "front end," it is actually more akin to execution engineering than it is to planning. FEED entails completing all of the engineering drawings that will be picked up and detailed in the next phase. The plot plans, the equipment layouts, the piping and instrumentation diagrams, line sizes, the electrical (single) lines, and the heat and material balances are all part of this work. The break between FEED and execution is largely artificial when considered only from the engineering perspective. When contractors are changed at the FEED-to-execution gate, for whatever reason, the new contractor needs to thoroughly review the work of the FEED contractor and almost always finds it deficient in a large number of respects. This finding seems to be completely independent of the actual quality of that FEED package! The result is lots of changes, sometimes important and sometimes cosmetic, and a slowing of the project. This transition costs the owner money and time and is thoroughly disliked by most project teams.

If the owner has not planned to change contractors after FEED, the change is very disruptive because new contractors have to be prequalified, and a tendering process has to be initiated.[10] Alternatively, a contractor is selected as a sole source,

---

[10]There should have been an exit strategy for the owner with alternative contractors already explored. That off-ramp should have been planned as a risk mitigation step, but in reality it is rarely done.

but that is not a good solution either.[11] So, the most important advantage of F-EPCM is that it avoids the FEED-to-execution transition.

There are reasons other than the avoidance of transition for owners to like EPCM. As an EPC contractual form, EPCM is a "one-stop shopping" exercise. Only one contracting decision has to be made; all the others are usually the responsibility of the EPCM, including the selection of the construction contractors. In practice, this means that owners feel like they require little or no construction expertise. Decisions such as when to start work in the field, selection of subcontractors, interface management, controls, and so forth are all considered responsibilities of the EPCM, with the owner providing guidance and consultation but not active management. The owner avoids all of the inspection challenges associated with EPC-LS. EPCM reflects the reality of today's industrial company projects organization: profound weakness in knowledge of construction and field management practices. The out-sourcing of construction management that started in Western countries in the late 1980s made contractual approaches such as EPCM inevitable in the 21st century.

The other positive of EPCM is that contractors really like the form, even more than EPC-reimbursable. Contractors generally tout the form to owners as the best contracting strategy for any and all projects. Contractors' preference for EPCM is understandable: it provides them work with essentially no risk but with a number of avenues for profit, which we will discuss a bit later. The EPCM form also relieves the contractor of having to do direct-hire of construction labor[12] and the full and complete construction management that goes with it. EPCM has significant

---

[11]I will discuss the importance of prequalification for EPCM and other contractors in Chapter 7.

[12]Direct hire of construction labor is when the EPC contractor hires individual craft laborers to execute most construction activities except so-called specialty contracts—scaffolding, heavy lift, etc.—which are generally subcontracted in all cases.

pluses for both owners and EPCM contractors. But when owners are saying "EPCM is the best way to go!" and contractors are saying "EPCM is the best way to go!" somebody ought to be asking "What's wrong with this picture?" So in keeping with the mantra of "there's no free lunch," what are the downsides of EPCM?

The Downsides of EPCM

As discussed earlier, EPCM is an expensive contractual approach for owners. At any project size, EPCM is less cost-competitive than EPC lump-sum by 5 to 10 percent, depending on project size.[13] And this is despite that, unlike EPC-LS, EPCM is transferring little or no risk to the contractor! The EPCM form is much less cost effective than the split forms—more than 13 percent on average. The EPCM form has more cost growth than EPC-LS (Pr.|t|<.006), and there is no difference in schedule slip. Therefore, the desire for predictability is not a reason for owners to prefer EPCM over EPC-LS. Cycle time[14] is about 9 percent shorter for EPCM than EPC-LS (Pr.|t|<.01) due to the long bid cycle associated with traditional EPC-LS between the completion of FEED and start of execution. There is no difference in average execution time.[15]

The biggest problem with EPCM from an owner's perspective is that cost performance degrades very rapidly with project size. Figure 4.3 provides the relationship between

---

[13]EPCM is on average (without controlling any other factor) 6.5 percent more expensive than EPC-LS. The result is very robust statistically: Pr.|t|<.005. The reader needs to be clear that 6.5 percent is a lot of money; for the average, my project in our sample, the premium is more than $30 million, and it only gets larger *as a percentage* with project size. If we control for the completeness of front-end loading, the premium paid for EPCM over EPC-LS *increases* to 9.4 percent on average. The typical EPCM is actually better prepared at FID than EPC lump-sum projects. With that said, remember that EPC-LS is often not an available alternative when EPCM is selected. But other strategies discussed later in this chapter are.

[14]Time from start of scope development through to the end of production startup.

[15]Time from FID to mechanical completion of facilities.

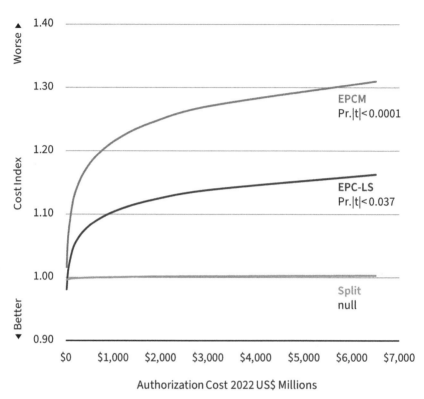

FIGURE 4.3 The scalability of cost performance varies greatly by contracting strategy.

cost effectiveness and project cost for three types of contract approaches: EPCM, EPC-LS, and the split forms. Both EPC-LS and EPCM degrade with project size, but EPCM degrades at a much faster rate. The split forms, however, show no relationship between cost effectiveness and size at all; they maintain their superior cost effectiveness as well for megaprojects as for smaller projects. Ironically, EPCM becomes *more* common as projects get larger, while split forms become *less* common.

Why EPCM Contracting Is Problematic

When I say that EPCM contracting is problematic, it is only problematic for owners. It has probably been instrumental in keeping

EPC contractors afloat financially over the past decade. But why is EPCM so problematic for owners, and what, if anything, can be done about it?

Because FEED is almost always included in the remit of the EPCM, the project's cost estimate and schedule are developed by the EPCM. It is the cost estimate that is key. When contractors who are going to execute develop the cost estimate, they are strongly incentivized to estimate high rather than 50/50. This is not a matter of evil intent; this is just a matter of common sense. As a contractor, would I rather underrun or overrun? Would I rather have more money in the engineering and construction management and construction accounts or less? Figure 4.4 provides the obvious answer to this obvious question.

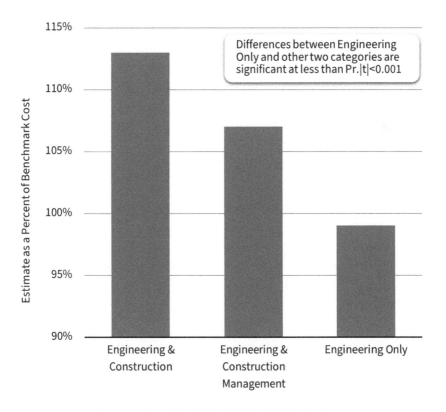

FIGURE 4.4   Contractors make higher estimates for themselves.

When contractors make the estimates for projects in which they are going to execute engineering and construction, the estimate is 13 percent higher than the expected value of the estimate or engineering and construction management, and the estimates contain 8 percent more money for the total project than cases in which the contractor is going to execute engineering only.

Why doesn't owner estimate validation remove the excess money in the contractor's estimate? When owners went through a validation process on EPC-R and EPCM contractor estimates, they removed little or none or the overestimated amounts. When the FEED contractor was going to execute engineering only, owner validation resulted in systematic improvement of the estimate (Pr.|t|<.02). What this tells us is pretty simple: when contractors have a very strong incentive to fatten up cost estimates, they will likely to do so and will do so in ways that are difficult for owner validation to find. This phenomenon is merely the principal-agent problem at work. It is also worth mentioning that the desire to plump up the estimates will occur regardless of whether additional incentive payments are employed. It is just a fact of the situation, and it erodes the cost effectiveness of EPC-R and EPCM strategies. The owner weakness that makes this process possible is the inability of most owner estimating functions to generate a bottom-up detailed material takeoff-based estimate. Because they do not know how to make such an estimate, they do not know how to find fat and errors in such estimates whether they are "open book" or not.

Owners' interests and contractors' interests do not, cannot, and never will fully align. As discussed in Chapter 3, even *owner* functions are often not fully aligned. There is another fact that really seals this issue. When owner personnel do EPCM, the projects results do not look like EPCM projects. Instead, the results look just like Re/Re or Re/LS projects, depending on how construction is contracted. A few owners maintain detailed engineering capability in-house, and those owners usually execute F-EPCM on their projects. They do not overestimate the projects.

The projects are much more cost effective than EPCM, but the work structure is otherwise identical to an EPCM. The only thing missing is the principal-agent problem.

Another disturbing aspect of EPCM from an owner's viewpoint is that the form becomes progressively more expensive with project size (Pr.|t|.004). This is a tendency more pronounced in EPCM than any other contract form.[16] Part, but only part, of the explanation is that the estimates are fatter with size. Given the incentive structures at work and the decreasing efficacy of validation as a function of size and complexity (there are more places to hide money subtly), this result is not surprising.

The big difficulty with EPCM is not the F-EP portion of the work; that is clear enough. However, the CM part frequently is not. Construction management is a general term that applies to a broad array of field activities, ranging from very high-level progress reporting to very detailed hands-on management responsibilities. The following is a short list of activities and functions that fall under the rubric of CM:

- Planning and sequencing of construction
- Ensuring timely completion systems for turnovers to ops
- Interface management (mostly between construction contractors on-site)
- Work package planning: primary and backup tasks planning and tools
- Quantity surveying
- Progress measurement and reporting
- Change management
- Review and approval of submittals to the engineer
- Taking of questions for design and tracking responses
- Safety program—planning and execution

---

[16]Although it is present for GMP contracts as well.

- QC
- Inspection and testing, such as weld tests, hydro testing, etc.
- Construction equipment leasing, maintenance shops, sometimes provision of certain equipment operators as well
- First-line gang supervision
- General foreperson
- Materials management
- Receipt of equipment and materials inspection
- Yard management
- Lift planning
- Specialty contractor management

  ○ Scaffold

  ○ Paint and insulation

  ○ Dining areas

  ○ Labor camp

This list is not exhaustive, but the point should be clear. CM can range from just a few of these at a high level to every one of these activities. How much CM is required depends very much on the strength of the general construction contractor or the disciplinary contractors who are hired to construct the facilities. When the EPCM contract is signed, generally prior to the start of FEED, none of the actual constructors have usually been identified and qualified. If they have been identified and qualified, they may turn out to be unavailable or uninterested in bidding when the time comes later in the project. The contract may list and the contractor may promise every CM service imaginable. But that doesn't govern the contractor's assumptions about what will really have to be staffed. If the EPCM underestimates the range and depth of CM that will be required, the contractor will need very good bench strength to be able to meet the unexpected challenge. This is where the type of economic entity contractors must be remembered: carrying a strong bench in a professional services organization is a recipe for bankruptcy.

If the EPCM that was selected at the beginning of FEED assumed that the level of CM required would be relatively shallow, the contractor may be woefully unprepared if the construction contractors selected are not able to carry most of their own CM. This sort of mismatch of expectations about the depth of CM that will be required is the single most intractable problem that we see in this contracting form. As projects get larger and more complex, the probability of a mismatch of expectations and reality seems to become almost a certainty. As the number of construction contractors increases on the site, the interface management challenges increase exponentially, and it always seems that at least one of a large number of constructors will turn out to be less competent than expected. The EPCM firm is often not equipped to rescue the situation.

Constructors Prime to Whom?

Another issue that comes up repeatedly in EPCM is whether the construction contractors should be prime to the owner or subcontractors of the EPCM. There are arguments to be made both ways. Some argue, quite plausibly, that the constructors should be subs to the EPCM because they will be supervised by the EPCM, not the owner. Having the constructors prime to the owner could introduce a confusion of authority and accountability. The EPCM directs subs on behalf of the owner as the owner's agent. But the owner must often have direct contact and direction authority over the subs, especially when they are working at the site of a pre-existing asset.

Both the owners and EPCM sometimes make counterarguments to the constructors being subs. The EPCMs argue that if the constructors are subcontractors to them, it could create some liability for them around construction quality and operability that they do not want. The EPCMs often are resisting that potential liability for causing delay or disruption to constructors' work, wanting theirs to be an entirely risk-free contract. The owners sometimes complain that when the constructors are sub to the EPCM, they are not allowed to interact effectively with the constructors. The EPCM structure can facilitate playing the blame-game—shifting responsibility away. When the construction contractors are prime to the owner, they have no links to the construction management entity. Any poor management by the EPCM relieves the constructors of responsibility but creates little risk for the EPCM. Any direction provided by the owner to whom the constructors are legally linked carries no risk for the EPCM and can be used to shift blame. The data do not provide us with any guidance here, which is another way of saying it doesn't make much difference. But expect it to be an issue.

Making EPCM Work Better

After reviewing the detailed histories of more than 300 EPCM projects, I see nine steps that owners can take that will systematically improve the outcomes of these projects. These steps will not eliminate the problems but at least will mitigate them.

1. As we will discuss in more detail in Chapter 7, it is important to prequalify potential F-EPCM contractors. EPCM contractors are selected without prequalification more than in any other contractual form. Be clear that this is not a recommendation to have a formal competitive bidding process for F-EPCM work; it is rather to fully review the field before you make a selection of the F-EPCM contractor. Owners learn important things during the prequalification process that may cause them to look beyond the contractor they were intending to hire sole-source.

2. Finish FEED *completely* before mobilizing design. That means completing all of the P&IDs, not just the inside battery limits portion. It means all the line sizes have been checked, the heat and material balances are fully closed, and all utility requirements are fully known and specified. The failure to complete FEED, which occurs in nearly 40 percent of EPCM projects, adds 10 percent to total installed cost (Pr.|t|<.0001) and is completely unnecessary. Because the FEED contractor will carry on into execution, it is too easy not to complete the FEED; it seems unnecessary. But without completed FEED, there is no quantities baseline for the project, maintaining control of engineering hours becomes more difficult, and work will be done out of order and therefore done more than once.

3. Validate the estimate made by your FEED-EPCM thoroughly. Challenge the bulk material quantities—it is the most common and insidious place to hide money. Benchmark the engineering hours by discipline. Carefully look at all the key ratios by material: bulks-to-equipment, engineering hours to bulks, engineering hours per piece of major equipment, labor hours to bulks, CM hours and cost to field hours, etc. If your EPCM balks at giving you complete access to the estimating information, you have selected a predatory EPCM.[17]

4. Work with the contractor at the start of FEED (or even before) to assess the construction market and the capabilities of the general contractors (GCs) and disciplinary construction contractors to understand what depth of construction management will be required for the project. Make the decision about whether a GC will be needed early and start the

---

[17]Do not forget to include access to all such information in the terms and conditions of the contract. There can be no ambiguity about the owner's right to the reimbursable cost information and the cost estimate they have paid for. If the contractor pushes back during negotiation, drop them and move to your second choice, which of course you will have maintained as an option as a matter of good practice.

prequalification process for GCs. If deep CM will be needed by your EPCM contractor, start discussing the staffing requirements during FEED, not later.

5. Again work with your assessment of the construction contractor market, and decide what construction contracting strategy will be used if a GC is not going to be employed. For EPCMs, unit rate contracts are the most cost effective—about 8 percent more cost effective on a whole project basis (Pr.|t|<.04). Lump-sums are directionally cheaper as well. Straight reimbursable and T&M contracts are the most expensive. Recall the principle that says that risks should be assigned to the party most capable of managing those risks. The construction firms doing the work are more capable of handling field productivity risks than any owner as long as the engineering and materials are available.

6. Do not attempt to do EPCM by directly contracting disciplinary subs if the disciplinary construction contractor market is so thin that many subs will be required to get the work done on any one EPCM contract. The EPCM will be overwhelmed with interface management problems. When you have a large number of contractors working side by side doing construction, it is almost certain something will go badly wrong. Go with a GC instead, preferably with a unit rate or lump-sum contract where available. Then allow the GC to manage and coordinate any disciplinary constructors as needed.

7. As discussed earlier in this chapter, when smart owners use EPC-LS strategies, they do very detailed and complete reviews of risk and risk assignments with the EPC during the negotiation process. Unfortunately, we rarely go through the same exercise with EPCM contractors. Part of the reason we do not do so is because the EPCM contract is usually negotiated before the start of FEED when project execution risks seem far in the future. Go through the same risk assignment exercise for EPCMs. Owners should not automatically

be agreeing to a zero-risk-to-the-contractor EPCM form. At a minimum there should be target hours for engineering and CM (separately) that result in a loss of overhead contributions if those hours are exceeded without owner changes.

8. If the owner chooses to be schedule-driven when using an EPCM form, be clear that there is a very sizeable penalty for being so—an average of 8.5 percent of total installed cost. The penalty for being schedule-driven is higher for EPCM than any other form except EPC-R.

9. Finally, owners have to exercise more discipline about allowing work to go to the field or fabrication yard too early. My advice would be never go to the field until after the final HAZOP is complete and changes incorporated and second model review is completed and changes incorporated. Then do a full review of procurement status. Understand exactly what is going on in the shops fabricating steel and pipe for the project. Then and only then, if everything looks sound, trigger field start. Owner project teams need to explain to the business sponsor that if the contractor attempts to go around the team to the business sponsor to suggest getting the field start sanctioned, they are doing so for their benefit, not the owner's.

EPCM is the single most popular industrial project contracting strategy in the world. Despite its many drawbacks, that is probably not going to change anytime soon. Therefore, it behooves all of us to do the things necessary to make EPCM as effective a strategy as possible.

Understanding the Split Strategies

Just as a reminder, there are four split strategies: Re/LS, Re/Re, LS/LS, and LS/Re. The last of the set is not used very often (about 2 percent of projects) and sometimes came about when the LS/

LS strategy unraveled because construction contractors would not work lump-sum. However, the LS/Re was nonetheless more cost effective (97 percent of industry average) than any of the EPC strategies. Because LS/Re is employed so rarely, we will not bother discussing it as a separate strategy.

The common feature of all split form strategies is the contractual break between engineering and procurement on the one hand and construction on the other. That break has a profound effect on the cost effectiveness of projects. For industrial companies making commodity products, the cost advantage of the split forms can over time provide a substantial boost to their return on capital employed (ROCE), which is one of the core financial measures of company success. Furthermore, as we saw in Chapter 3, the split forms can deliver on schedule-driven projects as fast as or faster than the EPC strategies. In this section, we will explore the advantages, disadvantages, and challenges of using these generally superior contract strategies.

Split Form Advantages

There are a number of advantages in using split form contracting beyond superior project performance. Perhaps most important, owners are able to maintain control of key project decisions. Most important, when a split strategy is used, owners really do control the decision about when to start construction or fabrication work. In today's industrial projects world, engineering is chronically late. That means that the planned start of construction dates are assuming more complete engineering and procurement than are actually achieved most of the time. Overly early start of construction drives labor productivity into the ground because materials availability and design will not support the intended pace of construction. That makes the decision about construction start date very important to healthy projects.

In EPC forms, the owners think they control the field-start decision, but they rarely really do. The incentive situation for an

EPC or EPCM contractor is clear enough: getting into the field benefits their cash flow. When the contractor says "We are ready to start construction," it is very difficult for the owner to say otherwise. There is a fundamental information asymmetry. In more than a few cases, we know of EPC-R and EPCM contractors who went around owner project teams who were resisting starting in the field to tell the business sponsor that the project team was "dragging its feet" and costing the project "precious time." In split forms, that pressure from the contractor is not there, although the pressure from the business sponsor may be.

In split forms, owners control the selection of construction contractors. That can be good or bad depending on the construction knowledge of the owner, but generally I believe that encouraging owners to have more and better understanding of construction is a good thing.

Split forms offer more flexibility than EPC forms. Better use can be made of whatever construction capability exists in the market. One can go with disciplinary contractors, a general contractor, or a mix of GC and subs. Usually, we can avoid the worst construction contract approaches—reimbursable and time and materials—and select lump-sum or unit rates. They have the advantage of making craft productivity the responsibility of the constructor instead of the owner. In EPC-R and EPCM forms, reimbursable or T&M is used most of the time. With their great flexibility and owner control, split forms offer a lot more opportunities to use local contractors.

Split Forms and Modularization

There is another benefit that we at IPA did not understand until looking at these data: split forms using a heavy degree of modular construction are significantly cheaper than EPC forms using modular construction. When looking at modular construction in the past, our conclusion was always that modular construction cost a bit more than stick build except in cases in which labor was abnormally expensive or not available in sufficient supply to do the job in a timely way.[18] When we look at the EPC options (LS, R, and CM), modular construction is about 4 percent *more* than industry average cost, and the result is significant even controlling for FEL (Pr.|t|<.04). But looking only at the split forms using substantial modularization, the cost index is almost 6 percent *below* industry average, even controlling for FEL, and the result is very robust statistically (Pr.|t|<.0001).

We can only conclude that intrinsically a high degree of modularization usually results in a less expensive project *for someone.* When the engineering firm contracts with the fabrication yard, it appears that more than 100 percent of the savings associated with modularization goes to the EPC. When the fabrication yard is prime to the owner, the savings go to the owner. The delta is a hefty 10 percent of total installed cost. The engineer's role should only be answering questions about their own design. Then have the setting and finishing contractor prime to the owner with your own CM, with a GC, or with a hired CM firm.

Finally, and probably the biggest advantage to the owner, the split forms avoid having an EPC set their own cost estimate. As we showed in Figure 4.4, when a firm doing EPC-R or EPCM does FEED, the cost estimate is 8 to 12 percent higher for the whole project. Most of the time, all of that money gets spent.

Disadvantages and Challenges of the Split Strategies

The largest burden of the split strategies is that the owner team and owner project organization must understand construction management. This does not imply that the owner team must do the construction management in split form projects. The owner

---

[18]We also find that modular construction had no effect on execution time regardless of any factors being controlled.

can hire a firm that will do the CM work or the owner can hire a GC who will do overall CM, execute part of the work with their own organization, and subcontract the things the GC does not want to self-perform. But the owner needs to understand CM deeply enough to orchestrate the different scenarios. It is very likely that the exact implementation of split strategies will change from project to project.

This is not a matter of having a cadre of good construction managers, although it is part of the calculus. This is a matter of understanding how construction of complex engineered facilities actually works and the things that will be necessary to generate a smooth construction process for a project. Unfortunately, a good many owners think they know construction management more deeply than they actually do. For example, we have seen too many owners who require that the constructors follow the Primavera® schedule that was laid out in front-end loading. But Primavera® does not reflect the way construction is actually done.[19] We have seen owners who dabble in some part of CM. For example, they decide they can do materials management for construction contractors because that will be more cost effective. The result is no one can find anything. We have seen procurement organizations that involved themselves repeatedly in a project for which the engineering contractor is responsible for procurement. Sometimes owners decide to do a "bit" of interface management. When the owner internally is not coherent, the owner/contractor interface cannot be either.

Owners must understand how constructors effectively monitor their progress, usually by the use of material installation

---

[19]This does not mean that the master schedule developed in FEL is not critically important for a successful complex project; it decidedly is. However, the master schedule is for the purpose of understanding whether the project schedule is feasible, for deciding whether the peak labor requirements by craft are sustainable at the site, and for laying out the systems turnovers in the proper order to commission and start up the facilities.

rates, so the owner can understand whether the constructor he is prequalifying for the project is actually competent. When using split strategies, the owner will be responsible for selecting the constructors, not the engineering firm. In many cases, the owner will be responsible for doing CM and in others selecting a competent CM or CM/GC. Unless a GC is going to be used, the owner must know how to select the support and specialty contractors as well—scaffolding, heavy lift, etc. All of this takes knowledgeable people. However, the advantages of being able to use the split contracting strategies are so great that it is well worth the investment in people.

To manage split strategy projects effectively, the owner must know how to manage the transition between engineering and engineered material procurement on the one hand and construction on the other. In split strategy projects, the engineering firm (or in-house detailed engineering organization) will be developing packages for the purposes of bidding the construction work, usually by discipline—civil, mechanical, E&I.[20] The owner must then evaluate those bids and select the constructors.

One of the issues that actually comes up in every form of contracting is how to get good construction input into the engineering design of the project and into the FEED where engineering work should be sequenced. A clever way of doing this that we have seen practiced on split forms more often than in other forms is to invite the potential constructors to comment on design and sequencing as part of the prequalification process. We have seen the same process used with fabricators in modular and offshore construction as well. The constructor/fabricators appear willing and even eager to cooperate with this process because out of sequence design and design features that will

---

[20]The word *bidding* does not necessarily imply lump-sum construction. Predominantly lump-sum construction is used on about half of split form contracting projects, with reimbursable, T&M, and unit rates making up the remainder.

create constructability challenges are among their chief complaints about engineering firms.[21]

Owners using split form contracting must also understand the constructor markets in which the project will be executed. Like politics, construction is always local. If an owner works in many places around the world, an in-house infrastructure will have to be built to maintain knowledge of local construction markets and local norms with regard to construction contracting. The upshot of all this is that owner teams need to be somewhat larger in execution for split strategies than for EPC approaches.

The greater burden that the split strategies place on owner organizations is why the paradox of more effectiveness and less use exists. Given the size of the savings involved, however, the owner would come out well ahead to hire and retain the staff needed to execute split forms well. Split strategies are becoming more popular at a rate of about 1.4 percent higher use per year since 2000 (Pr.>|t|.0001). But that doesn't mean they are popular or that all owner users of the strategy are competent to execute it. Increasing use of split forms in the future will require strengthening more owner project organizations in the area of construction management.

Differences Among Re/Re, Re/LS, and LS/LS

There are some important differences in how the various split forms work. Re/Re is the most robust of the three forms. It

---

[21]One might imagine that the integration of engineering and construction would not be a significant problem when using an EPC strategy. It is. Often the engineering and construction organizations of EPC firms are not well integrated. In most EPC firms, the engineers are in charge because the engineers make the sales. The constructors often do not have a strong position at the management tables of EPC firms and little way to force good integration.

provides very good cost and schedule performance, very little cost growth (4 percent), and less schedule slip than average (15 percent, which is a lot but still less than average). Re/Re is especially cost effective when unit rate construction contracts are used but are cost effective on average in any case. The overall performance is dependent only on completing front-end loading with good quality. When speed in execution is important, Re/Re becomes the fastest of all contracting strategies (82 percent of industry average) with no degradation of cost performance. By contrast, the Re/LS and LS/LS forms are more sensitive to site knowledge and to team continuity than Re/Re. Because it does not use lump-sum construction, there are fewer "gotcha" items.

Under schedule pressure, the Re/LS responds just as well as the Re/Re, but LS/LS does not. When schedule-driven, the LS/LS form gathers very little speed, and the cost performance degrades from .92 in the non-schedule driven case to .98. Re/Re and Re/LS show no cost degradation at all. The culprit is the poor flexibility under schedule-driven conditions of the lump-sum engineering. In case after case, we saw that the engineering firm was unwilling to accelerate because they were working lump-sum and were seeking to maximize profits. Lump-sum engineering tends to experience more slip than reimbursable engineering and not respond well to any attempt to increase speed. This should not be a surprise. Engineering tends to slip because the engineer does not have readily available the engineering disciplines needed in the right order. On a reimbursable, he can hire from the street to fill gaps. On lump-sum engineering, that is a recipe to lose money unless the fee formula is altered, which we discuss in Chapter 8.

Why So Much Reimbursable Construction?

Outside EPC-LS contracts, only about 40 percent of projects in the process industries use lump-sum contracts for construction.

Straight reimbursable (fixed-fee) and T&M together are more common despite generating inferior results. The amount of reimbursable and T&M construction goes up as projects get larger. Fewer than a third of projects more than $200 million have predominantly lump-sum construction.

Some owners tell us that the construction companies resist lump-sum construction, and some tell us they resist unit rates as well. But that is not really my experience in talking to construction firms. A friend of mine was CEO of a first-rate construction company. He was adamant that lump-sum construction was better for his firm because it kept them sharp and focused. "Reimbursable makes you sloppy." I suspect what is actually going on is the construction firms resist lump-sum with owners who don't understand construction management and with engineers that will not sequence their work to ensure that design and materials are available when needed.

When constructors work on a reimbursable or T&M basis rather than lump-sum or unit rates, the owner is taking responsibility for risk associated with craft labor productivity. That violates a basic principle of contracting: when a risk is assigned to a party who does not control the risk, the risk goes unmanaged. Owners do not have the skills needed to control labor productivity. Therefore, they need to ensure the project is set up properly in front-end loading and that the detailed engineering will support transfer of that risk to those who do.

Summary

The contracting strategies that we have reviewed in Chapters 3 and 4 are the standard approaches for industrial projects. Each strategy is appropriate in some circumstances, depending on the project, the strength of the owner, and the contractor market. Most industrial owners are able to use only one or two of the standard strategies effectively, and most often those are the EPC strategies. The reluctance of owners to employ the split strategies costs industrial owners massive amounts of money. Developing the capability needed to employ split strategies on a wide variety of projects would be a very profitable investment.

Many owners, however, are not satisfied that the standard approaches produce the best possible outcomes and look to other strategies to deliver better results. We discuss a number of those less common strategies in the next two chapters.

CHAPTER 5

The Unusual EPC Lump-Sum Strategies

As discussed in Chapter 3, the primary contracting strategies account for about 90 percent of industrial projects. But there some other strategies that have been developed to address some of the problems that bedevil the standard EPC and split forms. Most of these strategies are FEPC strategies that take single contractors all the way from the beginning of FEED (or even a bit earlier) through the end of construction (and may include startup as well). All of these unusual strategies are "continuity strategies," which is a feature that makes them attractive to owners who worry about being capable of managing transitions.

The following are the unusual EPC-LS strategies:

- Functional specification contracts (also called *duty specification* or *performance specification contracts*)
- Design competitions
- Convert to EPC lump-sum (also called convertible contracts)
- Guaranteed Maximum Price (GMP, also called *not-to-exceed* [NTE] contracts)

Of course, there are compelling reasons why these contract approaches have remained niche applications in the industrial sectors rather than mainstream. Some relate to difficulty of use and others to very specific market situations. All of these unusual strategies have some strong advocates, even in situations in which they are not appropriate. Because they will be recommended from time to time, it is important to understand what the approaches entail and their strengths and weaknesses. That is our task in this chapter.

Functional Specification Contracting (Duty Spec)

At the beginning of Chapter 2, we described the typical owner stage-gated front-end development process. After the business case for a capital project was developed, an owner team is assigned to develop the scope of the project. In duty spec contracting, the owner team does a very basic description of the need and requirements that the capital project is intended to fill. The team specifies all needed details about location of facilities and in the case of on-shore projects may, provide any site-specific soils and logistics information available, but usually not as Rely Upon.[1]

In duty spec contracting, the owner must be very clear about what the functionality requirements are for the facility, including capacities, precise product requirements and detailed specifications, range of feedstock specifications, operational performance, operating personnel and other operating costs, uptime requirements, turn-down requirements, startup and shutdown, etc. Any needed feature of a facility that is not included in the

---

[1]*Rely Upon* is a legal term of art indicating that the contractor need not verify the information for purposes of making their bid and that risk associated with any errors in the information remains with the owner. In the event that the Rely Upon information is incorrect, the contract ceiling will be adjusted to reflect the higher costs. In general, more extensive Rely Upon information lowers the risk profile of a project for the contractors bidding lump-sum.

specification document will become a potentially expensive change later. At the same time, the owner must take care that all of the hoped for bidders can deliver a facility with the specified characteristics. Specifications that can be realistically met by only one or two providers defeat the purpose of a functional specification approach by creating a noncompetitive bidding situation.

When the specification is complete, the owner issues an invitation to bid to the providers of this sort of facility in the market. As implied in the last sentence, this entire approach to industrial contracting is premised on there being a developed set of providers in the market. As a consequence, duty spec contracting is generally confined to very standard facilities, such as air separation, nitric and sulfuric acid plants, natural gas cleanup facilities where the gas composition is very common, hydrogen manufacturing units, certain petrochemical units such as ethylene, plain vanilla office buildings, and so forth. It is also commonly employed in a set of offshore oil and gas production facilities called *floating production, storage, and off-loading* (FPSO) platforms.

The bidders respond with a lump-sum price for delivering a project that fully meets the duty spec requirements in a given period of time. In their bids they provide the details of their offering and often how and why it is superior to others in the particular application at hand. Beyond the requirements of the ITB, the owner has no rights to stipulate the technology, equipment, or execution and development approach. Duty spec contracts will often include performance warranties with penalties associated with underperformance. Duty spec is the most "owner hands-off" of all contracting approaches.

Duty spec projects can be very large or quite small. In oil and gas production, the average FPSO duty spec contract is more than $1 billion. So too are ethylene plants done on duty spec. At the other end of the spectrum, many "package plants" done on a duty spec basis are less than $50 million. Duty spec projects are also more likely to be "build-operate-transfer" projects than nonduty specs. The contractor may operate such a project for a year or more to shake out any bugs before transferring the asset to the owner. And some projects are leased assets or even build-operate contracts in which the owner pays a fee for product on a unit basis and never owns and operates the asset.

Results for all of the contract types discussed in this chapter and the next will be presented in the format shown in Figure 5.1. The first three bars show the competitiveness of the contract approach in terms of capital cost effectiveness, execution schedule effectiveness, and cycle time effectiveness, along with the variation around each outcome. The fourth and fifth bars show the cost growth and schedule slip outcomes for the contract type and the variation for each. The measure for those two outcomes is on the right-hand vertical axis. We maintain the same axes throughout all in order to provide easier comparison.

As shown in Figure 5.1, the term *average* doesn't mean very much for duty spec projects—their results are all over the place. The most cost-effective duty spec projects in our database were less than 70 percent of industry average cost. One of those projects was $3.8 billion project, meaning that the owner saved a billion dollars relative to industry average. Another duty spec

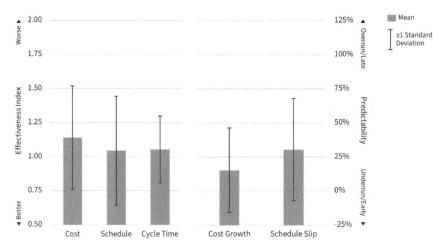

FIGURE 5.1 Functional specification project results are highly variable.

was a $2.7 billion project that cost more than double the industry average. Almost all of the lack of cost competitiveness in functional specification projects was associated with cost growth (Pr.|t|<.001), and cost growth was very strongly associated with schedule slip (Pr.|t|<.0001).

The point is that from the owner's perspective, there are very good duty spec projects, and there are horrible duty spec projects. So what determines which is which? Changes are the key problem. A duty spec contract is premised on the assumption that the market provides a complete solution for the given owner requirement. If it does not, duty spec is not an appropriate strategy for the need. Second, duty spec contracting assumes that the owner will be *satisfied* with the solution put forward by the winner of the duty spec competition as long as it fulfills the requirements in the specification document. However, one of the things we have learned over the years is that some owners are *never* satisfied with *any* solution that does not have their fingerprints all over it. I plead with such owners to not use duty spec contracting, but they don't always listen. They never end up happy.

When examining the outcomes shown in Figure 5.1, note that the duty spec projects end up at about industry average speed, but feature a 30 percent slip in execution. This tells us that when owners use duty spec contracting, they believe (or at least hope) that the project will be much faster than industry average. Sometimes the owner believes the contractor will skip FEED, but in fact they have to do the FEED. But there is some basis for believing duty specs should be faster. If a contractor is offering a technology solution they have executed many times before, that should provide much better speed than the usual development process. It often does. But if the owner changes the requirements, much of that speed is lost, which creates much of the schedule slip. And, of course, duty spec projects are as subject to unpleasant surprises in the market conditions as any other type of project.

Finally, if a duty spec project is to be a part of a larger project, which is often the case, it is important to try to shield the duty spec project from any interference from the larger effort. This is often difficult to do. The contract terms and conditions become important in such cases in determining who loses money—the owner or the contractor. If the contract does not clearly state that interference is the owner's risk, the contractor can face a sizeable loss. It is my impression that duty spec contracts end up in arbitration or court more than any other contractual form.

So, duty spec is a workable and even efficient contracting strategy if *all* of the following apply:

- The market offers a complete solution to the owner's need with at least three or more providers of solutions.
- The functional specification document has been carefully crafted to include all owner requirements.
- The owner is disciplined enough not to "dabble" with the winning contractor's solution.
- It is reasonably certain that the duty spec project can be isolated from other owner or third-party projects and activities going on around the duty spec scope.
- Finally, at the end of the project, it must be straightforward to measure and test whether the project has achieved the functionality required in the specification. Any ambiguity here opens the door to endless wrangling about whether the facilities are acceptable.

Design Competitions

Design competitions are the most elegant of all EPC-LS strategies for industrial projects. A design competition has the owner develop the scope in FEL-2 in the normal fashion, but then instead of selecting a contractor to execute FEED and prepare an ITB for bidding the project competitively, the owner hires two or

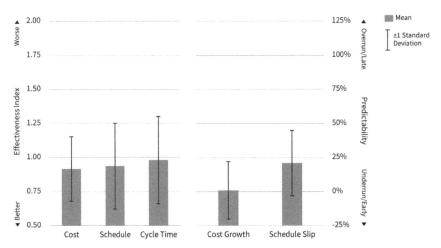

FIGURE 5.2   Design competitions produce excellent projects.

more contractors to develop FEED that will result in competing EPC-LS bids by those contractors. The winning FEED contractor will then execute the EPC-LS.[2] We have only 24 true design competitions in our sample, but their results are so uniform that statistical significance of the results in not in question. Like functional specification, design competitions are often used for large projects. The largest in our dataset is in excess of $10 billion.

Figure 5.2 shows the results of the design competitions. The projects were highly cost effective.[3] Only 3 of the 24 projects cost more than industry average, and only 1 of the 24 projects cost more than 20 percent above the industry average. They average no cost growth, and most projects underran by a few percent— just part of owner's contingency not used. They were execution schedule effective and cycle time effective. Their only flaw as a

---

[2]Depending on the procurement rules in effect, the winner can be selected on the basis of low bid or best value. It is important, however, to detail the selection criteria in the terms and conditions at the start of the contest to ensure fairness and in some cases compliance with law.

[3]The capital costs of the design competitions include 100 percent of the money paid to all of the contractors for their FEED work. There are no costs excluded in the calculation of the cost effectiveness index for these projects.

group is that they average a 20 percent slip in execution schedule, about 3 percent more than the overall average.

To progress a design competition, the owner needs to prequalify the EPC contractors that have the capability to execute his project. Rather than the standard prequalification routine, the owner usually enters into direct discussion with the contractor about whether they are willing to enter the design competition and the rules that will apply. One of the important rules is that the contractors must be willing to sign a contract that will bind the contractor to the terms and conditions for both FEED and execution and startup if the project is turnkey. After the competing FEED contractors have been selected, the owner provides a separate fully staffed owner team to each FEED competitor. There is supposed to be full separation of the teams from each other—the term *Chinese* wall is often used. This is so that any ideas or technology that a FEED competitor considers proprietary will be protected.[4]

The provision of separate owner teams is a necessity for design competitions and sometimes induces the owner to have only two competitors. As shown in Figure 5.3, more than two competitors is the rule, and sometimes as many as five have been used.

There are several important advantages to design competitions. First, they eliminate one of the worst features of EPC-LS projects—the long bidding cycle between the end of FEED and the start of execution. In FEED competitions, the winner starts execution immediately; there is not even a negotiation of the contractual provisions needed because they have all been agreed to when the original contract was signed.

Second, design competitions usually meet the legal requirements in those countries where competitive bidding is required for contracting. In those cases, at least three FEED competitors

---

[4]It does sometimes appear that those Chinese walls are more akin to "Japanese walls"—that is, not as thick as advertised.

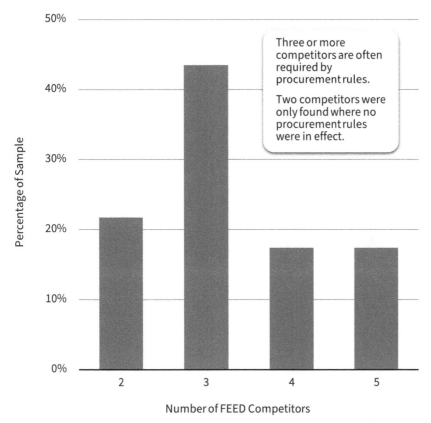

FIGURE 5.3   Most design competitions include three or more competitors.

are required and occasionally more. As shown in Figure 5.4, having more competitors is associated with better cost and execution schedule performance even though it means footing the bill for more FEEDs. Recall that the FEED costs for all competitors are included in the capital costs in our analysis.

Third, in almost all cases, design competitions result in very complete FEEDs, which is one of the keys to project effectiveness. And there is no two- to three-month FEED review period at the start of execution. The period the owner needs to review and compare FEED packages is minimal as the owner project team has been working closely with each contractor as the FEED work progressed. This ensures that the bids will follow a uniform

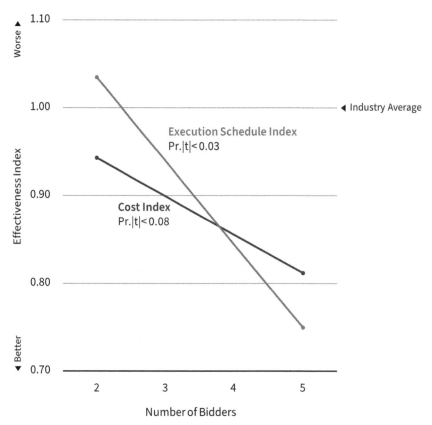

FIGURE 5.4   More players improve design competition results.

format making bid tabulation easy. Finally, there is no possibility of the execution contractor having any basis for change orders or claims based on the inadequacy of the FEED work.

There were two bad projects in the set of design competitions, and both projects illustrate some of the things that can go wrong. The first was a project of about $400 million. The owner employed only two FEED competitors but with the stipulation that the loser would be reimbursed for only $1.5 million of his costs while the winner would be fully reimbursed.[5] For reasons unexplained (and perhaps inexplicable), this was thought to be

---

[5]Typical FEED costs for a $400 million process facility would be between $8 million and $12 million. The amount provided could not possibly cover costs.

an incentive. But the project was schedule driven by the owner who cut the FEED competition short and told the competitors to produce a bid, which they did. The project was awarded to the lower bidder, but the fact that the FEED work was not complete meant that the contractor had justifiable change orders and claims. The project ended up very late with a great deal of cost growth and was about 16 percent more expensive than industry average.

The other failed project was far worse. Unlike the previous bad project, this one was a megaproject. It is also the one project with very poor cost results among the design competitions. Again, the owner decided to go with only two FEED competitors. Toward the end of FEED, one of the competitors withdrew from the competition, citing too much other work. The remaining competitor was now sole source and declined to continue on an EPC-LS basis, demanding and getting an EPC reimbursable instead. The owner decided they were better off going reimbursable because putting the project out for bid would cost them at least 18 months and they would have to depend on their remaining contractor to prepare the ITB. The project proceeded to overrun by nearly 50 percent and ended up 80 percent over industry average cost. It was a debacle for the owner but a huge windfall for the contractor.

What are the lessons? For both projects, go with three or more competitors, not two. For the first project, however, FEED competitions are not suitable for schedule-driven projects! The whole purpose of a design competition is to get a rock-solid EPC-LS bid based on a rock-solid FEED. Cutting FEED short undermines the entire rationale. I almost think the lesson learned for the project is the old lesson "Don't be stupid anymore!" For the second project, the owner did experience some bad luck. But failing to take the time needed to develop a third and possibly a fourth competitor was very short-sighted. Ironically, one of the potential competitors they excluded "because they don't do FEED" was the winning competitor in a FEED competition two years later for a similar scope and performed very well. Alas, it was for a different owner.

Should the owner pay 100 percent of the losers' costs? Some owners try to run design competitions without fully paying the losers. There is no reason to believe that paying only the winner's full cost acts as an effective incentive. More importantly, when the contractors are spending out of pocket, they are much more likely to skimp rather than do the work thoroughly. We see this problem repeatedly in public-sector infrastructure projects in which competing contractors are given a "stipend" that is far less than the needed cost to complete the equivalent of FEED. The slight added cost of fully paying for the work (up to a ceiling, obviously) seems like an excellent investment. Remember the principle: owners are from Mars; contractors are from Venus. Owners are heavily capitalized; contractors are not.

If design competitions are so effective, why are they so uncommon? Two reasons have been offered when we ask that question—one a pretty solid reason and the other moronic. The solid reason is the owner just does not have the needed personnel to field three FEED teams for a single project. Owner organizations are often too lean to staff the projects in their portfolio even once, much less more than once. For the 9 to 18 months of FEED, design competitions do consume a lot of owner talent. That puts design competitions out of reach for many owners except during down cycles.

The moronic objection we hear much more often than one would hope is when the business sponsor rejects the idea of a design competition saying "I'm not paying those [expletive] contractors more than one time to do FEED. Do you take me for an idiot?" It's probably best to bite your tongue.

Design competitions are the most underemployed of contract strategies. Just like the split strategies, they do not degrade as projects get larger. Unlike the split strategies, they do not require the owner to deeply understand construction management. And unlike traditional EPC-LS, they have good cycle time performance while providing excellent cost, schedule, and quality results.

Convert to EPC Lump-Sum (Convertibles)

Convert to EPC lump-sum is a form of FEPC contract that starts as a reimbursable contract in FEED and contains the option contractually to convert at one or more points to EPC-LS. Generally, when an owner selects a convertible form, it is with the expectation that conversion will occur at the designated point. The most common expected conversion point is after "second model review" when final HAZOP[6] has been completed and any changes from the HAZOP are incorporated into the design. This is at about 60 to 70 percent design complete. At that point in the development of a project there should be essentially no further change. It is, therefore, a good point at which to ask the contractor to provide a lump-sum amount to complete the project. In almost all cases, the contractor's estimate is to be "open book."[7] The convertible contract could have the conversion to lump-sum occur at other points as well. We have examples of intended conversion at the end of FEED and intended conversion at the end of detailed engineering.

This convertible strategy should not be confused with the practice of bidding construction packages on unit rates and then converting those bids to lump-sum when the quantities to be installed are fully defined after the given area of engineering is

---

[6]HAZOP is a methodology to review all facets of process design to ensure that it will perform safely under all operating conditions including startup, shutdown, and emergency upsets. HAZOP analyses should be first done late in FEED as soon as the P&IDs are complete and done in final form at about 60 percent design complete. HAZOP analyses frequently find needed changes to design that are not otherwise apparent.

[7]In our experience, the "open book" provision, which means that the contractor's estimate calculations are supposed to be fully transparent, has no effect on the course of convertible contracts. It does not appear to constrain contractors' ability to set the estimate as they want.

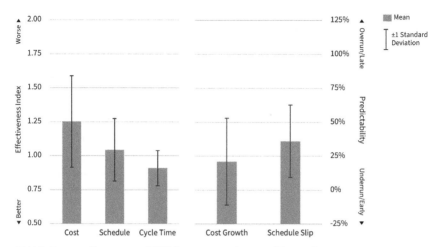

FIGURE 5.5 Convert to EPC lump-sum is a problematic strategy.

complete. The construction contractor knows that conversion to lump-sum is possible or certain and that it will be done by formula. The bidding of unit rates to convert to lump-sum construction is done to reduce the bid-to-award time and mitigate any delay.

Figure 5.5 shows the results of convertible contracts in our data and reflects our general experience with convertibles as well. Convertibles tend to produce very expensive projects. They also suffer a good deal of cost growth, which tends to occur early in a project if the conversion ultimately happens and later if it does not. The convertible projects tend to have good cycle time performance, which is generated from abnormally fast front-end loading.

Convertibles display more execution schedule slip than any other form at over 36 percent. Much of the slip is generated by grossly unrealistic execution schedules. The schedule forecast at FID was about 80 percent of industry average, but ironically the convertibles were not made up of schedule-driven projects; they are about average in that regard with only about a third being schedule-driven. Very poor front-end loading facilitated the optimism in the schedules.[8] Convertibles were less likely than other contract approaches to complete FEED (Pr.|t|<.03). Poor FEL also generates part (but only part) of the cost growth.

Key Problems in Convertible Contracting

The principal-agent problem comes to the forefront when we think about convertible contracts. The principal-agent problem is the reality that the interests of owners and the interests of contractors are never, I mean *never*, perfectly aligned. Convertibles are an FEPC contracting model. The contractor who will execute the project executes FEED and with it the estimate and schedule for execution. Control of the FID estimates and schedules is no different than the situation in EPC-R and EPCM contracting approaches.

The big issue with convertibles is that the contractor always in fact controls the conversion decision. The contract provisions say that the owner controls the decision. The contractor, who has been with the project from the end of scope development, understands the owner's "pain point" for conversion. Above a certain amount, the owner will consider the conversion amount too high. But in most cases the owner is not in a position to either control the field execution as a reimbursable or exercise its "off-ramp" to switch to a different contractor. The result is that the project proceeds to convert to lump-sum at a high cost point or

---

[8]Paradoxically, poor project preparation routinely accompanies unrealistic optimism. The poor preparation should make those involved pessimistic about the project's chances of achieving good outcomes. But it is the nature of projects that what you don't know about a project is free and takes no time. There is nothing like a detailed carefully crafted critical path analysis to blow up the expectation that a particular project can be done in a fraction of industry-average time.

continues on as a reimbursable with poor controls. Either result is poor for the owner.

Exercising the "off-ramp" option is really difficult. If conversion was supposed to occur at second model review, but the owner wants to switch to different contractors for construction, the contract normally requires that the original contractor complete engineering and procurement of engineered materials. That means the contract must have fully defined all of the engineering and procurement deliverables to a very complete degree, and the owner has devised a mechanism to encourage or require that the contractor complete the engineering and procurement work in a timely fashion. That would require, for example, target hours for engineering and procurement after which contributions to overheads would be withdrawn plus provisions such as forfeiture of a letter of credit for abandoning the project.

In our experience, owners rarely have written the convertible contracts well enough for the off-ramp to be taken gracefully. The owner is often in the unenviable position of having to select the least bad of a set of bad options. Devising an effective off-ramp at the end of FEED would be relatively easy but rarely would the owner want to exercise at that point. Any later exit is very problematic, including at the end of detailed engineering because work in the field should have already begun in earnest. That would then require an awkward field construction hand-over.

Owners entertain the possibility of using convertible contracting because it appears to offer the best of all worlds—complete contractor continuity for the project plus an EPC lump-sum. It appears very plausible but on close inspection rarely works out the way the owner expects. All this is especially painful because convertible contracting is most often employed on difficult large projects, which are already prone to failure. Often the owner had tried to secure contractor interest in an EPC-LS competition, found no takers, and went to a convertible as a backup strategy. It should not be considered a viable fallback strategy. Convert to

EPC-LS is the only contracting strategy that I would never recommend to an owner under any circumstances. They are just too difficult to control.

Guaranteed Maximum Price (GMP)

A GMP is an FEPC form with a ceiling on cost excluding cost generated by owner changes or contract-specified additional items. It is an (F)EPC reimbursable on the downside of the agreed price and an EPC-LS on the high-side of the strike price. Outside of payment scheme, GMPs usually carry the terms and conditions associated with reimbursable contracts, rather than EPC-LS. For example, liquidated damages for delays are not used, and the liability framework is like a reimbursable.

GMP is an uncommon industrial project strategy; we have only 32 in our dataset. Three quarters of those projects come from pharmaceuticals or consumer products. The contract form is only common in those sectors. The GMP projects in our dataset are the smallest with the median cost of only $50 million. No megaprojects employed the form. Most of the GMP projects were relatively simple projects.

The immediate question that one normally gets about GMP is why would a sane contractor accept a contract with only downside risk? The simple answer is they wouldn't on any project they deem significantly risky from a cost perspective. The outcomes of GMPs in Figure 5.6 support this view.

The GMPs were slightly expensive with an average cost index at 1.07, and they were unusually predictable in cost. The average project had no cost growth or underrun with a modest 10 percent standard deviation. When the projects did overrun, it was mostly for things that would be added to the cost ceiling, such as owner changes. Owners must remember that the GMP cost ceiling gets raised for every owner change made after the "maximum price" is set. There were no reports of contractors losing money on

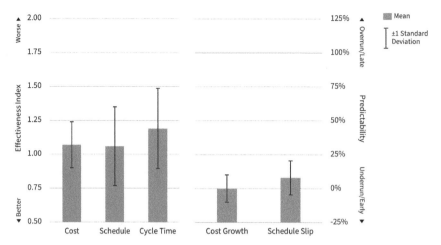

FIGURE 5.6 GMP is cost predictable.

GMPs, which is very different from EPC-LS. The projects were also efficient users of time, with reasonable schedule competitiveness and relatively little schedule slip.

There is an aspect to our set of GMPs, however, that is a bit misleading. Most of the projects were done by contractors that had a very close long-term relationship with the owner. In addition, this is an FEPC form, which is to say that the contractor developed the cost estimate. Like most other FEPC forms, the estimates were somewhat generous, and the contractor was quite confident that the project could be done for the amount in the GMP or they lobbied for a different contract type. In other words, there is a substantial amount of self-selection going on in this form. Because the GMP projects were often repetitive, the projects (and the contractual relationship) likely benefit from some degree of learning curve.

Because a GMP is an FEPC form, there is at least opportunity for the contractor to take advantage of the situation, so why is the principal-agent problem not costing the owner more money? First, remember that the GMP projects are small by industrial standards. Smaller projects are more transparent to the owner and therefore less subject to the principal-agent problem. The second important reason is because of the long-term owner/contractor relationships. When an owner and a contractor work together on projects over a number of projects, a "normal" relationship between a supplier and a buyer of professional services can take hold. By a normal relationship, I mean a relationship in which the contracts are self-enforcing. Neither owner nor contractor seek to take advantage because the relationship is working for both parties, and the only way for it to keep working is for neither to take unfair advantage. That is the way things are supposed to work. Engineering and construction service relationships are the exception in the world of professional services generally. Engineering and construction services contracts are often not mutually self-enforcing because the provider (the contractor) feels that every assignment is a "one-off" engagement and that the quality of work on this project will have only the slightest effect on whether the next assignment is won. This situation is the norm on large projects in particular.

The tendency for large project contracting to be one-off and therefore not a self-enforcing relationship has not always been the case in industrial projects. Thirty years ago when owners had much stronger in-house project organizations, those organizations kept careful track of the performance of the various contractors with whom they worked. Every engagement was carefully rated, and those ratings played a key role in the selection for the next project. As owner project organizations weakened and other functions, such as procurement, encroached on contractor selection decisions, the relationships between owner and contractor became progressively transactional. The transactional nature of industrial contracting substantially exacerbates the principal-agent problem by removing from the contractor the single most important incentive to do the best possible work and not exploit the situation: the desire for more work.

Summary

The unusual EPC lump-sum contracting options run the full gamut in terms of outcomes, from very good in the case of design competitions to distressingly awful in the case of convert to lump-sum. How they turn out is largely governed by the way the principal-agent problem plays out for the different strategies. Among the unusual EPC-LS strategies, the only one that does not suffer from the one-off transaction problem is GMP. It is important to remember, however, that GMP, when not employed in the context of an ongoing owner/contractor relationship, will also be subject to the principal-agent problem, especially for large projects.

I believe that most owner project organization managers are acutely aware of the non-self-enforcing nature of most contract forms and have tried various alternative approaches to mitigating the problem, but with only limited success. The use of incentives in contracts is one example, which we will discuss in Chapter 8. Another is the use of "collaborative contracting" approaches such as integrated project delivery/alliancing, long-term partnering, and what we dub "repeat supply chain." We discuss those in the next chapter.

CHAPTER 6

Collaborative and Relational Contracting Strategies

I define *collaborative contracting* as attempts to foster better working relationships between parties through the terms and conditions of the contract itself. Not included in this contracting strategy is the use of conventional incentive clauses. I define *relational contracting* as attempts by owners and contractors to establish long-term working relationships without changing the contract terms and conditions—a conventional contracting form is employed.

There are two types of collaborative contracting: alliancing/ integrated project delivery (IPD) and partnering alliances. One type of relational contracting is discussed that we call *repeat supply chain*. These three types of contracting strategies are associated with very different project outcomes.

IPD/Alliancing: In Search of Collaboration Through Contracting

Projects are joint products of owners and contractors. Collaboration—which means "to work together"—is important to project success. Collaboration at the working level is essential. Collaboration all the way up to the owner and contractor top managements is desirable. Some contracting approaches, in particular integrated project delivery/alliancing and partnering alliances, were developed with the goal of maximizing the potential for collaboration.

Integrated project delivery, which is usually called *alliancing* in the petroleum sector, is aimed at aligning the objectives of owner, contractors, licensors, and even major vendors by creating an incentive pool that will be shared if the project achieves designated targets.[1] Sometimes, failure to meet those targets may create a "pain-share" pool, in which overruns are distributed. Strictly speaking, IPD is an incentivized (usually) EPC (usually) reimbursable strategy. IPD seeks to go much further than the typical incentivized reimbursable to generate teamwork and align objectives with all players.

According to Phillip Barutha, who was the lead researcher for the Construction Industry Institute team on IPD, there are "six cardinal pillars" of IPD that are essential to the contract form.

- The integration of project participants early on, including those who do not normally join a project until halfway through the project cycle or later, e.g., constructors, fabricators, module, or facility transporters (in the case of modular on-shore or offshore platforms), and installers
- Risk and reward sharing among all the members of the alliance, including the owner
- Collaborative, if not consensus, decision-making
- Jointly developed and validated targets

---

[1] In this discussion, I am only referring to the use of IPD in a "one-off" project situation. When collaborative strategies are used with contractors on a long-term, multi-project basis, those are considered "partnering alliance" situations, not IPD.

- Liability waivers amongst the alliance members
- Multiparty agreements[2]

These key characteristics of IPD as a contract strategy are interesting in that a number of them conflict directly with the central elements of other contracting approaches. We will discuss these points after reviewing the performance of the strategy. We consider the multiparty incentive pooling arrangement as an essential feature of this contracting approach. We would not classify a project as IPD without it.

IPD has become somewhat popular in some regions, such as Australia, for publicly owned infrastructure project delivery. IPD has been tried from time to time in petroleum development projects in the U.K. North Sea and very occasionally for refining and chemicals projects in the United States and elsewhere. It has repeatedly been touted as the contracting form of the future, especially in the United Kingdom, but has never taken hold in industrial projects.[3]

There is a mistaken belief that IPD/alliancing has not been tested for industrial projects[4] and is therefore something new. In fact, the approach has been tried on many industrial projects starting at least as long ago as 1994 with BP's Andrew Project. IPA has evaluated more than major 30 industrial projects using IPD/ alliancing as the contracting methodology. Petroleum production, refining, petrochemicals, minerals processing, and industrial infrastructure projects are included in our IPD/alliancing set. The projects tend to be large with a median cost of more than

[2]Philip James Barutha, *Integrated Project Delivery for Industrial Projects*, Dissertation, Iowa State University, Department of Civil Engineering, 2018. A very similar set of criteria were developed much earlier by the European Construction Institute study of Alliancing published in 2000. See Bob Scott, et al., *Partnering in Europe,* Thomas Telford Publishing, London, 2000.
[3]B. Scott, op. cit. 2000.
[4]See "Integrated Project Delivery for Industrial Projects," Construction Industry Institute Research Team 341, Final Report 341, July 2019.

$1 billion. The smallest project in this set is more than $250 million. All of the IPD projects we examined had multiparty agreements in place, the element that is most often missing from the "pillars" cited previously.

When looking at the history of IPD/alliancing since it was introduced nearly 30 years ago, it has caught on in some project sectors, but not in industrial projects where economic profit is the ultimate goal. IPD/alliancing has generally been used much more often in sectors and for projects in which cost-competitiveness is not paramount, such as hospital design and construction in the United States. It has never caught on in industrial sectors as a mainstream contracting approach and I strongly suspect it never will. We have only one company in our database that has used IPD/alliancing more than twice; the modal number of uses is one. The basic reason is quite straightforward: IPD/alliancing has very few true "successes" when capital cost *competitiveness* is an important measure of success.

As shown in Figure 6.1, IPD/alliancing had the poorest outcomes of all contracting strategies in IPA's databases, even worse than convert to EPC-LS. Of particular note is their lack of cost competitiveness with the average project at 126 percent of

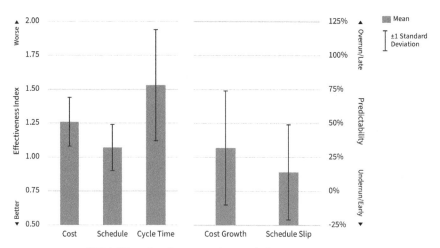

FIGURE 6.1 IPD/alliancing is expensive and slow.

industry average. Cost growth was highly variable but averaged over 30 percent real.[5] A number of projects underran their FID budgets (while usually being expensive), and a number were cost blow-outs.

Conceptually, IPD/alliancing makes sense. One of the biggest problems in project execution is the management of the interfaces between the many organizations involved. If only all organizations could be motivated via the incentive pool and good communication to cooperate more fully, many of the pain points and much of the friction might be avoided.

When IPD/alliancing is chosen, it is often accompanied by a great deal of owner effort to integrate with the contractors and suppliers. "One team, one voice, one outcome, one shared destiny" are typical of the slogans and sentiments that accompany the form. Team-building sessions and the like are quite common. The use of the contracting form is often the subject of publicity around the project as well, especially if it is a large and prominent project. IPD requires a good deal of owner work in its implementation.

When owners used IPD/alliancing, they selected the strategy early in front-end loading and formed the pool of contractors no later than FEED (FEL 3). The owners and contractors were very aware that they were trying something different, which might have led to a "Hawthorne effect" but judging from the results clearly did not.[6] The owners put more thought and work into the contracting strategy for these projects than any other strategy I have seen. The owner personnel were often personally invested in making the strategy successful. This sometimes resulted in

---

[5]The term *real* is used because the effects of any escalation and foreign currency changes have been removed.

[6]The Hawthorne effect derives from a series of industrial "scientific management" experiments conducted by Elton Mayo and Associates at the Hawthorne, New York, facility of the General Electric Company in the early 20th century. Because the company personnel involved in the experiments knew that they were being watched and measured, their performance was far better than expected.

very intense denial when the failures of the projects were documented. There was even one project that was a complete disappointment including a large overrun, significant schedule slip, and very poor plant operability in which the owner PM and contractor leads wrote an effusive trade magazine article praising the contracting strategy used on the project while omitting the project results.[7]

Case Studies of One-Off IPD/Alliances

To better understand the dynamics of integrated project delivery in industrial projects, I want to offer two case studies that are quite typical of two groups of IPD/alliancing projects: the first represents what was considered a successful application of the strategy, while the second represents what can only be described as very disappointing. Almost all IPD/alliancing projects in our dataset are represented in one of these two cases. I am disguising the projects as needed to protect confidentiality as well as the innocent and the guilty.

A Successful IPD/Alliance

This was an off-shore petroleum development project in European waters. It was to increase production at an existing asset by tapping into some adjacent reserves that could not be reached from the original project. The project cost was just over $500 million, which included drilling, making it a modest-sized project by offshore standards. The project incorporated no new technology, and the scopes were quite standard and familiar to all involved. As is typical of an offshore project, there were lots of

---

[7]One common characteristic of IPD/alliances is that the final alliance contracts were often significantly delayed.

players involved—several contractors, heavy lift company, major suppliers, and a field service firm. Eight companies in all signed the alliance agreement. Lots of players, of course, means lots of interfaces to manage.

The idea for forming an alliance to implement the project came from "lots of calls from contractors" to the business sponsor at the operating company encouraging an IPD form. The host government was also actively encouraging the strategy as well as a way of supporting EPC contractors. The contracting strategy was embraced by most (not all) of the project team but viewed with some suspicion by the nonoperating partners. As is usually the case, the operating partner's views prevailed.

The alliance agreement detailed a complex incentive structure that included a base fee as negotiated in individual contracts between the owner and contractor plus a variety of performance fees and pots of contingency money, some of which would be entirely kept by the contractor if not expended and some of which would add to the alliance incentive account to be shared among the members. There were provisions for "pain-sharing," but in most instances when pain would result, the owner stepped in with its contingency funds to bail out those situations. The incentive fees were in aggregate considerably larger than the base fees contained in the individual contracts.

Project Drivers

The project practices were generally as good as or better than the industry average. The objectives were clearly and fully defined; the team included all the needed disciplines, including operations and maintenance; roles and responsibilities were fully defined; and an active risk management program was in place. The front-end loading was industry average. The drivers, taken as a whole, would lead us to expect a better-than-average project with fairly good cost and schedule performance. The FEL could and should have been better, but it was at least industry average.

The alliance members were encouraged (and incentivized) to bring cost-savings ideas to the fore and did so, but the savings suggested were modest, which is not surprising considering the very conventional nature of the project.

Execution proceeded smoothly, especially considering that a significant number of major changes were required, in fact more than double the industry average.[8] The alliance mostly operated as intended, but the lead owner operator was surprised at the amount of active intervention it had to provide, especially with regard to cost controls.

Project Results

Construction safety was very poor. Both DART and recordable injuries were double industry average. Interestingly, the safety provisions of the alliance contract were written in a way to make it extremely unlikely that the contractors would suffer any loss of incentive fees due to safety problems. Only a fatality or a single catastrophic event would cause any loss. Merely being double the industry average for injuries caused no loss of incentive.[9]

Costs underran by 12 percent, while **cost competitiveness** was very poor at 30 percent over industry average. That means that the starting authorization (FID) estimate was a whopping 40+ percent over a competitive number! This is the story of "successful" IPD projects: generous estimates, underruns, and poor competitiveness.

The **schedule** slipped by about seven months amounting to a 15 percent slip in the execution schedule. Like cost, the schedule

---

[8]We define a major change as any change (design or scope) that changes the expected total costs by more than one-half of 1 percent or the schedule by more than one month. In this case, any change of more than $3.5 million would qualify as a major change.

[9]This is unfortunately rather common in incentivized contracts. As we will discuss in Chapter 7, safety gets a great deal of play in that process and then is often forgotten when it comes to actual selection of contractors.

was not aggressive at the start with a planned schedule competitiveness index of 1.10. Therefore, the project eroded some business value due to schedule but much less than the effect of the overspend. **Startup** experienced a few hiccups but nothing out of the ordinary.

So, was this a successful project? It would seem that success, like beauty, is often in the eye of the beholder. The team and the business sponsor considered the project a brilliant success and attributed that success to the alliance. I strongly suspect that some of the contractors (not all) did as well. The contractor who arguably performed worst by a considerable margin scored a profit in excess of 15 percent of their costs. The contractor who arguably performed best took home less than 1 percent of the base cost and probably lost money overall. This underscores the difficulty of devising an incentive payment scheme ex ante that will faithfully represent performance ex post. In this case, the relationships among alliance partners remained functional throughout the project. However, that was surely facilitated by the generous budget for the project.

An Unsuccessful Alliance

The second case is a $300 million commodity chemicals project using an innovative technology route for a standard product. The alliance was formed in front-end loading and included the technology developer and two engineering contractors, the constructor, and the owner. The constructor was able to make input into the constructability of the design and design and procurement sequencing. A pooled gain/pain-share incentive was established for the alliance members.

The primary impetus for the alliance arrangement was the hope that it would facilitate communication and cooperation, especially between the technology developer and the engineering contractors. In particular, it was expected that the licensor and engineering contractors would work seamlessly and that the constructor's input would mitigate the effects of late engineering input should that occur. The owner was experienced with IPD, and the alliance had good top management support.

Drivers

The drivers were very strong for this project: a fully integrated and fully staffed owner team and best practical front-end loading. However, unlike our prior case study, the targets for this project were tight. Cost was set at 98 percent of industry average, and schedule was 96 percent. Planned operability was very high at 100 percent of nameplate in the first year. The gain/pain share was aimed at both cost and schedule, but schedule was the key driver with $75,000 *per day* gainshare available for earlier than planned mechanical completion.

Execution

The engineering was a nightmare. The technology developer and engineering firms fought constantly. Their systems were not compatible, and their attitudes were not either. They fought over roles and ownership of improvements. The alliance contract provided no practical conflict resolution. Engineering was quite late, which extended procurement and resulted in poor labor productivity for the constructor in the field. The constructor was in a zero-profit situation before even starting his work.

Project Outcomes

Cost grew by 10 percent, which was really pretty good, all things considered, but this wiped out all cost-related incentives. Schedule, however, slipped 17 percent. The project was from a capital cost and schedule perspective not too bad, but no incentives were paid, and the contractors made little or no money, depending on whether they had hidden profit in their multiplier. The real problem was startup and operability. The plant produced only about 30 percent of nameplate in the first six months and then finally came to steady-state at about 65 percent of nameplate in the second year. The poor operability was clearly a product of the poor working relationships among the technology developer and engineers and wiped out all business value for the venture. This was a negative returns project.

Why did this project fail? It failed because the owner expected the contractual form to induce the contractors to do what the contractors really did not want to do: trust each other and cooperate and freely share information. They had fundamentally misaligned objectives, and the incentives in the contract did not change that. More importantly, the alliance form did not provide the sort of clearly delineated roles and responsibilities that would have assisted in conflict resolution. Instead, shared risks became nobody's risk. The constructor, of course, being last in line bore the brunt.

The Meaning of "Success" in IPD

A single handful of IPD/alliancing projects in our database were considered successes by the owners. Those projects look remarkably similar. The projects either underran or came in close to their FID budgets while being uncompetitive in cost by 20 to 30 percent. Their schedule results varied, but the cost underruns overrode any disappointments associated with schedule. The tendency to conflate cost underruns with success in projects, which we discussed in Chapter 3, is a near-universal phenomenon.

In sectors where cost-competitiveness is rarely measured, a cost-ineffective contracting strategy can thrive if it is routinely associated with not overrunning the budget. When projects go badly, it is quite possible that everybody involved loses money—owner and contractor alike—regardless of the compensation scheme. But when a project goes smoothly, underruns its budget, but is very expensive, somebody got rich, and it isn't the owner.

Collaborative contracting is often premised on everything going well. It envisions projects without significant surprises and without substantial conflict. Perhaps the hope is that the contracting form can alter the project reality.

There are several things wrong with this premise. First, contracting is always a second-order driver of outcomes at best. Project realities are unaltered by contracting form except in cases where contracting makes a project worse. Contracts have little ability to alter poor fundamentals. This is not pessimistic thinking. This is just reality.

Second, collaborative contracting tends to submerge conflict under a haze of good feeling. But it is still there. Contractor management does not tell their project team "Oh, don't worry about us making a profit on this one." So rather than clearly marking, understanding, and *managing* the principal-agent fault lines, potential conflicts are not seen until they have erupted and caused damage to the project. For example, in one large chemical project using IPD/alliancing, despite lots of team building, alliance sessions, and discussions, it did not emerge until FID that one joint venture partner in the project would not approve any project with any form of reimbursable construction. The constructor had already been brought on to the project and signed a contract on a reimbursable compensation basis. The project was delayed three months by the need to renegotiate the contract to lump-sum for construction. We can all agree that conflict is bad for projects, but unseen, and therefore unmanageable, conflict is much worse.

Third, IPD seems premised on the notion that there is an enormous amount of money to be saved via better collaboration among all players. Good collaboration, however achieved, will certainly save some time and money, but it cannot possibly create a breakthrough in construction productivity. Only massive substitution of capital for labor can do that, and collaboration doesn't touch that issue.

Fourth, one-off collaborative contracting approaches always suffer from a lack of time. When I have asked contractor and owner engagement leaders for partnering alliance relationships (discussed later in the chapter) how long it takes for the organizations to understand each other, no one has ever said less than two years, and most have said three. Yet with one-off IPD we expect a number of organizations to learn how to work smoothly with each other in a matter of weeks or a couple of months, not years. Workable levels of collaboration between owners and contractors can develop quickly if the conditions are there. But deep collaboration takes a good deal of time to develop. Because they are multiproject and multiyear arrangements, partnering alliances and repeat supply chain strategies discussed later in this chapter do not suffer from this time constraint defect.

Finally, the most mistaken aspect of one-off IPD/alliancing is the belief that collaboration requires contractual help. Unless the organizations have worked to create barriers, most owner and contractor personnel expect to work collaboratively to complete a project. There are important prerequisites—clear objectives, clear delineation of roles and responsibilities, competence, and mutual respect. Those things are both necessary and sufficient for a collaborative work environment to develop. Things beyond those conditions are window dressing or distractions.

The Six Pillars in Context of Results

Now let us return to the six "pillars" introduced at the start of this chapter and discuss each in light of the results of industrial IPD. The first pillar is the integration of all key project players early on. This is a compelling goal: managing the early involvement of the contractors and important service providers who start their work late in the project cycle. The most prominent of these are the constructors. For the typical process facility, more than 60 percent of the cycle time has expired before a constructor starts work. If brought into the project shortly before their work is to start, none of their requirements and preferences have been heard. None of their ideas for how to improve construction have been incorporated into the engineering and procurement efforts for the project.

One rationale for the EPC forms of contracting is that the constructors are embedded in the principal contractor and therefore will be fully represented in the front end. It is remarkable, however, how often that does not happen in EPC-R contracting. Construction professionals in many EPCs complain that their inputs are not really welcomed by the engineers in their firm and that the engineers, as the point of sales, call all the shots. In EPCM contracting, as we discussed in Chapter 4, the construction management component is often not fully defined up front in FEED where it will count the most.

Bringing the constructors, fabricators, heavy-lift companies, and other providers on the project *contractually* during front-end loading creates a host of problems and sharply limits the contract options available. It renders Re/LS, one of the most effective of all strategies, essentially impossible to implement. I believe the best practical solution to this problem is to bring potential constructors and others in to review the project toward the end of FEED as part of the prequalification process. Let them fully inspect and critique the project execution plan, engineering sequencing and packaging, and the procurement approach. That will mitigate the problem of not hearing those who join late, provided that the owner and engineering firm are listening. This does not entail or require an IPD form but will accomplish a key goal.

The second pillar of IPD is risk and reward sharing. I believe this element of IPD is highly problematic. There is an old saying in contracts: "Shared risk is *your* risk." As I will discuss in more detail in Chapter 9, contracting is all about risk assignment. One of the key purposes of a contract is to clearly articulate which risk belongs to which party. Fans of IPD often argue that other contracting strategies constitute "risk shedding" by owners. It is surely true that some owners in some circumstances seek to dump as much risk onto their contractors as they possibly can. As we have noted, that doesn't really work, but some do try it. But most contracting strategies seek to assign risks according to who best controls a risk, not simply shed risk. And a great many industrial projects today are done under no-risk-to-contractor contractual approaches. EPCM is the most popular of all industrial contracting strategies, and it is usually a low-risk or no-risk to contractor form. It hardly represents a "risk-shedding" strategy.

The third pillar of IPD is "collaborative decision-making." If collaborative is taken to mean that owners fully and carefully listen to the input of their contractors, then I am a firm supporter. If it means what it suggests, that decisions are made jointly, it is borderline insane for complex projects. The asset being created is being funded by and will be used for as much as a generation by the owner, not the contractors. Capital projects need strong owners.[10] Listening well is a key attribute of project leadership, but sharing decision-making is an attribute of weak leaders.[11]

The fourth pillar of IPD is jointly developed targets for cost and schedule. Target-setting is one of the most difficult things to do well in capital projects.[12] Setting aggressive targets without a clear path to achieve them is a fool's game. Setting soft targets means you will achieve soft results. Jointly developing and validating targets is common enough on incentivized contract arrangements, but it doesn't make the principal-agent problem go away.

The fifth pillar of IPD is liability waivers for all alliance members. The waiver of liability means that no member of the alliance has legal recourse against another for damages they may suffer in the execution of the project. I have not seen a blanket waiver of liability in alliance agreements and have not seen a waiver

---

[10]See Graham M. Winch and Roine Leiringer (2016). "Owner Project Capabilities for Infrastructure Development: A Review and Development of the 'Strong Owner' Concept." *International Journal of Project Management*, 34(2), 271–281.

[11]For a discussion of project leadership skills including the importance of listening, see E.W. Merrow and Neeraj Nandurdikar, *Leading Complex Projects*, Hoboken: John Wiley & Sons, 2018.

[12]See Paul H. Barshop, *Capital Projects*, Hoboken: John Wiley & Sons, 2016.

litigated for gross negligence.[13] What is peculiar about the waiver provision is that the alliance members normally sign individual contracts with the owner and those contracts contain conventional liability frameworks. If a large failed IPD project did end up in litigation, I would expect a bonanza for the legal profession. Baratha finds that the liability waiver provision is the least agreed upon of the IPD pillars.[14] It is easy to understand why.

Finally, to have a true alliance, there needs to be an agreement among all the participants to define and memorialize the intended relationships among all the players. The agreement always calls for collaboration and a "no blame" culture. The multiparty agreement acts as a kind of "no fault insurance" arrangement. But the problem with this is that many of the parties, especially the owner, want actual insurance in place. Insurance, however, is fault-based, and if no one is at fault, then how does it work?

In our experience with IPD/alliancing, getting the multiparty agreement signed by all intended participants is often difficult. Securing agreement from all about the risk-sharing formula is most problematic. The usual multiparty agreement is not signed and final until execution is well under way. It is particularly difficult to get those who will start their work late to agree to a situation in which they could start their work in a loss position on the project. Often, specialty contractors refuse to join the alliance at all, arguing that their profits should not depend on the performance of others. As one of my colleagues put it, "Alliancing is a bit like those dreaded graduate school class projects where everyone receives the same grade even though the work performance is never uniform."

It is my conclusion that although well intentioned, IPD/alliancing has a very small niche in industrial project contracting and probably no place in complex industrial projects. In its attempt to eliminate the principal-agent problem in contracting,

---

[13]In most engineering and construction contracts, caps on liability can be lifted if gross negligence or fraud is proven.
[14]Baratha, op. cit., p. 43.

it merely submerges it. When it does resurface, the contract offers no assistance. If an owner is not cost-conscious, IPD may appear to be workable, but only at the expense of shareholders somewhere. There is no free lunch. Virtually all industrial owners are in fact cost-conscious.

Partnering/Long-Term Alliances

Partnering refers to long-term, multiproject relationships between an owner and a contractor. The relationships are often dubbed "alliances," but the form is quite different from one-off IPD/alliancing. This model of contracting involves signing a multiyear multiproject contract between an owner and a contractor, usually an EPC. The typical contract length is five years and is renewable by mutual consent. The contractor is usually involved in front-end loading and carries on to do detailed engineering and construction. Some agreements guarantee the contractor a minimum level of work each year, but most do not.

The partnering form became popular for major industrial projects during the 1990s in the United States. At that time, there was an over-supply of EPC contractors in the market, and most contractors were very hungry for work. When the industrial projects market started to accelerate after 2003, the approach was largely abandoned except for site-based small project systems where it continues to be a staple. Our sample of major industrial projects from this century has no examples of partnering form projects.

When the contracting approach was in use during the 1990s, IPA conducted a series of studies trying to understand whether it was a superior form.[15] Some examples were indeed spectacular performers. One large chemical company executed all of its

---

[15]E.W. Merrow, "Partnering Alliances and Project Outcomes," *Industry Benchmarking Consortium Annual Meeting*, 1996; and see E.W. Merrow, "Contracting Strategy," *Industry Benchmarking Consortium Annual Meeting Proceedings*, March 2000.

projects in the United States and Europe with three partner EPC contractors in long-term partner alliances. The owner maintained a strong engineering and projects organization that followed strong practices. Five-year contracts were executed with the three partner contractors, and projects were allocated among the three based on expertise. A certain amount of competitive tension was maintained in the three-contractor arrangement.

We also found that for every partnership like the previous one, there was one that produced poor project results. For example, another major chemical company had a long-term relationship with a single contractor that produced projects that averaged more than 30 percent more than industry average cost while producing persistent underruns! That systematic over-capitalization contributed to the demise of the company. The partnerships were a study in extreme contrasts; some brilliant project results were obtained, and some very poor project results were produced.

The differences in the two sets were clear. The strong partnerships had strong owner project organizations with a very strong focus on front-end loading excellence. The partnerships producing poor project results had been used as a vehicle for downsizing and outsourcing engineering and project skills by the owners. It left the owners easy prey for contractors who overestimated projects, brought in underruns, and pocketed out-sized profits. Second, the strong partnerships had very active relationship management on both sides. This was relational contracting at its best. Both owner and contractor understood that maintaining the partnership was going to take significant work. Third, the owners in successful partnerships always stayed in touch with the market. They would bid the occasional project out on an EPC-LS basis to see if the partner EPCs were producing competitive results. When more than one partner contractor was involved, they would introduce a measure of competition between them, giving more work at the margin to the contractor performing better. Finally, the owner in successful partnering relationships had reasonably stable project workloads and modest expectations. In the unsuccessful cases, there were sometimes grossly misaligned objectives: the owner was looking for the contractor to smooth the peaks and valleys in their project portfolio while the contractor was looking for steady work. What could go wrong?

The period from about 1984 to 2003 was a period of relatively low work in the process industries around the world. The petroleum industry was in a period of low and very low prices, and the minerals industry was mostly in an overcapacity situation. Chemicals growth was mostly in line with global economic growth, but margins were being eroded by globalization of the industry. This was also a period of overcapacity in the engineering and construction industry because the rapid growth of the 1970s and early 1980s had spawned a much larger EPC industry that was then devastated by the collapse of oil prices in 1984. This made the period quite a benign one for owners (and a miserable one for contractors) and facilitated the functionality of partnership arrangements.

When the demand for engineering and construction services suddenly accelerated in 2004, the EPC industry was at low-ebb and had significantly consolidated. The partnerships were largely abandoned as the shortage of EPC services took hold. If project markets in a region are in an extended low period and surplus EPC capacity exists, partnership arrangements are clearly workable. But all of the lessons from the 1990's experience still pertain: strong partnerships need strong owners and strong relationship management to work along with some mechanism to maintain contact with the market.

Repeat Supply Chain Contracting

We end our discussion of unusual contracting strategies with repeat supply chain (RSC) contracting. All of our RSC projects are drawn from petroleum production projects, but there is no obvious reason why equivalent results would not occur in other industrial sectors. Our databases contain more than 70 RSC projects in 17 separate series that range from 2 to 9 projects. The average capital cost of the projects is just under $2 billion, although they range downward to about $100 million. Virtually all of the projects were contracted as lump-sums.

A repeat supply chain occurs when the same set of suppliers—engineering firm, substructure vendor/yard, topsides fabricator, and systems integrator—is used for sequential projects with an owner on a sole source basis. What differentiates RSC from partnering contracting is that each project is governed by a separate contract with no guarantee of future work. RSC contracting is always accompanied by some degree of standardization. In some respects, standardization is a necessary condition because the contractors and suppliers must be capable of performing over a series of projects, so the projects cannot be too dissimilar. A large amount of heterogeneity of project scopes would make that all but impossible. The degree of standardization varied from series to series, and none of the series of projects were characterized by highly (greater than 80 percent) standardized scope.

As shown in Figure 6.2, RSC contracting produces excellent value for owners—the best overall results of any particular

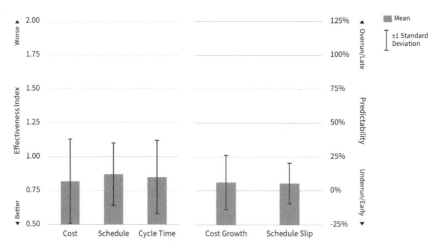

FIGURE 6.2 Repeat supply chains provide the best value overall.

contracting form.[16] In addition to excellent cost, schedule, and cycle time results, RSC contracted projects experienced the fewest operability problem in the first year after startup of any contracting approach.[17] But in keeping with the principle that there is never a free lunch, RSC contracting is quite difficult to manage and may be limited in potential application.

Repeat supply chains usually started as a matter of serendipity rather than design. An owner would develop a project in some region and select via competitive bidding a set of contractors and service providers to perform the work. After the project went unusually well, the owner decided that rather than competitively bidding the next project in the same geography, he would invite the contractors and other suppliers on the first project to join the next project on a sole source basis, agree on a cost estimate and schedule, and execute the second project. There is no "all-party agreement" in this form. This process is repeated until there are no more projects for the owner or one of the parties loses interest. As soon as the contractors and other suppliers accept that this will continue, the relationships and contracts become self-enforcing. Exploiting the situation for monetary gain or doing demonstrably poor work would mean that the next project would go to a competitor.

The best known RSC in the petroleum industry was the series of deep water spar production platform projects led by Don Vardeman, first at Oryx Petroleum and then carried to Kerr-McGee and finally Anadarko through acquisition. As Vardeman explained, the key to the contracting strategy was the careful maintenance of the relationships over time.[18] Not every project

---

[16]There are two sources of cost efficiency at work in RSC contracting: standardization and the contracting strategy. Sorting out the contribution of each discretely is difficult because standardization of industrial projects is almost always accompanied by a contracting approach that is in effect RSC.

[17]E.W. Merrow and J.A. Walker, "The Efficacy of Unusual Contracting Approaches in Petroleum Production Projects," *Proceedings of the Upstream Industry Benchmarking Consortium Annual Meeting*, November 2019.

[18]See Edward W. Merrow and Neeraj S. Nandurdikar, op. cit., pp. 130 ff.

went perfectly, and not every contractor performance was exemplary, but the relationships were managed by frank discussions of performance, give and take, and constant learning. There were never any formal guarantees, but there was the guarantee that if the suppliers were faithful to the relationship by doing solid work, they would always be rewarded with the next job. The average platform in that series of megaprojects cost 75 percent of industry average, which is astounding performance.

The benefits of RSC are obvious. As the set of suppliers work together on sequential projects, the management of the interfaces becomes progressively easier. The repeat nature of the work means that low cost could be maintained, while profitability for the contractors and suppliers improved because the work was being done more efficiently. The self-enforcing nature of the relationships means that senior leadership is aligned on both the buyer and seller sides.[19]

All of the RSC series that we have seen were confined to a particular region of the world. In principle, it may be possible to run an RSC across regions, but we have not seen it done. In some companies, RSC contracting generates strenuous objections from the procurement organization or the legal department due to the sole source nature of the strategy. Some engineering organizations and business functions also object to the high degree of standardization that is often necessary to make RSC contracting work. And, of course, in some jurisdictions such sole source contracting is illegal because open bidding competitions are required for projects.

What I find most interesting is that RSC contracting appears to generate all of the advantages sought by IPD/alliancing—excellent collaboration, early involvement of all parties, better

---

[19]Of note, the RSCs did not show learning curves in which each project was more cost competitive than the one before. I believe there are two reasons for this. First, the RSCs were only started because the first project was cost effective, which had the effect of lowering the Y-intercept on the learning curve. Second, the suppliers could improve their profitability, which may well have been on the low side for the initial projects, by being more efficient in the subsequent projects.

management of interfaces, and better alignment of incentives. But RSC contracting does this without gimmick and without asking the *contracts* to generate the collaboration, which clearly does not work. The contracts for the RSC projects were standard fixed-price contracts. They were also mostly irrelevant, which is the best contract of all.

The Effects of Scale on the Unusual Contracting Forms

One of the most important attributes of a contracting strategy is how its effectiveness changes with project size and complexity. As we noted in Chapter 4, EPC reimbursable and EPCM scale quite poorly. As owners lose line-of-sight control, the forms become progressively more expensive and slow. EPC lump-sum degrades with size, but not as severely as the two reimbursable forms. The split forms Re/LS and Re/Re do not degrade at all with increased size and complexity.

The unusual forms differ in how they respond to size and complexity:

- **Duty spec** contracts remain relatively constant with respect to size as long as standard solutions are available at the size and complexity sought. There may be some tendency for operability to degrade with complexity.
- **Design competitions** are unaffected by size and complexity. Some of the most successful complex megaprojects resulted from well-run design competitions.
- **Convert to lump-sum** are also unaffected by size and complexity, but that is not a good thing! They tend to be very expensive for owners at all sizes.
- Because **GMPs** are usually on the smaller size, there is not enough variation to understand how they scale.

- **IPD/alliancing** does not scale well. IPD megaprojects were not only disproportionately failures; IPD/alliancing appears to be a *causal factor* in increasing their chances to fail even in a group of projects that do not tend to do very well.[20] Smaller IPDs tend to be expensive but are more likely to go smoothly than megaproject alliances. IPD is a complex contractual form that often does a poor job assigning risk. That is a poor match for projects with a large number of participants and built-in problems for good risk assignment.

- **Partnering arrangements** were rarely used with projects over about $250 million. Owners that had partnering contractors tended to go to market outside the partnerships for the big projects and contract them on a one-off basis. I believe the reason for this is that a very large project could upset the partnership arrangements by overwhelming the staffing capability of the partner contractor within the relationship. In most partner arrangements, the contractor staffing for the partner owner was quite stable as personnel would be assigned long term. For these reasons we can't know how the form would scale.

- **Repeat supply chain** scales very well as a contracting form. We cannot tell how scale would affect any single supply chain series because the projects tended to be of fairly uniform size. RSCs that started large remained large, and those that started with small projects tended to remain small. The RSC contracting dataset, however, had a disproportionate number of megaprojects. Provided that sufficient standardization can be sustained, RSC is a capable contracting strategy for megaprojects.

---

[20]See E. Merrow, *Industrial Megaprojects*, op. cit. p. 260.

CHAPTER 7

Prequalification

As we are closing out a disappointing project with one of our owner clients, one of the most common observations of the project team is "We selected the wrong contractor." Of course, sometimes this is just scapegoating, but often it reflects important realities. What kinds of things do we hear?

- The contractor didn't really have the experience we thought they did.
- They can't do direct-hire.
- We didn't get the people they promised.
- They didn't QC design; they didn't even do interference checks!
- They didn't have any bench strength when we needed more people.
- They didn't understand how to work with the labor around here.
- They didn't have the construction management talent we thought they did.

And so forth and so on. When we ask "Did you prequalify?" the answer is too often "We didn't really have time to do much. We needed to get FEED started ASAP."

The evolution of a project's contracting strategy should begin early in scope development, which we call FEL-2. However, in strong project systems, some contracting activities have been proceeding all along outside the realm of any individual project. Those activities are constant monitoring of the contracting market in all of the locations—sometimes around the world—where the company is likely to pursue capital projects. These activities, which we call elements of FEL-0, may be part of the work of a contracting group within the owner's projects organization or undertaken by corporate procurement or supply chain management as part of their ongoing market assessment activities.

Contracting Market Assessment

The assessment of the contracting market must answer a great many questions. What is the level of project activity in the area relative to historical norms? Is work accelerating or declining? What type of facilities are being built, and what contractors are involved in engineering and construction? How well are the projects going? When projects in an area are suffering due to an overheated market, the information is generally freely available in the press, in the regional contractor association meetings, from union halls where applicable, and from industry information and data providers.

If the market is hot or accelerating rapidly (or both), that fact will change the likelihood and cost effectiveness of lump-sum strategies, especially EPC-LS. If the market is trending down or is relatively cool, many more contractors will be interested in your projects. That is both a plus and a minus. It's a plus because it may mean that the strongest contractors will be interested when they otherwise might not be. It also means that sorting through the contractor in prequalification will be a bigger job. A down market also makes it more likely that some contractors will be having "quiet chats" with owner businesspeople, often on the golf course, about what a good job they can do on any upcoming projects. The contractors may also be suggesting what would be "the best" contracting strategy for any project. If you recall our "successful" IPD project in Chapter 6, that project's contracting strategy was created in that fashion in a down market. It is not uncommon, but it is extraordinarily risky, for an owner business to start deciding contracting strategies.

If an owner's "market watchers" are good, they will be listening carefully to understand if any contractors are in financial trouble. In much of the world, the past decade has been a very difficult one for contractors and for EPC and engineering contractors in particular. The contractors, really through no fault of their own, have been caught in a demographic trap that has made effective management of the firms and of projects very difficult. This has resulted in some notable failures of even prominent firms and struggles in projects for many others. Looking at the financial health of a contractor will be part of the prequalification process, but more knowledge earlier and more nuanced information is always helpful.

In some industrial sectors, and for very large projects regardless of sector, the market assessments must be global rather than region-specific. In oil and gas production projects, for example, the EPC market is fully global. A contractor's capability to do work in the U.S. Gulf of Mexico may affect its work in Malaysia or the North Sea almost as much as their work for others in the Gulf of Mexico. A Korean EPC contractor's work in the Middle East may dictate his level of interest in a project in Southeast Asia and so forth. Information is available, but an owner must have an active market assessment capability, or the contractor selection process will be less reliable.

The Purposes of Prequalification

As mentioned, contracting strategy and prequalification must start early in the scope development process—really as soon as we know what kind of facility we are going to build, roughly how large it will be in terms of cost, and where it will be. The early start is dictated by the fact that before FEL-2 ends, prequalification of FEED contractors is a must, and for some contracting strategies, prequalification of all engineering or EPC contractors who will be considered for the project is essential. If we do not complete prequalification early, some good contracting strategies will become impracticable, and the selection of the FEED contractor will often end up a sole source selection. That sole source selection then often goes on to execute the entire project without a careful comparative look at their qualifications ever occurring. As we will see, that is often a costly error of omission.

Prequalification reduces the set of contractors who will be considered for a project to a manageable number. What is a considered a "manageable number" varies by project characteristics and contractor market situation. If a project is large and complex and likely to have multiple prime contractors, the number of contractors to be considered and ultimately qualified to bid should be larger. Hot markets mean that there will be more "dropouts" along the way, so a larger number should be considered.

In addition to reducing the number, prequalification is directly aimed at *dis*qualifying contractors that we do not want bidding on the project.[1] Contractors lacking the skills needed to do the defined work must be eliminated from contention. Unqualified contractors often end up with the job if they are not eliminated. In bidding contests, they often provide the lowest bid, sometimes because they do not understand the scope and its difficulty. Sometimes they provide the low bid because they are desperate for work. Desperation is not a qualification.

In situations in which owners have complete latitude in their selection process, they are tempted to allow unqualified contractors into the game because they know they can eliminate them later. That is a dangerous and unethical game. The danger is that when the owner or businesspeople see that low bid or low hourly

---

[1]Remember the term *bidding* does not imply a bidding contest, although a formal bidding contest may result.

rate, the discretion that the team thought it had disappears and pressure mounts to take on that suboptimal contractor. If the goal is simply to try to force down the bids of the qualified contractors by including more players who have no chance of success, that unethically uses the unqualified contractor's time and money in preparing a bid for your own purposes. In contracting, unethical owner behavior shapes reputation. In contracting, reputation ultimately plays a significant role in how much you pay and who you get to participate.

In most situations, a pool of four to six qualified contractors for any particular scope of work is sufficient. In EPC lump-sum bidding contests, four or more generally provides a strong market response. Including too many in a pool regardless of contracting strategy tends to dilute everyone's interest because the probability of a successful effort by the contractor declines.[2]

Forced Changes of Contracting Strategy

When prequalification and the marketing studies that should accompany it are done correctly, the chances that an owner will be forced to change strategy late in front-end loading are minimal. This is very important because late changes in contracting strategy are strongly associated with project failures—large cost overruns and slips in execution schedule.

The most common type of forced strategy change is the discovery after issuance of the invitations to bid that EPC lump-sum is not a viable strategy. This takes several forms. The most common is that the contractors who had indicated that they

---

[2] Owners sometimes believe that contractors will not know how many contractors are in contention for a project. That belief is almost always mistaken. The contracting industry is characterized by extensive movement of personnel from contractor to contractor. With personnel movement goes information movement.

intended to bid decline to do so, and the owner is stuck with perhaps one bid. That one bid may be too high to be acceptable. That sometimes leads the owners to attempt a "convert to lump-sum" strategy with that remaining bidder, which we discussed in Chapter 5. As you will recall, that is not a happy option.

Another common situation is the one in which no responsive bids are received at all. This usually occurs when the bidders realize that the project is not sufficiently well defined for them to bid a lump-sum safely. The bids are then heavily qualified and therefore not actually EPC-LS bid at all. I remember reviewing a bid in which 1,500 exceptions and qualifications were made! The usual qualifications are that the cost and schedule are subject to completion of FEED work such as the P&IDs and development of a baseline cost estimate and schedule after which time a lump-sum price can be established. This is, of course, a backdoor convert to LS.

Sometimes the period for which the bids are valid is exceeded before the project can move forward. In those cases, a winner was often selected and negotiation of terms and conditions was complete, but when the period of validity expires, the contractor is now in control of the situation. The delays are sometimes caused by the owner's lack of decisiveness and sometimes by tardiness on the part of government regulators. Either way, it is a precarious situation for the owner.

Quite reasonably, contractors will resist extraordinarily long validity periods for bids. In a down-market period, six months or more may be acceptable, but in a hot market where escalation is high and the contractors' opportunity costs are high, shorter periods will be sought. If owners want a long period for bid validity, they need to be prepared to index the cost of commodities in periods of high escalation. Otherwise, they risk having no bidders for the work.

Being forced from an EPC-LS to an EPC-R, EPCM, or convert to LS strategy creates an untenable situation for the owner team. The team has been staffed for EPC-LS, which usually means a small owner staff geared to inspection. The team is not staffed and has little hope of being ready to control a reimbursable form for any part of the work, much less all of it.

Our recommendation to project teams in this situation of forced change in contracting strategy is either to postpone the project significantly while preparing the team for better controls or to switch to a split strategy in which they can proceed with engineering and procurement on a reimbursable basis while preparing to either bid the construction work lump-sum or prepare themselves to control some form of reimbursable construction. Given the lack of owner controls, the engineering should be expected to have difficulties, but if the construction can be salvaged with a split strategy, the damage will be limited. Far better is to avoid the situation in the first place.

The Prequalification Process

The prequalification process starts with a solicitation of interest from the contractors identified by the market assessment team. The request includes little more than a basic description of the project, its location, and the role that the contractor might play—FEED only, engineering, construction, or EPC/EPCM—and the type of competition that will ensue. Sometimes the request for information will provide either a short list of *disqualifying* criteria or a list of required qualifications.

A positive response from a contractor prompts a written questionnaire. The written questionnaire asks for a good deal of mundane business information, including information about certifications, workload, recent jobs, references, and so forth. If construction activities may be included, the owner usually requests a great deal of construction safety information. Usually, the owner also asks a great many questions about the financial health of the firm.

From the list of contractors who pass the written questionnaire qualifications, a set is selected for visits by the owner team.

That team should be cross-functional with supply chain, legal, and various project functions represented, but should be led by someone from the project team, often the project manager or the contracts manager on the team.[3] The visits to the contractors will result in a final qualified list of candidates for the project.

The use of prequalification is not universal. It becomes more common as project size increases. Prequalification is most common when EPC-LS is being employed and is used more than 80 percent of the time. Prequalification occurs on less than 70 percent of large (greater than $75 million) EPC-R and EPCM strategies. Owners often do F-EPC-R and EPCM selection sole source. Prequalification of engineering contractors falls to 63 percent on the two most common split forms, Re/LS and Re/Re, but prequalification of engineering contractors on the lump-sum engineering split forms is almost 80 percent, just like EPC-LS. Prequalification of construction contractors by owners is very common for large split form strategy projects (greater than 75 percent) but much less common on all three EPC forms (less than 50 percent). This is not surprising. On the EPC forms, the constructor selection is either wholly up to the contractor (EPC-LS), or it is expected that the contractor will perform the function (EPC-R and EPCM). Recall that the owner's desire for "one-stop shopping" often influences the selection of the EPC forms so they can avoid the burden and knowledge requirements of constructor selection.

Does Prequalification Improve Contractor Selection?

It turns out that prequalification does make a difference, but the kind of difference it makes is a function of contract strategy. The

---

[3]This is a reason (among many others) to form the owner project team early and maintain core team continuity from FEL-2 forward.

prequalification of engineering contractors on EPC form contracts is a reduction in capital cost of about 7 percent (Pr.|t|<.03), a reduction in cost growth of about 3 percent (Pr.|t|<.001), and a slight decrease in schedule slip. The most striking aspect of the result is that the effects are the same for EPC-LS, EPC-R, and EPCM. Prequalification of the engineering contractor has no effect on execution schedule and no effect on engineering slip, which remains high across all the EPC forms.

The fact that prequalification has the same effect across all EPC forms makes the differences in frequency of prequalification very important. The fact that we are much more likely not to prequalify in EPCM than in EPC-LS plays a role in the performance gap we found between those two forms in Chapter 3. When we explicitly sole source EPCM contractors, we only prequalify before that sole source selection about 40 percent of the time. In other words, we never checked the market before, simply selecting the contractor that would carry the project from start to finish. Given the poor results, that does not appear to be a very wise decision.

Prequalification of constructors on the EPC forms had absolutely no effect on anything! We would expect that on EPC-LS where the EPC contractor is on the hook for project cost. But the owner preferences for constructors appears to be ignored on EPCM contracts as well.

The effects of prequalification in split-form contracting are quite different. Prequalifying the engineering contractor had no effect on project cost or cost growth for Re/LS and Re/Re contracting. However, prequalification of the engineering contractor was associated with a very beneficial effect on schedule: engineering time was 10 percent better, and execution time fully reflected that 10 percent improvement (Pr.|t|<.03).

The positive effects of prequalification of the engineering contractor in the split forms makes sense. For split-form contracting, it is very important that the engineer know how to develop effective disciplinary packages on which the constructors will bid. Timeliness of engineering becomes more critical to keeping the project from extending than in EPC forms because early field start is not possible without the constructors on board, and that requires the engineering packages. Therefore, owners are clearly testing schedule capabilities of the engineers as they do prequalification.

Prequalification of *constructors* in split-form contracting was essential to good cost performance. The prequalified cases show 15 percent better cost competitiveness—a huge difference (Pr.|t|<.02). However, and this is ironic, prequalification of constructors on split-form contracts was associated with 18 percent longer execution times, but no longer construction times! This strongly suggests that owners are prequalifying constructors too late in the process, probably well after detailed engineering has started rather than as part of front-end loading. As suggested in Chapter 7, we should be prequalifying constructors toward the end of FEED when we can get their input on FEED quality and engineering sequencing.

So, the data tell us that prequalification really does make a difference. In EPC situations the prequalification should focus on the engineering company and not worry about the constructors. In split-contracting cases, owners need to focus both on engineers and constructors, but need to be prequalifying constructors earlier in order not to pay a schedule penalty.

There basically are no cases in which prequalification is not justified. One can say prequalifying construction contractors on EPCM form contracts probably doesn't make any difference, but that's the problem of how we're doing the project and how we're controlling it, not a problem in principle.

The Key Prequalification Criteria

Now that we have established that prequalification supports better project outcomes, let's examine the most common and arguably important prequalification criteria. For EPC firms and constructors, there are five qualification criteria that are always or almost always used:

- Construction safety
- Financial health
- Technology experience
- Experience with local labor practices and norms
- Quality of the contractor team offered/promised

As we discuss these four criteria, I want to focus on some of the pitfalls we see repeatedly in the way these criteria are used to prequalify.

Safety First

Almost every EPC and constructor was quizzed, often in great detail, about their safety records. One prequalification protocol had more than 200 questions on safety! We had incident rates and types of accidents and injuries. In the United States, insurance rates for safety were generally requested as an indicator. Sometimes, the questionnaires were careful to inquire about safety experience for work closely aligned with the intended project, but sometimes that was not stipulated.

The most interesting feature of the safety criterion is that it was almost always used as a binary. The most common rule was to disqualify contractors when their safety performance was poorer than the company's average, even if the company's average was much poorer than their peers. Generally, however, if a contractor met the threshold to be qualified, safety performance did not figure at all in the actual selection process or figured in a minor way. This approach dilutes the importance of safety as a contractor selection criterion. There were contractors disqualified for poor safety performance, but not many.

Despite the load of questions addressed on safety in prequalification, *we can find no relationship at all between prequalification and actual safety performance on the ensuing project.* Projects with and without prequalification have the same safety outcomes. Further, the safety thresholds used had no relationship with safety achieved on the projects.

Although this may be discouraging, I do not think it is surprising. IPA has always found that owner behavior regarding construction safety is crucial to achieving construction safety. If the owner cares more about schedule than safety, safety will suffer regardless of contractor. Also, the nature of the market dampens differences in safety performance on industrial projects. Contractors cannot afford to allow their insurance premiums to go up and up. Contractors who are unsafe may quickly find themselves out of business. And, of course, the tendency of the owner to use their own safety performance averages as the threshold tends to depress any effect.

Few owners included substantial prequalification criteria around environmental and other sustainability concerns as well as safety. The exceptions were mostly mining companies for which sustainability issues are generally more salient. To date, very few owners have included questions around greenhouse gas emissions, but we expect this to change rapidly in the next few years.

Contractor Finances

Unlike industrial owners, contractors are thinly capitalized firms. They earn primarily through the sale of employee hours, not through the sales of products. Therefore, when business turns down, they are financially vulnerable. When they suffer losses, usually due to overruns on lump-sum contracts, they lack balance sheet resources to tide the firm over and instead must reduce costs. The only way to significantly reduce costs is to shed people, but the shedding of people makes them less capable and therefore less strong in the marketplace. Contractor bankruptcies are not uncommon, even among large players.

When a contractor is in financial trouble, the projects under way suffer, and every owner knows this. Therefore, prequalification routinely requests a good deal of information about the contractor's financial health. Because the balance sheet is not very meaningful—it is usually thin—owners tend to focus on current work levels and backlog, bondability and credit-worthiness, and timely payment of vendors and subcontractors.[4] Pending owner claims in dispute are also queried, but almost never secure a useful answer. A more useful question, because it is much harder to game, would be whether the contractor has initiated arbitration or litigation with an owner and whether an owner, subcontractor, or vendor has instigated arbitration or litigation against the contractor.

Although it is obviously important not to engage a financially ailing contractor on lump-sum work, it is also important to avoid situations in which vendors will shun the contractor as not credit-worthy and where subcontractors will not entertain work because of payment history issues. Owners tend to be less rigorous in the financial vetting of construction firms than EPCs, but still require that they be in good financial standing.

Despite all of this prequalification work, we still see projects (and often major projects) damaged by the poor financial health of a major contractor. The reason for this is that owners are not getting enough information about *ongoing* projects, especially large lump-sum projects. Most prequalification questionnaires do not even inquire about the status of ongoing projects other than they be listed for purposes of understanding workload. If a

---

[4]Auditors of EPC contractors are under enormous pressure to make the accounts look strong, which may also decrease the usefulness of financials. Note, for example, the scandal surrounding the audit of Carillion in the United Kingdom.

large project, even a reimbursable project, is going very poorly, it diverts management attention away from any other job. We even have cases where suppliers and subcontractors hear about payment problems on another project for an EPC and seek to bail on the one they are working on for fear of not being paid.

To counter this problem, owners need to not only get a list of current projects and their size; they also need to know the compensation scheme, and they should ask the contractor whether there are any significant problems on those projects. (They shouldn't expect to get entirely accurate answers.) Then they need to make discreet inquiries with the owner project teams on the large projects and especially those being done lump-sum.

Large owner firms are sometimes so incoherent they do not even ask their colleagues about how a project with a contractor is going within their own firm. We had a recent case in which while the EPC was making a complete hash of a company megaproject, they were signed up to take on an even larger project in another location. They made a complete mess of that as well. Of course, the owner role was large in both. We have cases in which one project team is prequalifying a contractor that is in massive litigation over a project with another team. This sort of incoherence occurs because multiple owner functions are often involved in the contractor qualification and selection process and do not talk to each other. In today's world, unlike times past, very few owners keep systematic track of the performance of contractors. The failure to carefully track contractor performance is both a symptom of the transactional, one-off nature of much of today's contracting and a cause as well. If the owner doesn't even keep track of performance, it sends a very clear message to contractors that their performance on this project will have no effect on their chances with the next. That undermines any positive self-enforcing nature of the relationship.

Technology Experience

One of the most limiting of prequalification requirements is direct experience with the technology that will be embedded in the project. If written narrowly, technology experience may knock out all but a few EPC contractors. For example, if the requirement is written "contractor must have design experience with major refinery processing units, including hydrotreaters," a great many contractors will qualify. If the requirement is written "must have design experience with Axens Prime-G+[®5] hydrotreating technology," the field is narrowed radically. Before using a narrow definition, owners should ask themselves whether very specific experience is really needed and why. Most engineering contractors can complete front-end and then detailed engineering on a licensor's basic engineering package. If the technology is open art, contractors experienced with similar technologies can usually perform well. If a technology is extraordinarily difficult or subject to extensive intellectual property protection, that may make an open solicitation to the market inappropriate.

We did find that owners are not at all careful in verifying contractor claims of experience with a technology. For example, one contractor claimed experience with a technology when their only role was as a project managing contractor (PMC) on a much larger project incorporating the given technology. A separate EPC-LS contractor actually did 100 percent of the work on that particular unit. Another contractor claimed engineering experience when all they really had was construction experience for a technology. Owners need to require that contractors detail the role they played in a prior project employing the technology or the requirement is meaningless.

---

[5]Prime G Plus is a registered trademark of the Axens Group.

Local Construction Experience

Even when most labor is imported, construction is always local. There are local norms for construction contracting, for compensation schemes, for use of union or nonunion labor, and for how different crafts expect to be treated and addressed. Because construction is always local, it is important that any firms that will be intimately involved with field work—EPCs, general contractors, and construction management firms—understand local norms.

When split-contracting forms are used, only the GC and any disciplinary constructors need to have local experience, and this is the case about 90 percent of the time. The more problematic cases are when EPC forms are being used. Local experience is less common (69 percent), and the absence of local experience is associated with a 5 percent hit to both cost and schedule. The problem is that when an EPC form is selected and the local EPC contractor market is thin, requiring local construction experience may seriously hamper the owner's ability to find a sufficient number of players.

One of the major advantages of split-form contracting is that the market for the project can be opened up to many more local constructors provided that market exists at all. We have cases in thin market areas where the local construction experience has narrowed the number of potential contractors from eight or nine to two or three. That changes the nature of the competition significantly.

Lack of local construction experience also dampens the enthusiasm of good contractors for work. For example, Asian EPC contractors cite their lack of local construction experience as the number-one reason they have been reluctant to enter the North American market. Joint ventures with local constructors are feasible in principle but difficult to develop in a timely way in practice.

Quality of the Contractor Team

During the site visit to contractor offices that follows the questionnaire screening round, the contractor usually presents the core team they are offering for the project. Most of the time the contractor is careful to caveat the offering as being less than an iron-clad promise, although it is often taken as such. In practice, there are lots of practical reasons why contractors cannot promise a particular team unless the project timeline is quite immediate. Because contractors sell hours, they cannot economically hold people on the hope they will win a particular project. To do so would be ruinous. The contracting industry is also beset with high rates of personnel turnover, especially during hot market periods. Some of the people presented six months ago are probably no longer with the firm.

When reviewing the results of prequalification of contractors, the "quality of the contractor team" came up often. However, it was usually very impressionistic: "we like them a lot," "easy to talk to," "good experience." Missing were hard to fudge and solid criteria like the following:

- Number of times the core team (project manager, lead engineer, disciplinary leads, estimator, planner schedule, construction manager, and controls lead) has *worked together on a project as a team* rarely appeared as a prequalification criterion. (References for those projects would be invaluable.)

- Minimum percent of personnel who will be working on the project who have been with the contracting firm for at least one year in their current role.

- Independent certification of personnel on contractor's key systems (CAD, construction progress reporting system, etc.)

These verifiable and fact-based criteria are largely absent despite their importance.

Projects are a "people business," but that should not mean that people attributes are not carefully measured. It is nice to find people likeable, but finding them competent and experienced is far better.

Location of Contractor's Home Office

When a project team selects a FEED and/or detailed engineering contractor on a major project, they are also selecting the place they will be living for the next 18 to 30 months. Most owner teams colocate to the home office location of their primary engineering contractor. In some cases this is an explicit prequalification criterion when there is a preference for a contractor local to the team and many such contractors are available. Often, however, the criterion is unstated, but it is often the most important screen for selecting an engineering contractor or EPC. Let's be honest, many of us wouldn't mind terribly being "stuck" in Paris, London, Perth, or Madrid for the next two years compared to a number of other places I won't bother to mention. Like it or not, Technip has unfair advantage!

Data Transparency, Transfer Methodologies, and Ownership

One of the topics we almost never see in prequalification questionnaires or site visit discussions is the treatment of project data. The last decade has seen a revolution in data development, storage, and system interoperability. Just a few years ago, the CAD model and database for a project would be of modest value to an owner because the platform on which the work was done would not be interoperable with any other. Our ability to measure and record and transmit data is many times better than just a few years ago. And at the same time, more owner companies are seeking to standardize their facilities.

All of this means that ownership of data, ability to access project information in real time, and how that will be done are becoming major issues in the negotiation of terms and conditions in contracts. If owners intend to push forward with technology standardization, they must take ownership and physical possession of the designs. If owners want to make use of latest technology to understand the state and progress of their capital projects, they must ensure that the contractors will have compatible systems in place and be willing to provide the data needed in real time. Waiting until you are ready to negotiate the terms and conditions for the contract to clarify requirements is a losing proposition. At that point, time pressures will make successful negotiation unlikely. However, if these issues are added to prequalification, are discussed, and it is made clear the requirements are non-negotiable, it is much more likely that the needed data transfer will actually occur down the road.

Selection

Prequalification sets the table for a high-quality selection process. A good selection process is not primarily focused on cost. Cost is almost always an important criterion, but when it is the dominant criterion, project results suffer. One of the distinct disadvantages of EPC-LS contracting is that cost is more likely to be used as the controlling factor for EPC-LS than in any other contracting approach. However, regardless of contracting strategy, cost as the primary selection criterion is associated with higher cost (Pr.|t|<.01) and longer execution schedules (Pr.|t|<.01).

A clearly superior approach is to employ a holistic set of selection criteria that are weighted according to the characteristics of the project. In addition to cost and schedule, technical capability and experience on the technologies to be employed are very important considerations. Experience in the project locale is important. The most important consideration, however, should be the strength of the team and depth of personnel that will be provided to the project. The team is more important than cost or schedule promises because the team, along with the owner's work, will determine whether those promises are met. Aspects of team and personnel strength that are not ambiguous or subjective should be given special attention.

- What was the experience of the team working together?
- Working together on a similar project is even better but not essential.
- What was the experience of team members working for the contractor on previous projects?
- There should be a limited number (less than half) of personnel with no experience working for this specific contractor; some positions such as cost controls must have worked for the contractor on previous projects (demonstrated understanding of contractor systems).
- Will the team be co-located?
- What percent of personnel have at least one year of experience with the contractor's systems in the proposed role?
- What is the company's competency assurance process? (Review competency tests. Secure test results for personnel to be assigned.)
- Review the proposed organization chart and job descriptions.
- Review the contractor staff retention history and retention policies.
- Review the project resource plan.
- If an engineering value center is going to be used, details of the home office (the particular home office, not the contractor generally) and the EVC working together should be obtained. How the home office/EVC interface will be managed should be provided in some detail.

Finally, the recent history of the contractor working with the owner should factor very heavily and formally in contractor selection. A recent history of good work should be rewarded with a leg up for more work.

Summary

As an owner, one must be clear about what you want from your contractors and start the process of getting that all the way back in prequalification. The earlier contractors understand owner expectations, the easier they will be to meet.

I don't think that prequalification is executed very well by most owners in the industry, but even with that, we can plainly see that it makes a difference in project quality. Unprequalified sole source contracting is not effective for owners unless they are in a partnering arrangement or repeat supply chain. (One could argue that the prequalification in those cases has actually been very deep.) Prequalification is often started too late, which makes it a more perfunctory exercise than it should be. There are some creative things that could be done with prequalification, such as incorporating constructor input in FEED, that are still unusual.

My advice to owners is to update and modernize your prequalification procedures. Stop asking for quite so much extraneous information about safety, hone down on the financial questions, and then focus on the new things that you will need going forward: data transparency, sustainability, and GHG emissions. Prequalification should be seen as an opportunity, not just another chore.

CHAPTER 8

The Use of Supplemental Incentives

A ll contracts contain an incentive structure for contractors. When we discuss "incentives" in contracting, we usually mean incentives that supplement and usually attempt to modify or augment the incentive structure that comes with the contractual form. For example, every EPC-LS contract is the fully cost incentivized contract. Every reimbursable contract carries within its structure the possibility of the contractor making more money through more hours charged whether or not those hours are strictly needed. In other words, every basic contractual form carries some version of the principal-agent problem. Supplemental incentives seek to ameliorate those problems. I emphasize the *supplemental* nature of incentive schemes because I find that many practitioners tend to forget the primary incentive structure as they approach incentive contracting. Supplemental incentives usually seek to "swim against the flow" of the contract's primary incentive scheme because it is believed that the primary incentive scheme contains some inherent misalignment of the principal (owner) and the agent (contractor). Often, the primary incentives overwhelm and render moot any of the supplemental incentives we seek to forge. At other times, the supplemental incentive may interact with the primary incentive to create unintended consequences.

For the analysis for this chapter, I have excluded the integrated project delivery/alliancing projects. They are incentivized contracts but are sufficiently different in their results that I do not want them distorting the results of the other contracting forms. I have also excluded the other unusual forms except guaranteed maximum price (GMP). Those other forms are rarely incentivized. Our focus will be on how incentives are used and their results for EPC-LS, EPC-R, EPCM, Re/LS, and Re/Re contracting forms. These five form encompass the great majority of industrial projects. For many parts of the analysis, the performance of EPC-R and EPCM is the same in their responses to incentives. In those cases I have combined them for ease of presentation.

Like IPD, incentive contracting often involves a lot of work in attempting to design the "perfect incentive." And like IPD, incentive schemes often invoke a good deal of passion. Here we will review what history has to tell us about supplemental incentives.

The Conceptual Basis for Incentive Contracting

The theoretical basis for incentive contracting stems from Fama and Jensen's seminal work on the principal-agent problem as it applies to business organizations.[1] Reimbursable contracts are behavior-based "fixed promised payoff" agreements. By contrast lump-sum contracts are "payoffs tied to specific measures of performance, namely, the agreed scope for the agreed price."[2] In lump-sum, the contractor's payoff is a function of execution

---

[1] Eugene F. Fama and Michael C. Jensen, "Separation of Ownership and Control," *Journal of Law and Economics*, Vol. XXVI, June 1983.
[2] op. cit., p. 302.

performance, provided the owner does not alter the agreement with changes. The virtue of lump-sum contracts is that they are simple outcome-based contracts, and the outcomes are reasonably measureable as long as the owner has an effective inspection organization to ensure that corners are not cut.

The disadvantages of EPC-LS are well known. When and where the market for engineering and construction management services is thin, which is often the case for large complex projects, EPC-LS is expensive for owners. When the project presents significant risks, the contractors will require a substantial cost premium for assuming those risks. For reasons we will discuss in Chapter 9, contractors are not efficient carriers of risk. So, although the incentive structures align well in EPC-LS, the form is often suboptimal for owners. This is where reimbursable plus supplemental incentive contracting appears to provide a better route for owners.[3]

However, reimbursable contracts are the area in which the fixed promised payoffs fail to align the interests of the principal (owner) and the agent (contractor). The payoff to the contractor under a reimbursable form is equivalent to a straight salaried employment agreement. As long as the person is employed, the promised payoff (salary) is guaranteed whether the employee's performance is deemed excellent or poor. The only remedy in the case of poor performance is termination. On a capital project, termination for poor performance is usually catastrophic for the capital asset being designed and constructed and is, therefore, not a real option.

The goal with most supplemental incentives is to add *outcome-based payoffs* to the fixed promised payoff and in doing so better align the principal and the agent goals. It is the equivalent of adding commissions to a salesperson's salary or providing stock options to an executive's salary. It appears to be a relatively simple and straightforward solution to the reimbursable dilemma.

---

[3]See T.C. Berends, "Cost Plus Incentive Fee Contracting—Experiences and Structuring," *International Journal of Project Management 18* (2000) pp.165–171.

But, of course, things are not really so simple in the world of employment or in the world of contracting.

The problems with the incentives formulation are the lack of transparency and measurability of the agent's behavior and the difficulty measuring outcomes. The reason that contracting strategy is much less important for smaller projects is that the owner has line-of-sight information to verify the performance of the contractor. Therefore, whether a behavior-based reimbursable contract or a lump-sum outcome-based form is used makes relatively little difference most of the time. But as projects get larger and more complex, behavior is less and less obvious, and the joint-product nature of projects becomes more prominent.

The performance of the principal (owner) on the front end of projects becomes progressively more critical to project outcomes as size and complexity increase. This point is demonstrated clearly in Figure 8.1. As project size increases, the detrimental

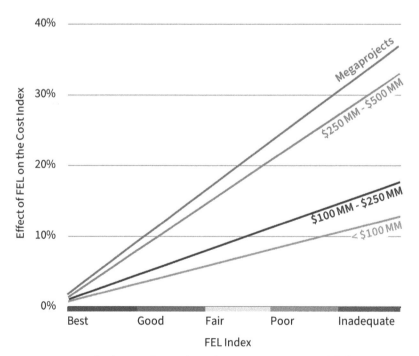

FIGURE 8.1   The larger the project, the more consequential the FEL.

effects of poor owner work on the front end become larger.[4] This figure shows the effect of poor owner work on cost competitiveness, but similar charts could be shown for cost overruns, execution schedule effectiveness, execution schedule slip, and facility operability.

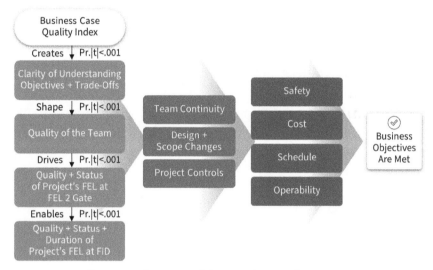

FIGURE 8.2   Owner performance drives project performance.

As shown in Figure 8.2, the owner's performance reverberates all the way through capital projects. The quality and completeness of the business case—a purely owner activity—drive the clarity of objectives, which in turn drives the completeness of the owner team, which facilitates closing of the scope in a timely way before FEED starts and ultimately results in a

---

[4]The FEL index is a numerical scale developed by IPA and used to evaluate more than 20,000 capital projects over the past 35 years. It measures engineering maturity, definition of the site-specific factors such as regulatory requirements and soil conditions, and project execution planning. The FEL index shown in Figure 8.1 was measured at full-funds authorization (final investment decision). Cost performance on the vertical axis is the competitiveness of a project versus projects of equivalent scope. What is shown is the incremental effects of FEL on cost competitiveness.

well-prepared project.[5] The well-prepared project is ultimately the successful project.

In practice, separating the effects of owner work and contractor work on project outcomes is progressively more difficult on larger and more complex projects, but it is precisely these projects on which we are more likely to see outcome-based incentive schemes. Outcome-based incentive schemes are problematic when who caused the outcome is hard to discern because they then encounter issues of fairness and rationality—fairness because it is obviously unfair for a contractor to lose an incentive due to the poor performance of the owner and rationality because the whole purpose of supplemental incentives is to line up contractor's behavior with performance to create an enhanced payoff.

When and What Incentives Are Used

The use of supplemental incentives is shaped by contracting strategy and by project size. As shown in Figure 8.3, the use of incentives becomes more common as projects get larger. This conforms to the principle that the principal-agent problem becomes more acute as behavior becomes less clear. Thus, the addition of outcome-based incentives on large projects is logical. By the time a project reaches $250 million in 2022 terms, more than half of the projects carry supplemental outcome-based incentives.

There are four major outcomes that are frequently addressed by incentives.

- Cost deviation from the authorization baseline
- Schedule deviation from baseline

---

[5]See Ed Merrow and Kate Rizor, "The Criticality of Gate 1—Making the Case for the Business Case," *Industry Benchmarking Consortium Annual Meeting*, IPA, March 2021.

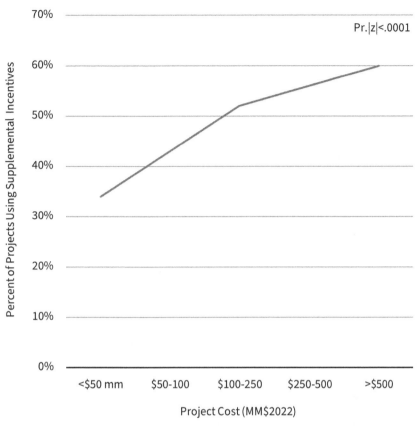

FIGURE 8.3   Incentive use increases with project size.

- Operability of plant, usually measured as percent of name-plate production in time
- Construction safety

As we at IPA evaluate a project, we inquire about the relative priority of outcomes. Logic would suggest that the frequency of incentivizing an outcome would be related to the importance attached to that outcome in the project objectives. However, we find much less pattern in the application of supplemental incentives than logic would suggest. When we consider cost, for example, projects in which low capital cost is the number-one objective apply cost incentives to 35 percent of projects, but

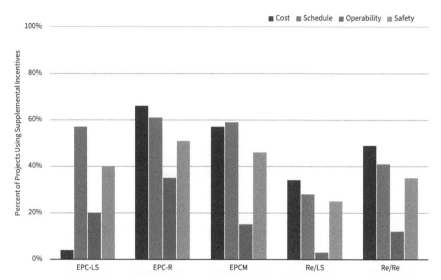

FIGURE 8.4   Incentives are most used on EPC-R and EPCM.

projects in which cost is not a high priority incentivize cost 30 percent of the time.[6] Even more peculiar is schedule. When project objectives place schedule attainment at number one, schedule is incentivized 33 percent of the time. When schedule is not top priority, owners incentivize schedule 38 percent of the time! Schedule is the most often incentivized outcome with incentives applied to 50 percent of projects. It is the norm in the industry (more than 80 percent) to employ both cost and schedule incentives to the same project despite the obvious observation that cost and schedule trade off against each other.

Figure 8.4 shows the frequency of incentives use for each of the big four project outcomes by the contract strategy employed. EPC-LS and Re/LS make the least use of incentives. In both cases, there is no consistent relationship between incentive use and size of project. The most commonly employed incentives in EPC-LS by far are for schedule with safety being second. Reasonably

---

[6]I excluded EPC-LS projects because they rarely carry a supplemental cost incentive as they are already fully cost incentivized.

enough, cost is not incentivized save for a few oddball schemes involving incentives for cost savings ideas presented during execution. (There were not many.) For Re/LS, schedule and safety are incentivized equally often. Note, however, that safety carries fewer incentive payments in Re/LS than any other form. Like EPC-LS, cost is less often incentivized in the Re/LS form because only engineering could be reasonably incentivized for cost and most owners realize that encouraging engineering contractors to skimp on engineering hours carries considerable risk to the owner of poor design, which in turn will vitiate the effectiveness of the planned lump-sum construction. When engineering was incentivized at all in the Re/LS form, it was for schedule. Constructors were most often incentivized for safety performance.

The most heavily incentivized contract forms are EPC-R and EPCM. Both forms are routinely incentivized for both cost *and* schedule. On large projects, cost and schedule are incentivized well over half of the time. Note the frequency of schedule incentives for these forms. This is despite not placing higher priority on schedule than average. The underlying owner assumption is that EPC-R and EPCM contractors will not turn in their best performance without incentives—lots of them. In EPC-R contracts, even operability is incentivized fairly often at more than 30 percent.[7] There is no discernible rhyme or reason for the frequency of operability incentives for EPC-R contracts. The owner has very good control of quality; there is no incentive to cut corners by the contractor. Even stranger, the EPC-R projects most likely to be incentivized for operability are those with *no* new technology whatsoever.

There is no consensus among owners in their philosophy toward using supplemental incentives. Some companies use them as a matter of policy. Many companies leave the issue up to individual project teams or to contracting groups within the projects or procurement organization. When a team or company decides to use incentives, they rarely decide to use a single incentive such

---

[7]Operability is very difficult to incentivize effectively for reasons we will discuss.

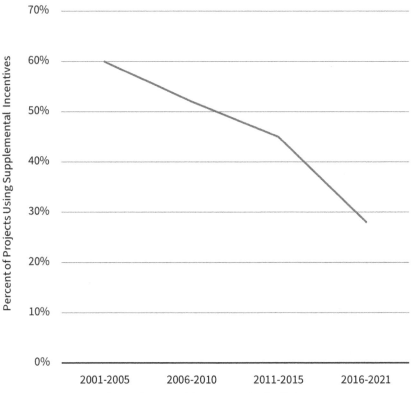

FIGURE 8.5 Use of supplemental incentives is declining.

as for schedule. Often contractors lobby for the use of incentives, although demanding incentives as a condition for taking a contract is rare. As shown in Figure 8.5, the use of incentives is declining among IPA clients. Supplemental incentives are used about half as often today as they were in 2001. This result may not be representative of the industry as IPA data have led us to question the efficacy of supplemental incentives for many years.

Cost Incentives and Outcomes

Cost-associated incentives are almost always based on deviations (underruns or overruns) from the owner's authorization estimate.[8] There are very few cost-based incentives associated with cost effectiveness because cost effectiveness is too difficult for all but the most sophisticated owners to measure. The fact that cost effectiveness rarely enters the discussion is very important. First, it means that the FEED-EPC-R or FEED-EPCM contractor who knows that cost-based incentives will be included in the execution contract is highly incentivized to inflate the cost estimate. As shown in Chapter 4, that is exactly what happens in F-EPC-R and EPCM reimbursable situations.

Cost deviation appears easy to measure in principle—just take the actual amount spent and divide it by the authorization estimate. It is, however, actually quite difficult to measure in a *meaningful* way in practice because so many unplanned things can happen during execution. Some of those things, such as a downturn in material prices, can generate a windfall for the incentivized contractor. Most of the things that can happen, however, increase the cost, and assigning responsibility for that in a reimbursable situation is usually difficult.[9]

Cost deviation incentives may come in the form of a fixed bonus amount for achieving a given cost result; a percent of fee at risk, which generally provides for a higher than normal potential fee; a percent of savings scheme; or a gain/pain-share arrangement. A fixed bonus amount is the most common, followed by percent of fee at risk, gainshare/painshare, and percent of savings.

---

[8]Recall that the "owner's" estimate was often developed by the FEED contractor. The degree to which it is really "an owner estimate" depends on the validation skills of the owner in such cases. Validation is actually quite difficult. See Melissa Mathews, "The Quality of Cost Estimates", Cost Engineering Committee Conference 2017, IPA.
[9]In lump-sums there are carefully written contract terms that clarify which things raise the contract ceiling and which do not. The contractor keeps a careful change log of everything that could raise the contract ceiling. In reimbursable contracts, even with substantial incentives in play, the contract terms are usually not nearly so clear, and the contractor is less likely to keep a good change log and may even be discouraged by the owner from spending the money needed to keep a good change log.

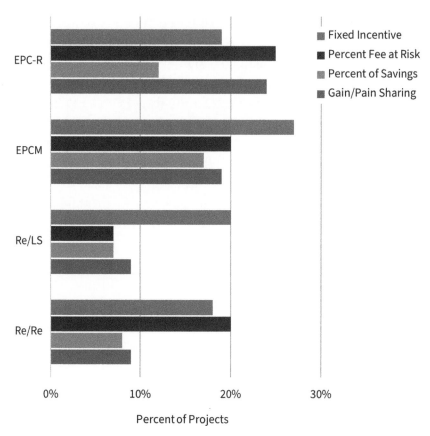

FIGURE 8.6   Types of cost incentives employed in different contracting settings.

Figure 8.6 shows the use of the different cost incentive approaches. Several things are noteworthy. The use of gain/pain sharing incentives is largely confined to EPC-R and EPCM. If Re/LS projects are incentivized at all for cost, it is usually with a simple fixed bonus payment amount and is usually made to the engineering company. For Re/Re forms, percent of fee at risk is used along with fixed bonuses.

Looking at EPC-R and EPCM contracting strategies, the use of cost incentives is associated with the project costing more money for the owner. The effect is 5 percent of total capital cost (Pr.|t|<.05). When we control for FEL quality, turnover of owner personnel, or the quality of controls, the result is unaffected.[10] Among EPC-R and EPCM projects, the cost-incentivized projects cost more. There is no relationship between cost incentives and more cost growth. This is to be expected, because incentivization is associated with inflated estimates, which tend to wash out any relationship with cost growth.

For the split-form contracting strategies, Re/LS and Re/Re, there is no relationship between incentivization for cost and cost of the project at all. Even after controlling for the same factors as discussed earlier, there is no relationship at all (Pr.|t|<.7). Cost incentives on EPC reimbursable forms damage the owner; on split forms they are just irrelevant. That makes it quite unfortunate for owners that they use incentives much more often on those reimbursable EPC forms.

Not all forms of cost incentives are equally damaging to owner interests on the EPC forms. By far the worst is the gain/painshare formulation of this incentive. Remember, gain/pain-share is where underruns are shared between the owner and contractor by formula, and overruns are shared as well. For EPC-R and EPCM strategies, gain/pain arrangements add *11 percent* to total capital cost (Pr.|t|<.005). Unlike cost incentives generally, gain/pain also tends to add to cost growth. The dynamic in gain/pain incentives is clear from reading the case studies. The pain-share provision adds substantially to the contractor's risk. It sometimes puts the contractor in the position of losing money on a reimbursable contract, which is generally considered a no-risk or low-risk contract type for contractors. If the positive incentive is lost and the pain portion approaching, the contractor often feels they are better off expending more hours as long as those hours include all of the multiplier. They will then fight

---

[10]Controlling for key practices that have major effects on project outcomes is essential if we are to avoid misplaced causation. If a particular contract type is associated with better or worse practices, those practices will usually have more effect on the results than the contract type. (Of course, if a contract type is associated with systematically better or worse practices, it is interesting to ask why.)

with the owner later about whether the pain-share should be inflicted. Owners often relent, and the contractor may come out whole if not ahead.

The least bad form of cost incentive for EPC-R and EPCM is the percent of savings form. Cost is directionally a bit higher, but it is not significant. Percent of fee at risk and a fixed amount bonus for cost performance bring about a 4 to 6 percent cost penalty.

Why Cost Incentives Do Not Work

The data are clear that cost incentives do not work as the owner hoped and for EPC-R and EPCM forms make projects considerably less cost effective. Similarly, cost incentives do nothing to reduce cost growth on projects. There are several reasons that cost incentives are not helpful.

Cost incentives do not change any project fundamentals. Cost incentives are unrelated to clear project objectives or the quality and completeness of the owner team. Incentives do not improve the quality of front-end loading or project controls. Therefore, a null effect of cost incentives on cost is not surprising.

What may be surprising to many is the detrimental effect on cost in precisely those reimbursable EPC/EPCM situations where owners feel they need cost incentives most to align owner and contractor objectives. The higher cost estimates associated with FEED contractors carrying over into execution on these forms is part of the problem. When cost will be incentivized, the FEED contractors need to ensure a generous cost estimate is reinforced.

I suspect that the owner tendency to incentivize multiple outcomes (and often in multiple ways) tends to reduce the effectiveness of all the incentives employed. In particular, the combined incentivization of cost and schedule leaves it to the contractor to try to figure out what the owner really wants.

Also, when cost incentives are broached during negotiation of contract provisions, they are frequently negotiated between the owner and contractor. Often, the contractors are highly skilled negotiators in these situations. Incentives are, of course, subject to gaming, and contractors are inevitably going to be more skilled than owners in playing contracting games. They have far more at stake in sharpening their skills.[11]

However, the worst problem is that cost incentives often turn out to be a "paper tiger." As a project progresses and if the contractor is increasingly at risk of losing his cost incentive, owners often re-baseline the incentive to keep the incentive active. Re-baselining takes the form of increasing the cost overrun level that will still generate a bonus payment. Think through the situation: you believe as an owner that the key ingredients in getting good work from this contractor are the supplemental incentives in the contract. If the contractor is in jeopardy of losing all incentives, they therefore will not do a good job. The logic is inescapable. In particular, with cost incentives, you fear that the contractor is going to "crank hours," which was precisely the behavior you were hoping to avoid in the first place by using cost incentives. This leads almost inevitably to the sense that re-baselining is necessary to success. The owner is caught in a trap of their own making.

It may be, of course, that owner changes and inefficiencies are the reason that costs have increased in which case it feels fundamentally unfair to penalize the contractor. It may be that the sources of cost growth are ambiguous, which renders the loss of the incentive ethically ambiguous. But if we regularly re-baseline when incentives are being lost, what meaning did the incentives have to start with?

---

[11]For a discussion of contracting games, see James G. Zack, "Claimsmanship: Current Perspective," *Journal of Construction Engineering and Management* 119 (September 1993).

An Exception That Tests the Rule

I am aware of one very effective process plant constructor that always negotiates a *single* incentive in their reimbursable work—an incentive around labor productivity. At a number of points I have reminded readers that owners should not assume construction labor productivity risk. It is a risk over which owners have limited control and lack the staff competence to manage.

The owner and contractor would agree to target hours for the work that could be modified only for scope changes. Sometimes a small dead band around that target will be included. Then deviations from that band would create a gain for the contractor on a per-hour saved basis or a loss on the high side. As this was a very high-productivity constructor, it is hard to argue that the incentives did not work even though it could not be proven definitively without a controlled experiment.

There are several appealing features of this incentive scheme. First, it was not a general cost incentive. Cost incentives create a moral hazard around wanting (or hiding) markups elsewhere that will generate an incentive gain even if productivity is poor. The incentive also was not for hourly cost *paid* to and for craft but an incentive paid or not on the number of hours consumed. Second, it was generally the *only* incentive provided and always the only incentive that the constructor wanted. The constructor made the point that the owners usually wanted schedule incentives as well, and that would create a difficult optimization problem. The schedule incentive was unnecessary because if labor productivity is good, schedule usually follows. Third, any incentive bonus was shared with the construction management team.

On reflection, I am not surprised that an incentive set up in the previous manner was successful. It was simple and direct. It sought a *particular* change over which the construction firm had a significant degree of direct control. It is also so unusual that it would never show up in the data!

Schedule Incentives and Schedule Outcomes

Schedule and schedule slip are big issues for industrial projects. If projects were faster, there would be less chance of bleeding in the business case between the decision to move forward and the realization of the result. For industrial projects generally, slip in execution schedules averages 18 percent from FID to mechanical completion, and slip in engineering is far worse, which means that the overlap of detailed engineering and construction is routinely larger than expected.[12] As shown in Figure 8.7, slip is common to all contract approaches. EPC-LS suffers the least engineering slip, and along with the other EPC strategies has less execution slip. The split forms average a lot of slip in engineering and execution. Engineering slip is problematic across the board save in EPC-LS. We are showing the medians (half more/half less). The mean (i.e., average) engineering slip is far worse! Note that although Re/Re has quite a bit of slip, the resulting schedules are still comparable to the EPC-R and EPCM forms and faster than EPC-LS. Re/LS, however, delivers the longest execution schedules on average, although by only a small amount.

Owners use schedule incentives in half of their projects. The goal of a schedule incentive is to improve the chances of the project coming in on time or to accelerate the schedule from the promised date. If, after controlling for project practices,

---

[12]We measure engineering slip as the actual time from the start of detailed engineering to demobilization of the contractor's design team divided by the planned time. Slip in engineering is a key cause of project failure, especially in larger projects. Engineering slip causes slip in equipment and engineered material procurement. Even though the start of construction is usually delayed somewhat, construction often outruns engineering and procurement when engineering slip is large. This in turn causes labor productivity to plummet as the constructors have no materials to install. As engineering slips, the engineering errors increase, which means that the design that reaches the field is often of poorer quality.

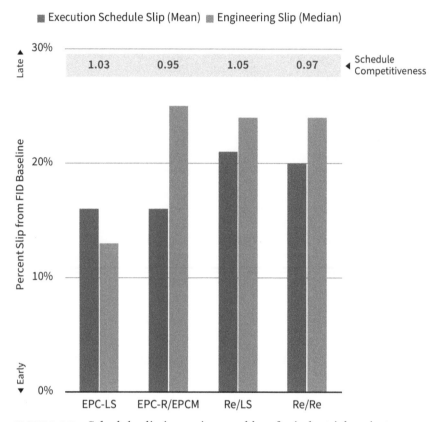

■ Execution Schedule Slip (Mean) ■ Engineering Slip (Median)

FIGURE 8.7 Schedule slip is a serious problem for industrial projects.

schedule-incentivized projects are not faster in execution than their non-schedule-incentivized counterparts and they are not subject to less slip in schedule, then I think we must agree that the incentives are not effective.

Schedule Incentives in the EPC Forms

Let's look first at the EPC-LS projects. Referring to Figure 8.4, more than 50 percent of EPC-LS projects are schedule-incentivized. Remembering that EPC-LS contracts are intrinsically strongly cost-incentivized, it is rather surprising that owners attempt to modify that incentive structure with schedule incentives. It is even more surprising when one notes that every EPC-LS contractor is already cost-incentivized to get done as quickly as reasonably possible. The EPC-LS contractor wants to finish the job, get the retained funds, and be on to the next project. There is no incentive to dawdle. But there is a powerful *dis*incentive to attempt to accelerate the project to be faster than the lowest cost region of schedule. The disincentive is largest in large EPC-LS projects because the lowest cost region of schedule is a narrower window, and the marginal costs of acceleration increase rapidly with project size.

The data confirm what common sense suggested: there is no relationship whatsoever between the use of schedule incentives and faster schedule in EPC-LS. The difference with and without incentives is 2 percent and not nearly significant. The execution and engineering slip are actually worse when schedule incentives were involved. That result disappears when we control for FEED quality. The lack of relationship between schedule incentives and schedule results does not mean that schedule incentives were never paid on EPC-LS; they often were. But they were paid on a completely random result. If the contractor was lucky enough to complete the project in the bonus payment period, the contractor got a bonus. If not, there was no bonus. (If there were cost penalties for late completion, those are usually in the form of liquidated damages, and I will speak to them later in the chapter.) The problem is that in those cases in which the project was incentivized for schedule and came in within the bonus time, the owner too often believes that the incentive created the outcome. Misplaced causation is so common in incentive contracting that it is almost the norm.

Turning now to the EPC reimbursable forms, EPC-R and EPCM, schedule incentives were used on about 60 percent of projects in both groups. The schedule competitiveness for the reimbursable EPC forms is identical. Execution schedule slip is identical. There was a little less engineering slip in the incentivized. No statistical controls make a difference in these results.

The data on EPC forms and schedule incentives are crystal clear: they don't work. The irony is that schedule incentives are most frequently used on exactly these projects! Just like EPC-LS results, owners believe that incentives worked when the projects did not slip a lot, and when they do, it must have been something else, not the incentive.

Schedule Incentives on Split-Form Contracting

We now turn to looking at schedule incentives and the split forms Re/LS and Re/Re. Schedule incentives are used less often in these forms than any of the EPC strategies. Schedule incentives are used in only 25 percent of Re/LS projects and about a third of Re/Re projects. The lower use of schedule incentives on Re/LS projects is understandable when one recalls they are least likely to be schedule-driven projects. Less than one Re/LS project in five is schedule-driven, even less than EPC-LS. Re/Re projects are schedule-driven more often at 29 percent of projects, but still less than industry average. Schedule priority no doubt sometimes played a role in the decision to go with some form of reimbursable construction rather than lump-sum in the Re/Re strategy.

In another ironic twist, schedule incentives are most effective in the contracting strategies in which they are least used. Execution schedules are decreased 6 percent (Pr.|t|<.03) when schedule incentives are added to Re/LS contract approaches and by 8 percent when added to Re/Re projects (Pr.|t|<.01). Execution schedule slip declines by 9 percent (Pr.|t|<.01), and engineering slip declines by an impressive 12 percent (Pr.|t|<.004) on the Re/LS projects and by 6 and 11 percent, respectively, for Re/Re projects.[13] All results are statistically reliable.

---

[13]These results are unchanged when controlled for front-end loading and project size or other drivers.

In the Re/LS and Re/Re projects, the schedule incentives were almost all contained in the engineering contract, not the construction contracts. That reflects the reality that in split-form contracting, engineering dictates the pace almost completely.

Why do schedule incentives work in split forms when they fall so completely flat on EPC contracting forms? I believe the effectiveness of schedule incentives for engineering firms on split forms is due to the *salience* of the incentive and *clarity* about what is needed to earn the incentive. The salience is high because an incentive may double the fee earned by the engineer while having an undetectable effect on total installed cost.[14] The clarity is high because all the engineering has to do to increase speed is mobilize the staff by discipline faster. The engineering firm is not asked to speed up the entire project; they are tasked with speeding up *their* work, no one else's. Because their work is always critical path, improved speed translates to whole project speed. If the FEED work is complete, the primary reason that engineering tends to slip is because the engineering company does not have the right number of people in the right disciplines available at the right time. There are generally no downsides for the engineering contractor except annoying the owner team. The rules of credit generally reward the contractor for whatever work they do whether or not it slips and whether or not the work is in the proper sequence to serve construction. However, if the engineering contractor sees a significantly larger profit if the engineering can be completed sooner, they will work to make the right people available. This all needs to be set up by the owner early in the contracting process so the engineering company can make the needed arrangements without trying to brute-force accelerate engineering.

The problem with most incentives most of the time is that the connection between the incentive and the decisions and

---

[14]When schedule incentives are applied to split-form contracts, there is no negative impact on cost effectiveness. In fact, costs are directionally lower, not higher, but the result is not quite statistically reliable, controlling for FEL ($Pr.|t| < .09$).

actions needed to gain the incentive are usually not at all clear to the contractor people on the project who would have to implement any change in behavior. Achieving the incentives would often require a rethinking of the contractor's whole approach to the project, and that is not going to happen. In the split-form situation for the engineering firm, however, a relatively simply change can result in achieving the incentive without seriously altering anything else. We are not asking the engineering firm to spend more of their own money, and no more hours are actually needed to do the work expeditiously.

Contrast this with EPC situations. The EPC or EPCM contractor is incentivized to speed up the project but has a number of other things to worry about and a number of other areas in which profits may be made. The EPC-LS contractor is heavily incentivized for cost and so views any schedule incentives as strictly secondary. If they are won, fine. But any suggestion that an EPC-LS contractor would spend *money* to achieve a schedule incentive is borderline ridiculous. The EPC-LS contractor has so many subs, vendors, and other suppliers on which it depends that figuring out how to accelerate successfully is very challenging.

The EPC-R and EPCM contractor have profit potential throughout the entire project with schedule being only one element. The schedule incentive is much smaller as a percent of their contract than it is for the engineering contractor on a split form. It must be smaller because doubling the fees of the contractor on the whole project would be instantly noticeable in the total installed cost. So, both salience and clarity are lower in the EPC situations than in the split forms.

Figure 8.8 revisits the schedule results of different contracting strategies with and without schedule incentives. All of the changes with and without are minor in the EPC strategies, and none are statistically reliable. For the split strategies the differences are both large and statistically reliable. Note that the schedule incentivized Re/Re form is the fastest contracting approach at 89 percent of industry average. Also note that execution schedule

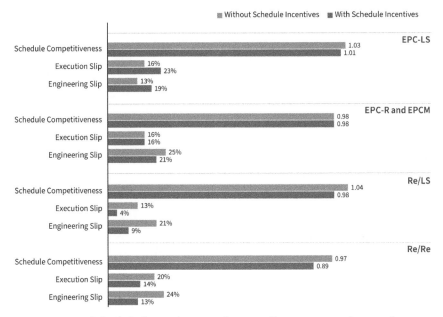

■ Without Schedule Incentives   ■ With Schedule Incentives

FIGURE 8.8 Schedule incentives accelerate split strategy projects only.

slip all but disappears on the schedule incentivized Re/LS form and that engineering slip is lowest of any contract form. Schedule incentives applied to the engineering contractor on split-form contracts are the only supplemental incentive that routinely works the way owners hope and expect.

Liquidated Damages (LDs) for Delay[15]

LDs are an agreed-upon amount in the contract terms and conditions that the contractor will pay the owner for unexcused delay

[15]Liquidated damages can in principle be used for a great many things. For example, LDs are sometimes included for replacement of key personnel by contractor during execution. Such use of LDs are intensely disliked by contractors, especially where the LDs seek to control their internal work processes. By far the most common use of LDs, however, is for delay. LDs for delay are normally confined to lump-sum situations, but other kinds of LDs might be used with any contractual form.

to a major project milestone, including mechanical completion and overall project completion.[16] The imposition of LDs often starts after a grace period following the milestone, as that milestone is extended to account for excusable delay. As a result, the contract's definition of excusable delay becomes very important here. Delay caused by the owner will almost always be excusable, as are delays explicitly covered by the force majeure clause in the contract. However, the consequences of delay caused by other events, particularly third parties and changes of law, are heavily negotiated and may be shifted to the contractor. In this case, the contractor may end up in jeopardy to pay LDs due to factors over which he had no real control.

As the name implies, LDs are usually (but not always) considered a wrap, that is, sole remedy for delay. LDs are not intended to be *penalties* for being late, even if it feels that way to the contractor. If the LDs are not tethered to specific costs borne by the owner for the delay or appear unreasonably high, courts and arbitrators may construe the LDs as penalties and reject the owner's imposition of LDs. LDs are an agreed-upon-in-advance formulaic *damage* claim by owner.

LDs are used almost exclusively on EPC-LS projects, rather than reimbursable forms of EPC or split forms. If non-recourse[17] lending is used on a project, the lenders often insist on EPC-LS contracts with LDs. LDs are occasionally used with lump-sum construction in split forms, but rarely. The reason that LDs are rarely tried on reimbursable contracts is that the notion of a contractually set and firm end date for which the contractor is responsible runs counter to the owner-controlled nature of

---

[16]Usually, the LDs are "paid" when the owner offsets the accrued LD amount from payment or retainage. LDs may also be included in contracts between a prime contractor and subs and usually are included if LDs are included in the prime contract as protection for the prime.

[17]Nonrecourse lending is money lent to finance the project with no access to the balance sheets of the owners or their parents. In other words, all repayment of loans must be made from project-generated revenue and not from other investor assets.

reimbursable projects. If the owner is in control, then the contractor cannot be made responsible for a firm completion date. We have seen a few examples of owners trying LDs on reimbursable contracts, but without success.

LDs can come in a number of forms. Contractors strongly prefer LDs that are intended to cover only *enumerated* owners' out-of-pocket costs associated with unexcused delay. This would be all of the direct time-related costs such as the owner project team, lease-extensions, individual contractors, agency staff, possibly the already hired operations team, and so forth. On large projects, a delay of a month could amount to millions of dollars in damages, especially if the owner team has a large number of ex-patriates working on the project site. Ideally, LDs provide some measure of protection to both owner and contractor. Owners feel that the LDs make slip in the schedule less likely. It is worth noting that the LDs, if limited to the owner's direct cost, cannot possibly offset the consequential damages of delayed production in most industrial projects. The direct costs recovered usually pale in comparison with the value of lost production and the loss of value associated with the time value of money.[18] When a project is late, almost the entire cost of the project is sitting on the ground generating no revenue, but generating large opportunity costs. When the project is externally financed, those costs are tangible as interest paid during construction. Sometimes the owner seeks to include that interest paid as a direct cost covered by the LDs, but that is rarely acceptable to the contractor because the amounts are so large. So the owner must be looking at the LDs as a form of supplemental incentive to reduce the probability of delay. It is not really a mechanism for recovery of all delay damages to the owner.

---

[18]There are counterexamples in our dataset where the LDs were far more valuable than the delays production because the market for the product had tanked during the project. In two cases, this resulted in the owners going into a "by the rules" slowdown in order to push the contractor into the LDs being paid. This is an example of a moral hazard inadvertently created. It is also highly unethical.

Although owners may want consequential damages, such as lost profit and perhaps even lost market share, from the contractor, the differences between owners and contractors as economic entities make consequential damages untenable for contractors. The contract rewards are simply not worth the potential risk. If production has been forward-sold at a specific price or, even better, at a fixed *margin*, LDs might be enforceable on the lost profit. LDs are in fact most often included when the product is forward-sold from an EPC-LS project. However, even in those cases, the LDs are usually confined to the owner's direct time-related losses rather than consequential damages. In today's contractor environment, very few contractors will accept *any* form of consequential damages and therefore will strongly resist anything but simple calculable direct costs in LDs.

The value of LDs to the contractor is that if they are properly written from the contractor's viewpoint, they provide a definable limit on liability for being late. When the LDs are capped to a percent of the contract value, they provide an absolute limit. When markets for contractor services are not depressed, the inclusion of LDs generally carries a risk premium in EPC-LS bids.

Do LDs Work?

For LDs to be considered effective from the owner's standpoint, they should be associated with less schedule slip and/or shorter projects. To say that LDs do not work as expected is an understatement. LDs are actually associated with projects being *longer* by 13 percent in execution (Pr.|t|<.05) and experiencing 15 percent *more* slip. The relationship is probably not causal, but it certainly does not support the use of the device. On projects with LDs we see more arguments between owner and contractor about what constitutes mechanical completion, with the owner wanting more pre-commissioning activities and punch list items completed than normal.[19] However, it is very clear that the projects are not shorter and do not experience less slip.

The schedule problems, however, are the minor problems. The use of LDs is associated with 75 percent *longer* startups (Pr.|t|<.03) and much poorer first-year operability! When the project is running late and the contractor sees the possibility of LDs being imposed, a mad dash ensues to complete the work within the required period. The result is sloppiness in construction that carries over into long startups and more mechanical failures in the first year. Despite the longer projects associated with LDs, we rarely see liquidated damages actually paid by the contractor. When LDs are included in the contract, contractors are careful to keep detailed logs of any owner or third-party created delays or to hurry to completion so the penalties are not imposed. The fact that those financing a project often mandate LDs for the EPC-LS projects they fund is another incentive irony. The only time that a bank may fail to get paid on a nonrecourse project loan is if the project does not produce and generate cash flow. The use of LDs is clearly associated with that being more rather than less likely.

From an economics perspective, incentives and penalties are the same thing. However, from the viewpoint of human psychology, they are very different. It is well known that people will struggle harder to avoid loss than to secure gain. The same applies in the contracting world. Any form of incentive that includes pain in the formula will be gamed with far more passion by contractors than those that contain only possibility of gain. Gain/painshare cost incentives, LDs for schedule, fee-at-risk, and operability penalties will receive focus by contractors, but usually at the expense of a good project.

---

[19]We define mechanical completion as the point when all facilities are ready to operate in principle. Practically speaking, startup may still be in the future due to commissioning activities. And a good many items not necessary for operation may still be pending.

So this leaves us in a conundrum. If there are no LDs, the owner may be damaged by the contractor's tardiness through no fault of their own. Also, if there are no LDs but the contractor is still liable for unexcused delay, the contractor may be subject to an owner claim anyway that is not capped or even fully defined.

LDs, unlike a good many other supplemental incentives, are not ignored by contractors. They clearly change behavior whenever the contractor is in jeopardy of their being triggered and the behavior is not good for the owner. Agreeing not to impose the LDs when the contractor is falling behind is just another form of incentive re-baselining.

A downside of LDs for owners is that when LDs are in place, contractors will be sticklers for each and every owner-caused delay. They will carefully document all such delays. Contractors will also document any owner behavior that *could* be considered owner-caused delay such as interference in the contractor's usual procedures.

On balance, my view is that owners are better off foregoing LDs and waiving most delay-related damages. Two avenues of thought lead me to this conclusion. First, the LDs are not working to reduce delay and are leading to unintended consequences that are quite damaging to owners. Second, the owner needs to remember that the contractor who is seriously late is already paying heavily for his tardiness. A mere 10 percent slip increases costs about 3 percent of contract value, which is very likely much of the contractor's profit. The contractor has every incentive to finish the job without the added concern of the LDs. In cases in which financing depends on the inclusion of LDs, they will be included, although efforts to educate bankers around the lack of effectiveness should probably be made.

Operability Incentives

Owners use operability incentives (i.e., bonus payments for facilities achieving a determined level of production over a defined period post startup) in only 12 percent of projects. Operability incentives can be tied to speed of completing startup activities or (and more usually) to facility uptime in the first year of production. Owners sometimes propose operability penalties as well in a gain/painshare type of arrangement but rarely include them due to vigorous opposition from EPC contractors. Operability incentives have no discernible relationship to operability outcomes in any contracting approach. That is just another way of saying that contractors ignore operability incentives. This is not at all surprising. Operability incentives are paid after the project is completed by the contractor, often a year or more. When a reward is distant in time, it will usually be ignored. Contractors also discount operability incentives and resist operability penalties because they believe the incentives depend on the performance of the owner's operating organization more than their performance.[20]

The most surprising aspect of operability incentives is they are only common (about 30 percent of projects) in EPC-reimbursable contracts. That is precisely where we would expect *not* to see them! Owner control is maximized in the EPC-R. The contractor is actually disincentivized to cut corners; cut corners mean fewer hours. Where we might expect to see operability incentives is in EPC-LS contracts, but they occur there at less than half the rate of EPC-R contracts. It does matter because when operability incentives are used, capital cost goes up. Even controlling for their higher use on EPC-R contracts, operability incentives are associated with 7 percent more expensive facilities $(Pr.|t| < .02)$.[21]

---

[20]Of course, in build-operate-transfer situations, the contractor will be automatically incentivized for operability because the contractor is often paid based on production amounts.

[21]We see a similar effect on capital cost when the owner places operability at the top of their priorities for a project. Incentivizing operability or giving operability highest priority appears to justify a more conservative approach to design, in other words, "gold-plating."

Safety Incentives

Safety incentives are amounts paid to the EPC or constructor based on achieving a specified DART and recordable injury rate on a project.[22] Owners include safety incentives in just over 30 percent of projects. Some owners incentivize safety routinely while some owners never do. Safety follows the pattern of all incentives in being used progressively less over time.

Safety incentives have no statistically significant relationship with better safety performance in industrial projects. The relationship is directionally negative but far too weak to be reliable. In light of contractor comments later in this chapter, we should dismiss the notion that incentives make a project safer. The quality of the owner team (Pr.|t|<.001) and the completeness of front-end loading (Pr.|t|<.04) are the primary drivers of construction safety.

What Contractors Think (But Often Don't Say) About Incentives

Several years ago, IPA surveyed a group of large EPC firms from around the world on their views of supplemental incentives. The group included European, North American, Korean, Australian, and Japanese firms. The most common respondent for the EPCs was their corporate contracting lead. The most surprising aspect of the results was the uniformity of reactions and comments about owner use of incentives. The candor of many respondents was disarming.

All contractors agreed that they like incentives because their base fees are too low for them to be financially healthy. Contractors like multiple outcomes subject to incentives as it increases their chances of capturing at least some of them. One wag said,

---

[22]Refer to Chapter 3 for the definitions of these terms.

"We particularly like incentives that pay early and pay often." Several said their favorite incentives were of the "feel good" variety.[23] As one contractor told me somewhat cynically, "Think of us as your psychiatrist; if you pay us, we will pretend to like you." They told us they often participate in setting incentives and argue for "holistic goal setting." That translates to multiple incentives. They rejected any suggestion that participation in incentive-setting amounted to a conflict of interest. The contractors expressed their disapproval of incentives aimed at changing the way they manage their staff. They especially dislike retention bonuses and even more especially penalties.

When asked about safety incentives, the contractor representatives were scathing in their comments. One simply called them "payments for underreporting." One comment was particularly persuasive: "Do the owners really believe that we won't bring our safety practices and safety culture to the job if they don't provide an incentive? Don't they realize that we have insurance premiums to pay? And if we don't have good safety practices, are we supposed to suddenly acquire them before construction starts? It's kind of idiotic."

Several contractors mentioned the owner tendency to re-baseline incentives that are being lost when the project is not going according to plan. They agreed that re-baselining undermines the rationale for incentives but felt it was often a matter of being fair.

When asked if they change anything in response to incentives, the contractors all said "no." One answer, however, was particularly telling: "We have developed our practices, procedures, and approaches to staffing and executing projects over the course of decades. We are always trying to improve, but improvement is a slow and continuous process. We will not and cannot

---

[23]These are payments for "teamwork," "responsiveness," "collaborative ways of working," and the like. Such incentives are not offered very often, and we have never found any connection to outcomes.

change the way we do a project because of some incentives. We are happy to get some incentives, but we won't change anything. Our way of doing projects has kept us in business a long time."

Conclusions About Supplemental Incentives

With the exception of schedule incentives for split-form contracts, supplemental incentives do not work the way owners hope they will. They often have unintended negative consequences and are generally associated with projects being poorer rather than better. The decline we see among our clients suggests that owners are slowly coming to agree.

Before an owner considers adding incentives to a contract, some hard questions need to be addressed.

- What *specifically* do we want this incentive to achieve? Answers such as "lower cost" or "faster schedule" are devoid of any real meaning.
- Specifically, what *actions* do we expect to be taken in response to this incentive and *by whom*?
- Does the person we expect to take action actually have personal control to take this action?
- Do we understand fully the relationship between taking the intended action and getting the intended result? Can we specify the causal chain?
- Can we imagine negative unintended consequences of employing the incentive?

I would submit that in most cases, owners cannot answer any of these questions, much less all of them. They expect the incentive will work in *unspecified ways* with *unspecified people* to achieve a *specified* improved result. It seems to me unlikely on its face.

I offer the following example of a successful supplemental incentive to underscore the importance of being able to answer the previous questions:

The owner project director on a large complex project established the following incentive with the contractor's project manager: "If at the end of the project, I can conclude in my sole discretion that you never withheld bad news from me even once during the project, I will pay your firm the entire bonus amount. If I conclude you withhold the bad news just once, you will get nothing. This is the only incentive in the contract. Are we clear?"

The owner director happily paid the incentive at the end of the project. But the interesting part is that the contractor's project manager said to him, "Your incentive forced me to tell and remind all of my key people that they must get the bad news to me quickly or we will lose our entire bonus."

The owner project director knew what he wanted, knew who could deliver that result, and challenged him to do so. The fact that it was the only incentive surely improved the chances of success. The tendency to add lots of supplemental incentives—for cost, for schedule, for teamwork, and so forth—works to decrease the probability of any of them working. Supplemental incentives that try to pull against the primary incentive in the contract form (e.g., schedule incentives in EPC-LS contracts) seem to me especially problematic.

The real problem with the use of incentives in contracting is that the underlying premise is fundamentally wrong. The underlying premise is that contractors will do their best only if they receive special incentives to do so. There is no support for this belief and lots of reasons to suspect that it is wrong. Engineers working for a contractor are no different than other professionals. They work to support themselves and their families and are deeply motivated by doing interesting and rewarding work well. If they are respected by the owner team and their views and involvement are solicited, they will never withhold their best because their firm is not receiving an incentive. Contractor people work best for intrinsic rewards, not for extrinsic rewards.[24] One might argue that is true for those on the workface but not necessarily for the contracting firm. That argument is an anthropomorphic fallacy. Contracting firms do not make any decisions; only people do.

When owners offer supplemental incentives, they are in effect offering a bribe and in doing so are disrespecting the professionalism of the contractors they have hired to assist with their project. They are attempting to manage at a distance rather than recognizing that projects are joint products in which their own active management is essential.

The trend toward using supplemental incentives was part of the movement away from relational contracting toward transactional contracting in the 1990s. That move toward contracting on a one-off basis undermined the self-enforcing nature of the professional services relationship and made the addition of incentives a logical, if flawed, adjunct. The weakening of owner project organizations was an essential part of the growth of transactional contracting because it became harder to maintain relationships with a weak owner entity and impossible to maintain relationships with owner procurement organizations that were focused on transactions. However, at the end of the day, adding incentive clauses to contracts was no solution to the problem.

---

[24]Alfie Kohn, "Science Confirms It: People are Not Pets—Research on the Efficacy of Rewards Tells Us That We Cannot Bribe Others into Doing What We Want," *New York Times*, October 28, 2018.

CHAPTER 9

It's All About Risk

Years ago, a VP of projects for one of the big oil companies complained to me, "Why do these darned [he used a different word] contractors take on risks they can't manage?" If it had been a real question instead of an outraged whine, I would have answered, "Because you make them, and they want to eat." But thinking about that incident led me to some insight into what contracting is really about: it's about risk allocation and assignment. At some level everybody on both sides of the table knows that, but we often do not behave as if we know it. During the awkward dance of contract negotiations, a forthright give and take around who is taking responsibility for which risks *and why* rarely happens.

In this chapter, I want to discuss what "risk" really means in projects. We often don't use the word very carefully or even in a manner that some would deem correctly. Second, I want to explore the principles of risk averseness and risk pricing and how those principles apply to owners and contractors. Then I will discuss the big areas of risk that need a careful look in every contract negotiation.

The Meaning of Risk

In its simplest form, *risk* refers to anything that is probabilistic rather than fully determined. By that definition almost everything is risky. When we speak of project risks, we are usually talking about things that could turn out *worse* than we expect. That doesn't narrow the field very much!

Strictly speaking, most of the things we call risks in projects are actually uncertainties. A true risk has a known probability distribution within a known range of possible outcomes.[1] Some refer to this as an actuarial risk. The distinction between risk and uncertainty is important because true risks can usually be at least mitigated by buying insurance of some form.

For example, there is a risk that a piece of equipment will be lost or damaged in transport. We can obtain insurance that will at least cover the cost of the equipment if not the consequential damages.[2] We can insure the piece of equipment because an insurance provider can figure out how likely damage in transport is and, therefore, what the insurance premium should be as a function of equipment cost. But note that we usually cannot insure against the damage that the now late piece of equipment did to our project. That is because the distribution of damages caused to projects from a late piece equipment is not known by an insurance company and varies greatly. Sometimes the damage to the project is essentially zero because the equipment was not on the critical path and the need to replace it doesn't put it on the critical path. Sometimes, a single piece of equipment can cause a project to be a year late and create large damage claims from contractors whose work is stopped.

There are relatively few true risks in projects compared with the number of uncertainties. Uncertainties come in different forms and sizes. In one form, the uncertainty is identified, the range of outcomes known, but the distribution of outcomes is unknown. For example, we might be trying a new piece of major equipment that has never been applied at scale in our intended

---

[1] See Frank Knight (1921). *Risk, Uncertainty and Profit*. New York: Houghton Mifflin.
[2] Another example of a true risk is foreign currency fluctuations that can add cost to a project. If we wish, we can insure against that possibility by buying derivatives in markets to keep currency values stable. (Of course, currency fluctuations can have an upside as well, which is not true for most project risks.)

use. The range of outcomes might be reasonably bounded: it will work as expected all the way to it doesn't work at all. Because the uncertainty is bounded, we may be able to hedge it by leaving space to replace the new equipment with the two pieces of equipment required in the past version of the process. Bounded uncertainties are more manageable than unbounded uncertainties, where we cannot define the range of possible outcomes. For example, engineering productivity is an unbounded uncertainty. While we can *imagine* how poor it could be, there is no natural limit. Finally, there are unknown uncertainties, those that never occurred to us as possible. They are fundamentally unmanageable.

In my experience with capital projects,

- True risks are few in number, which is unfortunate because they are easily managed via some form of insurance.
- Bounded uncertainties are plentiful but usually not too harmful. Much of what goes on a typical risk register are bounded uncertainties.
- Unbounded uncertainties are fewer in number but much more likely to cause significant damage.
- The unidentified uncertainties—the "unknown unknowns" as they are sometimes called—are either of the force majeure type[3] or are cascade failures that we didn't see coming. Force

---

[3] When I refer to "force majeure type" risks, I do not necessarily mean risks that would be covered in every force majeure clause in a contract. Rather, I am referring to risks that are external to the project over which no one associated with the project has control. For example, some contracts covered the COVID-19 pandemic under their force majeure clause because pandemics were listed as a force majeure event. Some contracts covered COVID-19, but more partially, under the acts of governments clause. Some contracts did not allow for any relief from the effects of COVID-19 (and are often now in dispute resolution). Another example would be a sudden increase in the price of fuel and other project inputs caused by the invasion of Ukraine. Such escalation is a "force majeure type" event but would almost never be included in a force majeure provision. It might be included in a materials escalation clause, but those clauses are unlikely until the bout of escalation has already become obvious to all in the market. The price of fuel could in principle be hedged—airlines used to hedge fuel prices routinely—but unless a market is already in disarray, such a hedge would rarely be in place for a project.

majeure events are simply a fact of life in projects and in life in general and are usually dealt with in contracts in whatever manner the parties negotiated, even if it is often an area of intense negotiation. The ugliest and most important uncertainties are the cascade failures.

The cascade failures are *amplifying knock-on effects*. These get more common as projects get larger and more complex but can occur on a project of any size.[4] For example, the owner team skipped preliminary HAZOP in front-end loading despite completing the P&IDs. When the HAZOP was done at about 60 percent design complete, major changes were indicated that set engineering and procurement back substantially, which caused materials to not arrive for the already mobilized mechanical contractor, which cratered piping productivity, which ended up with the E&I contractor invoking the cancellation clause in its contract due to the delay, and on and on until the project becomes an utter disaster in the field.

Contracts generally can do a decent job of assigning the bounded uncertainties but are less able to deal with the unbounded uncertainties. Where contracts really struggle is with the cascade failures. Going back to my homely HAZOP example: who would end up bearing the costs of the fiasco? On an EPC-LS, I am betting the contractor pays despite the owner being mostly to blame. After all, any FEED errors and omissions were supposed to be found in the first 60 days and so forth and so on. On a Re/LS, the piping contractor loses money and makes claims against the engineer and the owner, some of which may result

---

[4]Cascade failures become more common as projects get larger and more complex because large complex projects have many more hard-to-see interdependencies. Because the critical path for megaprojects is thick (many things on or close to the CP at any node), schedule knock-on effects are much more severe than in smaller projects with thin critical paths. This tendency for projects to tip into chaos has been noted by others as well. See John K. Hollmann, *Project Risk Quantification*, Probabilistic Publishing, 2016, pp. 279 ff.

in some recovery. And I can guarantee arguments all the way up and down the line about who the culprit really is. The cascade failures are where the interdependent nature of project activities and the joint product nature of owners and contractors come together. The lines of responsibility that contracts draw tend to be fuzzy and often unfair in dealing with the cascade failures because they are not anticipated.

Principles of Risk Assignment and Pricing

Jeff Bezos walks into a casino and places a $100,000 bet on 00 at the roulette wheel. He is followed by a poor man who puts the deed to his house on exactly the same bet. Both lose the bet. How do we respond? To Mr. Bezos we say it must be nice to be that rich. To the poor man we urgently refer him to a mental health clinic to deal with his gambling addiction. Same bet, different meaning. *The first principle of risk pricing is that the degree of risk averseness (if you are a rational person) is a function of one's wealth to the size of the bet.* This is why a great many people will flip a coin with you for a dollar, but very few will flip the same coin with the same expected pay-off (zero) for a million dollars. The downside of the bet has a very different meaning.

In the industrial projects world, the owners are Mr. Bezos, and the contractors are the poor bloke. That derives from owners and contractors being fundamentally different types of economic entities. Industrial owners are heavily capitalized, asset-heavy firms. Contractors are thinly capitalized, asset-light firms. Owners earn and are measured by earnings against capital assets. Contractors earn by selling the hours of their employees at a usually small markup.

Let's consider the different implications of a significant cost overrun on a project. If a contractor takes on a well-defined

EPC-LS project and the owner is disciplined, any cost overrun is *deducted* from the contractor's balance sheet. Given that the balance sheet is asset light, a major overrun on a large project may put even a large contractor in financial peril. But if the project were done on an EPC-R or Re/Re reimbursable basis and suffered the same cost overrun, that overrun is *added* to the owner's balance sheet as an asset. The owner doesn't like having to earn against a larger asset, but the overrun has very little effect on the company's financial health. *Owners are from Mars; contractors are from Venus.*

There are very practical implications of these differences for capital projects. Other things being equal, contractors will always want a larger premium (price) to take on a risk than the owner would. In my experience, owners often think that contractors gouge them with risk premiums on lump-sum contract bids. What they fail to understand is that from the contractor's perspective, the implications of taking on a risk are different than they are for the owner.

Does this mean that it is therefore inefficient to assign risks to contractors? No, it doesn't mean that at all, as we shall discuss. But it does mean that owners should expect contractors to be very careful about taking on risks. Given the tendency of contractors to price assignment of a risk higher than an owner, owners need to carefully examine whether any particular risk transfer is cost effective. Owners also need to examine whether the project circumstances make it easy for the contractor to shift the risk back to the owner. For example, if there is a reasonably high probability that government actions will slow a project, attempts to transfer delay risk to the contractor will probably not work out because actions of government risk are rarely accepted by a contractor. So any premium the owner pays in the contractor's bid for delay risk is probably money wasted. Owners should *expect* contractors to seek to shift risks back to the owner whenever owner behavior or circumstances makes that feasible. This is one of the fundamental flaws in "collaborative contracts."

The asymmetry in risk-carrying capability means that contractors will be sorely tempted to shift risk back to owners in risk-sharing contracts, and they do. The net result is that even successful integrated project delivery projects are expensive for owners.

The second principle of risk assignment and pricing is that the party most capable of managing and controlling a risk should be assigned the risk and with it the downside of failing to manage the risk successfully. This is a normative principle that accords with common sense. An alternative formulation is that assigning a risk to the party with greater control of the risk lowers the price of the risk, and vice versa.

Who is more capable of managing a risk may be a matter of skills or a matter of circumstance or both. Whenever a risk is assigned to a party that does not have control of the risk, a potential moral hazard is created in the party that does.[5] All contracting strategies create some moral hazards. EPC-LS creates a moral hazard that the contractor will cut corners in design or construction because the contractor may not bear the full consequences for those problems. Depending on how the contract is written, a moral hazard may be created by the owner not caring about flaws in their FEED package because the contract stipulates a transfer of responsibility.[6] Straight reimbursable or time and materials construction contracts may lead the constructor not to care about craft labor productivity because the risk is shifted to the owner.

Whatever moral hazard is created by a contract should become the focus of management by the other party. Smart owners using EPC-LS focus on a strong corps of inspectors; smart contractors doing EPC-LS focus on very deep evaluation of the FEED package in a short period of time; smart owners in reimbursable contracts focus on how they will manage productivity risks, and so forth.

---

[5]A moral hazard exists when a party lacks incentive to guard against a loss because they do not bear the consequences of that loss even though they control it.
[6]Owner beware, this may not work if an arbitrator finds it fundamentally unfair.

The third principle of risk assignment and pricing is that assignment of a risk to a party with little or no control over the risk means that risk will go unmanaged. When an owner dumps a risk on a contractor that the contractor cannot manage, the risk doesn't go away; it goes unmanaged. If the contractor cannot find a way to transfer the risk back to the owner or to a third party and the risk materializes, the contractor loses money. But if that risk results in a poor project or a low-quality asset, the risk all comes back to the owner and both the owner *and* the contractor lose money. Was that intelligent risk transfer? When working on contract terms and conditions with owners, I am sometimes quite amazed that owners believe that contractually transferring a risk actually solves the problem. Contracts do not change project reality. The reality is still there no matter what the contract says.

The fourth principle of risk assignment and pricing is there is no such thing as a shared risk. Risks must be assigned, not shared. That doesn't mean that the personnel of both owner and contractors may not be involved in the management of the risk, but the lead role in that management process will belong to the risk holder, and the consequences of failure to manage the risk successfully will accrue to the risk holder. Smart owners cooperate fully with contractors to assist in the management of risk that the contractor is assigned. Smart contractors cooperate fully with owners to manage risks the owner is assigned. But that is not a shared risk; that is good cooperative behavior and is normal.

One of the mistakes that owners and contractors sometimes make on EPC-LS projects is to exclude personnel from the other party from helping with the management of a risk. Owners need to be ready and willing to support contractors who are struggling on EPC-LS projects. This is why small execution owner teams are not positively indicated on EPC-LS. And recall the example of the brilliant project director with the "bring me the bad news incentive." That was an EPC-LS project, but he knew that he had to be in a position to help the contractor resolve problems, and the only way to do that was to know about them in real time. Shared risks are your risks, not mine!

So, what do the principles tell us about how to transfer risk in capital projects between the owner and the contractors? First, the principles tell us that owners who attempt to do wholesale, complete risk transfer to contractors are going to pay a higher price for their attempts than they probably realize in both the short and long term. Long term, owners who push all risk onto contractors get a market reputation that affects the bids they receive. For example, we work with a national oil company that always contracts EPC-LS and simply does not recognize as legitimate any project change. They require that dispute resolution be done locally and—*mirabile dictu*—they never seem to lose. What they do not seen to understand is that every contractor knows the game and bids 30 to 40 percent higher than they otherwise would. We see it in their benchmarks. Short term, owners who seek wholesale risk transfer will pay top dollar any time the market heats up. In the Middle East, for example, where most industrial projects are done EPC-LS, the swings in market prices for projects can be as much as 100 percent from market low to market high.

Second, risk transfer decisions (and negotiations) should be guided by who has the greater control over a risk. For example, I would never advise an owner to take on construction labor productivity risk. Owners simply lack the construction management chops needed to organize and supervise field labor except for small projects, and some owners cannot even manage that. Sometimes owners get away with straight reimbursable or time and materials construction arrangements, but they are carrying a risk they do not know how to manage. Lump-sum or unit rate construction is far more appropriate. Conversely, I would never advise a contractor to agree to some of the liability provisions that owners sometimes try to push into their contracts. For example, a provision that the contractor is fully liable for an

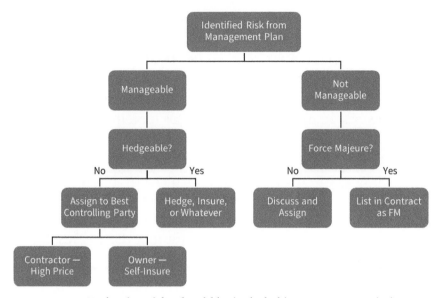

FIGURE 9.1 Evaluation risks should be included in contract negotiations.

event "in which owner is deemed to be primarily responsible" is a recipe for disaster unless the liability is capped at insurance, which many owners resist.

Third, contract negotiation should be done in the form of a "risk assignment workshop." As I discuss in the next chapter, this is where a solid construction lawyer can do a world of good for both sides. A logic diagram similar to the one found in Figure 9.1 should be used in conjunction with a risk register. Starting with an identified and defined risk from the risk register, the first question is the controllability of the risk. If the risk is not controllable within the project, the risk goes into a separate bucket that will also include all force majeure type events. Those will all have to be negotiated, but those risks follow a different path.

If a risk is considered controllable, is the risk hedgeable? For example, potential losses due to foreign currency exchange are hedgeable. If a contractor is going to accept those risks, then responsibility for hedging needs to be explicitly addressed in the contract.[7] If the owner is going to be responsible, the contract should stipulate that the owner will hedge or self-insure. If the risk is not hedgeable, who has the greater ability to control?

What are the underlying assumptions on the ability of the party to control? For example, the lump-sum construction contractor usually accepts responsibility for labor productivity, but there are a host of exceptions. For example, if engineered materials are incorrect, that is not the constructor's responsibility. If design has errors, the productivity loss normally ends up back with the owner or the engineer. If the mechanical contractor is working but the plot plan changes, all that comes back to the owner and/or the engineer. And what level of detail is assumed in the IFC design by the construction contractor? Rather than spelling out the conditions, many contracts leave it to later disputes to settle such issues.

In other words, contracts are risk-assignment documents and should be treated that way. That is really their primary purpose. However, the risk assignment is often not thorough because no systematic accounting of project risks is used. When risks are explicitly assigned to a party, it is rare that there is any discussion in the contract, or even in the negotiations, about *why* the party was assigned the risk. As a result, there is not deep agreement about the assignment of the risk. Making the risk assignments clear and discussing them fully is not just a matter of writing a more solid contract. It is also a matter of making it more likely that the assigned risks will be fully understood and fully managed by the party to whom they have been assigned. Disputes

---

[7]The currency risk area is interesting in that contractors and vendors often do not hedge the risk even if the contract explicitly passes the risk to them. Then, when they lose money on currency, they often complain bitterly that they didn't understand the risk and even try to claw back losses from owners. Given the small costs of hedging, I think owners would be smart to keep the risk and avoid the later hassles.

most often occur because the party assigned a risk in the contract did not fully appreciate or accept the risk they were taking on. Clarity in risk assignment is one of the few areas in which the contract itself can actually improve the reality of the project.

In a well-crafted contract, all of the true risks and all of known-unknowns—those things identified in the risk register—will be assigned a risk owner or otherwise accounted for. The unknown unknowns, of course, still remain. When an owner has done a solid job of preparing the project in front-end loading, most of the risks and known-unknowns have been identified, and the potential for unidentified uncertainties has been driven down as much as practically possible. In such cases, it is much more likely that any unidentified uncertainties—those ugly unknown unknowns—can be successfully managed should they arise. Projects fail when there are so many moving parts due to unpleasant surprises that project management simply cannot cope.

Key Risk Areas

I look at areas of risk not as a lawyer, because I am not, but from the perspective of project management and control. A good construction lawyer looks at how the allocation of risks in the terms and conditions combined with the compensation scheme affect the probability of disputes between owners and contractors (i.e., which Ts and Cs generate claims that will result in dispute resolution at the end of the project)?

My focus, however, is on how risk allocation combined with the contracting strategy generate better or worse projects measured primarily by cost and schedule results. Like the good construction lawyer working on the front end of the project, I hate to see projects end up in arbitration or litigation, but I hate to see an expensive, poor-quality asset produced even more.

In this regard, not all risks are equal. Inappropriate assignment of some risks tend to damage owners or contractors but have relatively little effect on the overall project. Other misassignments seriously damage projects and often take the contractor and its reputation as collateral damage.

For this discussion I am going to confine myself to a small subset of risk assignment areas that I see as especially problematic because they are associated with projects turning into complete disasters. As mentioned, these disasters are almost always due to the triggering of a cascade failure in the project. Often, the activity or failure to act that initiated the cascade had occurred before the contractor was even brought on board. Sometimes the five areas listed next are areas of contention and dispute between owners and contractors in the contracting process, but more often they are glossed over like the elephant in the room that no one wants to discuss for fear of getting the elephant upset.

- Schedule
- Site conditions
- Interface management responsibility
- Local content
- Labor shortages

When the contracts are lump-sum, complaints about the previous items mostly come from the contractor and are addressed to the owner. When the contracts are reimbursable, the complaints flow in the opposite direction. Either way, these are perennial areas of conflict.

Schedule

Three of four industrial projects are authorized on a schedule that will not be achieved. The average project starts with a schedule that is 85 percent of the time that the industry spends on average to complete that scope of work. This industry-wide tendency toward schedule aggressiveness is the trigger for more owner/contractor disputes and more project disasters than any other factor.

Schedule aggressiveness at FID means that delay will be the norm and the big issue becomes who pays for that delay. In my experience, who pays is often completely unhinged from who caused the delay. Therefore, the result is often unfair and comes down to who was more clever in negotiations on contract terms or who is better at playing "claimsmanship" games.[8]

Delay is never free, and in today's industrial projects world, delays in schedule are the sorest point in project performance. In the database underpinning this book, the average slip in the execution schedule from FID to mechanical completion was 18 percent. That contrasts with only 4 percent average cost growth. As is clear from Figure 9.2, incomplete front-end engineering design is the key driver of engineering slip, which in turn drives construction and total project execution slip.[9] Note that when FEED is complete, most of the slip in engineering can be accommodated, and the project ends up about 12 percent late. When FEED status is preliminary, the project slip jumps to more than 20 percent. Significant schedule slips are almost always cascade failures.[10]

---

[8]"Claimsmanship" is a term coined by James Zack, who defines it as "the art or practice of making and winning claims by questionable expedients without actually violating the rules." A good many claims games discussed by Zack center on schedule. See Zack, op. cit.

[9]The data for Fig. 9.2 have excluded projects with cash flow limitations and the high outliers have been removed. In other words the real picture is even worse. To remind the reader, IPA rates FEED as *complete* when heat material balances are closed and all piping and instrumentation diagrams are complete, reviewed, approved, and issued for (detailed) design (IFD). FEED is *preliminary* when P&IDs are not complete, reviewed, approved and IFD and *grossly deficient* when less than 50 percent of P&IDs are completed or when the heat and material balances have not been closed, which has the effect of potentially undermining the P&ID work. Because of its ability to detect flaws in the P&IDs, we would always recommend that the PI&Ds be subject to a HAZOP analysis prior to IFD.

[10]The only exceptions are major external shocks or getting cross-wise with the government.

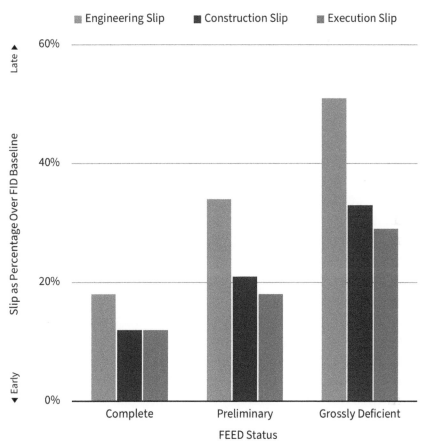

FIGURE 9.2 Incomplete FEED drives projects to slip.

The fact that FEED is the primary driver of slip is quite important for how we think about delays. FEED is always the owner's responsibility except in duty spec contracting. Even when the form is F-EP or F-EPC, the decision about whether to complete FEED prior to mobilizing detailed design is the owner's decision, not the contractor's. When FEED contractors who are going to continue into execution on a reimbursable basis encourage the owner to start detailed engineering with incomplete FEED, they are creating serious mischief, causing the whole project to slip, and likely enriching themselves with many extra hours in the process due to out-of-sequence work.

When owners cut FEED short, they are engaging in moronic behavior that will do the same.

Failure to complete the FEED work harms more than project duration. It also means that the FID estimate is not a quantities-based material take-off estimate[11] and therefore may be quite unreliable. It means the quantities baseline for project controls and, tellingly, control of engineering cannot be established, which makes setting target hours for engineering difficult if not impossible. Finally, it means that the project schedule is unlikely to be resource loaded. When FEED was not complete, fewer than one project in five had completed the schedule and execution planning work and two in five did not even have the critical path defined.

When the owner does not complete FEED on EPC lump-sums, they are passing a lot more risk to the contractor. Most of the time the contractors then price that risk into their bids. Sometimes, however, depending on the situation and their knowledge of the owner, the contractor will "bid their claims." That means when they see holes in the FEED package, they know that significant changes will be forthcoming, which enables them to bid lower, thereby winning the job and then recover cost with expensive changes. The cost competitiveness of EPC-LS with incomplete FEED is 13 percent poorer (higher cost) than the EPC-LS with completed FEED (Pr.|t|<.0001). Almost all cascade failures start with incomplete FEED and execution plans. One has to look hard and long to find a disaster project with completed FEED.

The risk mitigation strategy for owners in dealing with schedule problems with contractors is clear: complete FEED and construct a fully resource-loaded integrated schedule. The importance of FEED has been discussed, but the importance of the resource-loaded schedule is almost as great. The definition of

---

[11]One cannot realistically take off quantities without the P&IDs being issue for design.

the critical path establishes the floor on a project's duration but doesn't ensure that the duration is actually feasible. The resource loading combined with a probabilistic risk assessment does establish feasibility. For example, when a schedule is properly resource-loaded, it tells you how many engineers by discipline will be needed to achieve the planned engineering schedule. It tells you field labor requirements over time by trade. Those numbers can then be tested for reasonableness. If the schedule requires 400 pipe designers and the engineering firm has only 200 available, you are going to be late. We have seen projects in which, if they had resource-loaded the schedule, the owner would have realized they would need more qualified alloy welders than existed in the entire region. Realistic schedules do not ensure that delay will not occur, but unrealistic schedules ensure that it will.

The failure to complete the owner front-end work is perhaps the greatest confounding factor for contracting. I call it "the mother of failure." Some argue that the line demarcating the boundary between FEED and execution is fuzzy at best and nonexistent at worst. The line is, of course, artificial. But it is not arbitrary. Until the P&IDs are completed and a schedule is complete, there is no possibility of a definitive baseline from which to assess and control execution. Contracting is made more difficult because in the absence of a completed front end, it will be difficult to assign responsibilities (risks), and it will be difficult to separate causes and effects when it comes to reckoning results.

When a reimbursable FEED contractor who will continue on into detailed engineering whispers in the ear of the owner PM or business sponsor that completing FEED will cost the project time, they are factually incorrect, and their argument is very self-serving. When FEED is not complete, the control of engineering hours is all but impossible. The median (half above, half below) slip in detailed engineering is 27 percent for projects with incomplete FEED, and the mean is 52 percent. Many more total engineering hours are consumed than on completed FEED projects after controlling for size.

For EPC-LS contracts, the definition of excusable delay, ownership of float, the aggressiveness of the schedule, and the completeness of front-end loading must be considered together. If the contractor is going to be required to pay anything for delay through LDs, penalties, or through cost overruns to achieve schedule, it should not be for failing to achieve an unachievable schedule. Yet that is the situation in which we often find ourselves.

The owner's response is that the contractor agreed to a given schedule, so why should I provide relief? This response contains an important premise as well as a failure to acknowledge the asymmetry in the owner/contractor relationship. The unspoken premise is that the contractor actually knows how long the project will "normally" take. In fact, the contractor's view of how long the project will require is an estimate at best. Without a detailed integrated, networked, and resource-loaded schedule, the contractor does not know how long the project should take, and neither does the owner. The poorer the quality of the schedule at FID, the more aggressive that schedule is ($Pr.|t| < .02$). The asymmetry in the relationship is that contractors feel they must bid the owner's schedule or forego any real chance of winning the contract. A similar dynamic often plays out in reimbursable contracts as well, where the contractor must profess the belief that the owner's schedule ambitions are reasonable or risk losing the work. The root cause is the owner business sponsor's drive for speed, but the critical enabler of the problem is the lack of complete FEL.

There are a great many other examples of the same basic dynamic, such as time extensions for events beyond the contractor's reasonable control. I cannot begin to cover all of these circumstances, but holding contractors responsible for things they do not control can easily ruin a project. Things that happen early in execution are especially damaging.

Site Conditions

When thinking about site conditions, I am referring to much more than soils, although that is part of the set. I also include site access and logistics, laydown, the local regulatory and approvals process, the site health and safety requirements, local materials availability, and the nature of the local construction labor market.[12] Site conditions are a third of the front-end definition of projects.

Adverse site conditions that are not discovered as part of front-end loading are ideally suited to triggering cascade failures. Discovering hazardous materials in the soils at the start of digging foundations will in some countries, such as the United States, often shut the project down completely while soils remediation is done. Why is anyone ever shocked to find hydrocarbon contamination at a 100-year-old oil refinery?

We have a significant number of projects, usually large projects, where poor access to the site for construction labor led to hours-long delays. Workers either receive pay for the time or they walk. Sometimes site access requires the agreement of a third party, and when that is not forthcoming, the soils work cannot be completed. We have cases in which delayed site access meant that arriving equipment and materials had no laydown area and were dispatched to remote warehouses or left out to rust. Anything that disrupts construction just as it is starting usually triggers a cascade failure. But those things usually had their genesis in front-end errors or omissions.

In EPC-LS projects, the contract terms will determine who is charged with paying for the sorts of debacles cited earlier. The problem is that the consequences cascade failures are so large that the contractor cannot carry the risk, which means that one way or another the risk will return to the owner.

---

[12]For revamp projects, one might consider the verification of the as-built design and plant condition as part of the site conditions. We prefer to consider those as part of the Basic Data underpinning design rather than site conditions.

Site conditions are second only to schedule as a source of owner/contractor disputes. The effects of site conditions on cost growth are quite uniform across all contract forms. For each point on a 12-point site definition scale, cost growth increases about 2 percent for the EPC forms from the FID estimate and about 1 percent on split forms (Pr.|t|<.001). The effect of site conditions on execution schedule are more sensitive to contract form. Each point on the scale is associated with nearly 3 percent of schedule slip for the EPC-LS, EPC-R and EPCM forms (Pr.|t|<.0001) but has no association with slip on Re/LS and Re/Re (Pr.|t|<.87).

These differences in response between the EPC and split forms provide some richer insight into how these contracting approaches differ in practice. Inadequacies in defining the site-related issues are associated with finding more changes, and there is no reason to suppose the changes found are a function of contract type. However, in the EPC forms, the engineering and the field work are tied together in a single contractor, and the site definition deficiencies slow the project and construction in particular. The construction time on EPC forms increases at 3 percent per site definition point, right in line with overall execution. But in the split forms, the site issues are being caught and incorporated and have no effect on execution or construction time at all. On EPC forms, including EPCM, the EPC contractor, not the owner, decides when to go to the field, and they often decide to go too early. In the split forms, the changes translate into much less schedule slip than in the EPC forms because they are resolved before we move to the field or fabrication where they are more likely to be critical path. Split forms tend to be more robust against unpleasant surprises and reduce the possibilities of cascade failure.

Interface Management

There are interfaces to be managed on every project, large and small. The responsibilities for interface management are always divided in some fashion between the owner and the contractors. The assignment of interface responsibility should be part of the risk assignment process in the contract. Often, however, interfaces are left without clear assignment, or one of the parties doesn't want to live with the assignments made. And sometimes the assignments are joint, and that is akin to shared risk.

The contract terms should explicitly account for and assign the following interfaces:

- Dealing with government agencies at every level
- Community relations
- Site approvals
- Environment, health, and safety approvals
- Interface between project and site operations
- Partner investors and other external stakeholders
- Special transportation and logistics issues, especially those requiring extensive government interface, such as module transportation to site
- Equipment vendors and how owner frame agreements interact contractor vendor selection
- Subcontractors, especially owner-directed subs
- Third-party projects needed for successful startup, such as power and other infrastructure
- Specialty contractors such as scaffolding and heavy lift, etc.
- Disciplinary constructors on EPCM
- Prime-to-prime interfaces in multiprime arrangements

Regardless of contract form, every one of the previous interfaces needs to be assigned responsibility in the contract terms. Unassigned interfaces are likely to be unmanaged or managed poorly. The problem with interface management often starts with a failure to carefully and fully define the boundaries of the scope of work, which is where interfaces occur.

Obviously, the assignment should, like any risk, be based on the ability of the party to manage. Often, the assignments are assumed. For example, in EPCM, it is often assumed that interface with disciplinary constructors will be the responsibility of the EPCM. However, some owners believe the disciplinary subs should be responsive to *their* direction and the assumption proves wrong. Confusion follows.

There are some general rules of thumb in interface assignments. Government interfaces should be owner-managed because government officials often balk at dealing with contractors instead of the ultimately responsible party. Stakeholder management should be with owners because contractors have no role in the allocation of project value, which is the essence of stakeholder alignment and management. Prime-to-prime interfaces should be owner managed and not self-managed or PMC-managed. The interface with site operations should be owner managed because contractors lack influence within the company. Most of the other interfaces should have contractor leadership. However, for every case there is a counter-example.

The problems with interface management are usually created by owners. Sometimes, the owner team wants to minimize its involvement, even on reimbursable projects. The team is not adequately staffed to manage the usual owner-managed interfaces, and they are turned over to the contractor by default. The contractor did not anticipate being responsible for the interface because it was not clearly assigned or doesn't actually have the requisite skills to manage the interface. It is essential to remember that no prime contractor has contracts with other prime contractors and therefore lacks the wherewithal to manage them. On EPC-LS projects, some owners want essentially all interface management to be done by the contractor because they believe it helps maintain "the wrap" nature of the contract. That works only if the contractor knows he will be responsible and is able to marshal the skills to do it.

Owners can also go the other way—they dabble in everything. In one case I will never forget, the owner decided they would do management of the large multiconstructor laydown area for the project. Nobody could find anything in the laydown yard, and labor productivity plummeted. The owner generated an interface that didn't need to exist. Sometimes owner procurement dabbles in the contractor-to-vendor interfaces because they have an agreement with a vendor that supplies equipment and they want that agreement used. That can be done as long as it is clearly laid out at the beginning of the project, often in the ITB or even prequalification.[13]

The interface with third parties is a particularly difficult area. By definition, contractors have no control over third parties. Generally, the owner has more influence with a third party than the contractor and should therefore take the risk assignment. But if the third party fails to perform, that could open up major liability for the owner if the third party interferes with the contractor's work. In EPC-LS, that's a risk that smart contractors will price handsomely if it is passed to them. But this is perfect case of passing a risk that the assigned party cannot control and then imagining that the problem is solved. It may be priced by the contractor, but if the third party does not perform, the damage to the project will likely dwarf the damage to the contractor.

I have two recommendations in interface management, one obvious, one maybe not. First, do not attempt to dissolve interfaces that are really there. *Clarify* those interfaces and plan and assign their management instead. Second, network all of the interface managers, both owner and contractor, to promote cooperation, and inform and improve interface management. Above

---

[13]Whether a contractor will be allowed to source equipment as they wish from owner-approved vendors is very important to how some contractors bid a job. Some Asian contractors in particular pool risk with vendors who are part of their business association. They bid more aggressively when they control sourcing fully, subject only to owner's approved vendor list.

all, never dabble; either take on responsibility for an interface or fully and completely assign it to a contractor and then formally require all contractors to cooperate in its management.

Local Content

Local content is recognized as an important risk issue in large international projects in the developing world. However, local content is an issue for most projects, large and small, everywhere. On the large international projects in which local content is mandatory, onerous, and prescriptive, that is, very hard to meet, contractors add substantial risk premiums to their bids for EPC-LS work. In cool-to-normal markets, owners should expect all international bidders to add 10 to 20 percent to their bids when local content provisions are onerous. In hot markets, contractors will sometimes try to add enough to their bids for such projects that they will not be unlucky enough to win them. Onerous local content provisions on EPC-LS contracts are viewed by the contractors as almost untenable. In some locales, contractors view onerous local content as a "corruption required" provision.

I am not suggesting that local content provisions are automatically bad or not legitimate exercises of sovereignty. What I am suggesting is that local content provisions where local markets cannot provide the required content competitively and in a timely manner are enormously risky for contractors. Owners in such circumstances need to understand they are paying handsomely for the local content requirements. Host governments need to understand it as well.

What is often overlooked are informal local content provisions in projects everywhere. Every petroleum refinery, chemicals complex, or mining site has a need to keep the community in which they reside happy. One element of that process is to funnel work to local contractors and suppliers. Almost every directed subcontract by an owner is local content at work. And like local content elsewhere, it carries risks for the prime. Of course, overtly directing work carries risk for the owner as well, which is why local content motivated subs are often "encouraged" or "introduced" rather than directed. My view is that prime contractors should always fully review what goods and services can be provided locally in a competent way and bid or otherwise employ those providers. When an owner points to a particular supplier, that situation needs to be viewed with the same suspicion as onerous local content requirements on large international projects.

The most insidious local content situation is where government approvals, at any level, become contingent on the use of a particular contractor or a local contractor, however local is defined. This is rarely done in a transparent manner, but as an informal and unstated requirement. This is far more common in North America and Europe than generally recognized and acknowledged.

Contractors that have worked in a local market for any length of time have already learned to navigate the local content requirements. The contractor who is new to the market, however, is in real danger of being blindsided by requirements that do not even seem to be there.

Labor Availability

For every on-shore project, regardless of location, the availability of construction labor is a concern. Even for the fabrication of offshore platforms and modules, the availability of labor at the prequalified fab yards is an important issue. The labor situation for a project has a large effect on the choice of contracting strategy. When labor is tight, EPC-LS becomes more expensive or simply unavailable. Owners usually then resort to EPC-R or EPCM as their fallback. Rarely does the owner who was looking for an EPC-LS turn to one of the split forms. The things that pushed them to EPC-LS, primarily their own staffing weaknesses, push them to another EPC strategy with a different compensation scheme rather than to a split form. When an owner is forced to abandon EPC-LS as a strategy late in the front end or even after no acceptable bids are received, the resulting project is usually problematic because the project team has not prepared for a reimbursable strategy.

Poor labor availability rarely tanks projects, although it can play a role when other factors are in play. A tight labor situation extends execution and increases cost some, but by itself is not the cause of disaster. Depending on how it is handled, poor labor availability may drive poorer productivity. If, rather than slowing execution to accommodate the supply of productive labor, the owner (or contractor) attempts to maintain schedule by bringing in less qualified labor, productivity suffers substantially. Mixing high skill craft with low skill craft generally drags down the productivity of all. If the owner is smart enough to extend the schedule to keep craft competence high, the schedule slips, but the effect on cost is minimal as it affects only time-related costs. Planning a longer schedule to keep productivity up often leads to a faster project than staffing up with less productive labor.

The assessment of labor availability for a project is part of the owner's normal front-end loading requirements in execution planning. Owners completed what we at IPA deem a definitive labor assessment as part of FEL in only 55 percent of the projects in our sample of 1,148 projects. A definitive assessment includes a full craft labor survey. Somewhat perversely, owners did a better job assessing labor availability on smaller projects than larger projects, probably because it is easier. Unfortunately, it is more important for the larger projects.

To state the obvious, *assessing* the labor availability situation for a project does not change labor availability. We would expect the failure to assess the labor situation to affect predictability of cost and schedule more than competitiveness. It turns out that understanding labor availability does significantly improve cost and schedule predictability—less cost growth and less slip. But it also is associated with significantly better cost competitiveness, which suggests that intelligent adjustments are being made when labor is known to be tight.

During hot labor market periods, owners are not making optimal adjustments in contract strategies. Yes, they are responding by reducing EPC-LS, but that is undoubtedly more forced than by design. They run primarily to EPCM and actually reduce their use of Re/Re. But in hot market periods, Re/Re is far and away the most cost-effective contracting strategy available, even if construction is not done with unit rates. It also provides better schedule performance than EPCM. Even in hot markets, owners are better off hiring a construction management firm to supervise reimbursable construction on a Re/Re form than resorting to EPCM. It requires very little change in their staff capabilities to go that route.

The other recommendation I would make in hot labor markets is to discuss with the business sponsor the relaxation of the execution schedule requirements. I am not recommending slower projects. I am urging recognition that the project will be slower in a hot labor market so that it need not be a lot more expensive as well. I recognize that this hope is probably in vain because the circumstances that create a hot labor market are usually created by hot product markets.

CHAPTER 10

Who Should Control Contracting Strategy?

Ithin industrial owners there is no consensus about roles and responsibilities in contracting. The lack of clarity is not benign—it causes confusion and in some cases significant damage to capital projects. The following owner functions have some claim to control of contracting:

- The business sponsor
- The legal organization
- The procurement or supply chain management organization
- The capital projects organization
- An individual project team and its leader

The overlapping of responsibilities in these five entities has often resulted in turf fights and no one in charge of getting essential work done. The most common and heated of the disputes is usually between the procurement and projects organizations. In this chapter, I will argue that every function listed here can and perhaps should have a role in the contracting process for projects. The problem is that the best role is not always the role the function desires.

The Role of the Business Sponsor in Contracting

To be direct, the business sponsor of a project has no business in contracting. The business sponsor should not be selecting the contracting approach, should not be dictating terms and conditions, and certainly should not be deciding which particular contractors to select. Why? Because all of those activities require deep expertise that the business sponsor almost never has. With that said, the business sponsor has an indirect role in selecting contracting approach that must be respected by those selecting the strategy: the business sponsor sets the project objectives, and the project objectives may have an important role in contract strategy selection.

It is the business sponsor's remit and obligation to tell the project team the priorities for the project. For example, if the paramount goal for the project is getting to market as quickly as possible to beat a rival to the market, that should shape the contracting strategy. Conventional EPC-LS is probably off the table. A Re/Re strategy with schedule incentives for the engineering firm is probably the best solution as it is the fastest strategy generally available.

The most pernicious sort of business sponsor involvement is in contractor selection. Some EPCs make it a regular habit to cultivate owner businesspeople with the goal of winning work they would not be awarded by anyone else involved in the process. The business sponsors are wined and dined and taken out for golf. When the EPC is repaid for their kindness, the owner project teams respond by stuffing as much money into the cost estimate as they possibly can. That is a perfectly rational response to the wrong contractor being selected for a project. Business sponsors should be informed regarding the contracting strategy for the purpose of ensuring that it accords with project objectives. Beyond that, no further involvement is warranted.

Owner Legal Organization

Among project people, I may be a bit of an odd duck in that I believe that lawyers have an incredibly important role to play in contracting on both the owner and contractor sides. Alas, this is not the usual role they play. Lawyers, of course, have a role in writing or reviewing contract documents and advising their clients about proposing, accepting, or rejecting various terms and conditions in the engineering and construction contracts their clients must execute in the course of business.

Lawyers for contractors are much more likely to be construction lawyers than their owner counterparts. That is a distinct disadvantage for owners. If an owner has a substantial capital spend, bringing specialized construction attorneys in-house probably makes economic sense. If not, hiring outside construction counsel is probably a better option than turning the work over to corporate legal. The disadvantage of outside counsel is that they are likely to be used too late and too sparingly because they represent an out-of-pocket cost.

In my experience most owner and contractor lawyers view their remit of protecting their client's interests rather narrowly. Their goal is often to transfer as much responsibility and risk to the other side of the table as possible. Both owner and contractor lawyers seek to write an unbalanced contract with respect to risk; they just have diametrically opposing views of the proper balance. In the spirit of advocacy, they may suppose that a "fair and balanced" contract results, although experience tells us that often is not true. Lawyers are sometimes motivated to go for "the win" in contract negotiations in much the same way that they want to win in court. But if a "win" in contract negotiations is shifting all of the risks to the other side, the lawyer's win is usually the project's loss.

But what if lawyers for both sides viewed their client's interest in terms of generating the best possible project rather than narrowly interpreting their client's best interest as avoiding all risk? In other words, what if they were lawyers for the project in addition to their clients?[1] It is, after all, reasonable to suggest that the interests of both owners and contractors are usually met when a successful project results from their joint efforts. Of course, we have seen examples as discussed in Chapters 4, 5, and 6 in which owners gained at a contractor's expense and vice versa. And no amount of lawyering for the project will ever make the principal-agent misalignment of objectives go away. However, in the great majority of cases, good projects—projects that are delivered as promised—benefit both owner and contractor alike.

So what does it mean to be a lawyer for the project? To act as a lawyer for the benefit of the project requires that attorneys understand the costs as well as the obvious benefits of transferring risks to the other side. Risk transfer is never free. In the simplest case, the risk is priced by the contractor in their bid. Conversely, an owner keeping a risk that could have been transferred will result in lower bids. In some cases, a contractor may accept responsibility for a risk knowing full well that the risk will be transferred back to the owner. This happens, for example, when a contractor sees the holes in the ITB that will enable risks to be returned with ease. In the worst case for both owner and contractor, the contractor accepts a risk they cannot reasonably carry because they need the work too much to push back. Attorneys must really accept that there is no free lunch.

To be an effective lawyer for the project, the attorney must understand not only how projects work generally but the specifics of the project at hand. What may have been an appropriate term in the last project may not work for the current project at all. What was a reasonable term in a cool market may generate a lot of pushback or a very high price in the current market. Perhaps most important, the effective lawyer for the project knows the source of the primary risks in the project, who controls them, and who is best positioned to manage them effectively.

---

[1]For an extended discussion of this topic, see Andrew Ness and Edward W. Merrow, "Becoming a Lawyer for the Project," *Proceedings of the 33rd Annual Meeting of the American College of Construction Law,* Laguna Beach, CA, February 2022.

Lawyers for the project use the contract negotiation process as an opportunity to facilitate the risk management of the project. Contract negotiations are all about risk, but rather than clarifying risk assignment for a project, the contract terms and conditions and the negotiation process often obfuscate risk assignment. Having suffered through a number of these negotiations, I am led to suspect that muddying the water was sometimes the intent, perhaps thinking that a lack of clarity suits their client's interest. It never suits the interest of a good project.

I believe that contract clarity should be the first obligation of every lawyer working on project contracts. "Contracts should say what they mean and mean what they say." Projects are the joint product of many functions within many organizations working together to create an asset. Contracts should help sort out who is responsible for what and should be written in language understood by all. When contracts are written clearly, it is a little more likely that all concerned will see what is needed to make the project successful.

The most difficult task for attorneys working on projects is often figuring out who the client is. This can be especially difficult for owner attorneys. Is the client the corporation? Is it the business sponsor? Is it the supply chain director? Is it the project manager? All four "clients" have an interest in a successful project but are likely to have very different views of contracting and the lawyer's role. One can be a lawyer for the project while reporting to any of the four potential clients, but only if it is clear which one it is.

Very few IPA clients employ industry-wide standard contracts such as FIDIC or AIA. Some clients start with a standard contract and then modify it so extensively that the standard form all but disappears. Industry-standard contracts attempt to craft balanced terms and conditions, and that may be why they are not popular in industrial projects. The failure to adopt industry-standard contract provisions may be an opportunity lost as standard provisions might be understood more universally than bespoke terms.

The Proper Role of Procurement in Capital Project Contracting

If the role of the lawyer is often too small, the role of the corporate purchasing organization, which we will dub *procurement*, often has the opposite problem. Procurement is always an essential player in capital projects. Some owners have developed specialized capital project procurement organizations, but most have central procurement that performs some critical project functions. The ordering of long-lead equipment, for example, is generally procurement's remit. Many owners have standardization programs in their equipment selection across facilities, and the frame agreements that underpin these programs are usually run by procurement.

In some owner companies, the procurement organization has assumed responsibility for all or most contracting for engineering and construction services. Usually, that responsibility had to be wrestled away from the projects organization, most of which deeply oppose procurement taking contracting leadership. Procurement's argument is that they buy more or less everything for the company, they are deep experts in purchasing a whole range of goods and services, they know how to get the best deals, and that engineering and construction services are not fundamentally different than other things that they buy. The argument is certainly plausible, and in many owner organizations, procurement is a much more powerful corporate function than capital projects with much better access to the C-suite.

We have not undertaken a systematic study of our clientele in terms of who controls contracting and how that affects project outcomes. We do, however, have a great deal of anecdotal evidence that suggests that procurement's role in contracting should be carefully circumscribed. The following example suggests why.

The case was a very large greenfield megaproject. The competition for the utilities system, which was to be executed on an EPCM reimbursable, came down to two finalists. One of the two, a well-known Tier 1 contractor, had executed the FEED on the utility systems. The project director considered their FEED work excellent and preferred to continue with that contractor. The other, also a well-known Tier 1 contractor, was looking for entry into this regional market. The owner's chief procurement specialist on the project had the remit of making the decision. The contractor bids were extremely close, but the deciding factor was that the second contractor offered to execute the work with no fee. That "bargain" persuaded the procurement officer to award them the utilities contract. The result was an utter fiasco; the contractor's work on the utility systems was so bad that it prevented the startup of a multibillion-dollar complex for well over a year and hemorrhaged untold millions in net present value.

I submit that a competent projects person would not have made that mistake. The procurement specialist saw little danger in handing the contract to the firm that offered no fee because it was a well-known Tier 1 contractor (a "brand name" after all) and they were offering a bargain. If a solid, well-known vendor offers a lower price on a piece of equipment, one would be a fool not to take it! The difference, of course, is that a piece of equipment is easily inspected for quality; a contractor is not.

A project professional would also have known that Tier 1 contractor's offices are often anything but uniform in capability and that the office out of which this work was to be done was at best marginally competent. Sometimes, all that an office has in common with the headquarters office is a logo. A project professional would have been unimpressed by the offer to do the project at no fee, because a project professional would know that the fee is often the smallest source of profit for a contractor working on a reimbursable basis. A project professional would never look at EPCs and see interchangeable commodities. A procurement specialist is much more likely to.

We see this type of scenario play out on projects repeatedly where procurement rather than projects controls contractor selection. Like so many things, the difference in viewpoints between procurement and projects comes down to the incentive systems behind their organizations. The most important key performance indicator for procurement is cost savings. In many purchasing organizations, savings achieved on each transaction are carefully documented. Savings may be used to incentivize individuals and is almost always used to demonstrate the success and value of the procurement organization to the C-suite. This is not to say that many procurement organizations do not have more holistic, value-based KPIs. But savings as a percentage of transaction value is by far the easiest to measure, and easy-to-measure KPIs usually win out in the end. (Remember how the businesses love those cost underruns on projects; ease of measurement wins out.)

Indicators of value to procurement are not always indicators of value on projects. For example, procurement is likely to look favorably on lower hourly rates. But project professionals know that a contractor's hourly rates are indicative of almost nothing unless productivity is taken into account.[2] We see analogous problems with procurement controlling the purchase of major equipment on projects, where cost savings are often given priority over timely delivery despite timely delivery often being much more important to total project cost.[3]

What constitutes a good project is always more complex than what constitutes a good purchase. The quality component of value is always large with cost or schedule coming second. More

---

[2]In fact, higher rates are often indicators of higher value in contractors. IPA studies of productivity repeatedly show that contractors that command higher hourly prices can do so because they are more productive.

[3]Owner procurement of equipment and materials is the only example of maintaining a project activity in-house that is associated with poorer project performance. When in-house procurement buys all equipment and materials for a project, the projects are 8 percent slower in execution than when the purchasing is done by the engineering contractor (Pr.|t|<.01). There is no off-setting cost advantage. In fact, costs are directionally higher, but it is not statistically robust. When it comes to buying for projects, engineering contractors are better because they have much more buying power than even the largest owners, they have long-standing relationships with many more vendors, they bring inspection and expediting capability, and they are not incentivized to generate cost savings over timeliness.

important for contracting is to recognize the joint product nature of the owner/contractor relationship. Contracting for engineering and construction services takes deep knowledge of project management to do it well. If procurement had the level of project management expertise required to do a good job of hiring contractors, it would be the projects organization.

The Projects Organization Should Control Contracting

Contracting is very possibly the most difficult single aspect of project management. Contracting is sensitive to the particular challenges posed by a project. Contractor selection is sensitive to the strengths and weaknesses of the owner team. Contracting strategy, of course, is sensitive to the state of the market and the particulars of the location.

Projects should control the following:

- Contracting strategy decisions
- Prequalification
- Contractor selection
- Contract terms and conditions that affect the management of the project

The projects organization may have a contracts advisory group or may leave contracting entirely up to their project teams with the project manager playing the key role in the three previous activities. My experience is that leaving the tasks to the project manager/director works fine if the PM is familiar with the location in which the project is being executed and the specifics of the local markets. If the company has a geographically dispersed project portfolio and moves PMs to new locations frequently, a contracts advisory group may be essential.

Procurement can play a very useful role in contractor market assessment. Procurement usually has market assessment procedures and expertise that need not be fully replicated in the projects organization. Procurement sometimes has the responsibility for maintaining contract templates with standard terms and conditions. My only caveat with this last assignment is that procurement should not replace legal. The lawyers have a role to play in risk assignment as it pertains to the negotiation of terms and conditions that nonlawyers probably cannot fill. Furthermore, construction law is a constantly evolving area, and only legal is likely to stay abreast of developments. Despite all of the functions that have a role, contracting must stay firmly in the hands of the organization responsible and accountable for project success: the projects organization.

CHAPTER 11

The Effects of Scale

Large projects worry everyone involved because there is always a great deal at stake. They are very visible and can be career-breakers and even company-breakers. It is accepted wisdom in the projects literature and community that project outcomes tend to degrade as projects become larger and more complex.[1] There is much less agreement with regard to why larger and more complex projects tend to fail. Flyvbjerg et al. suggest that the optimism bias[2] and "strategic misrepresentation" are the primary causes.[3] Without denying the reality of the optimism bias and the capacity of humans to lie, my colleagues and I have demonstrated empirically that the same problems that lead smaller projects to go poorly cause large complex projects to fail miserably. Those problems start with objectives that are unreasonable, with owner teams that are missing key functions, and with front-end loading that is incomplete. Problems that would be damaging but manageable in smaller, simpler projects cause havoc in megaprojects

---

[1] E. Merrow, *Understanding the Outcomes of Megaprojects,* Rand Corporation, 1988; E. Merrow, *Industrial Megaprojects,* Wiley, 2011; Bent Flyvbjerg, et al., *Megaprojects and Risk,* Cambridge University Press, 2001.

[2] See Daniel Kahneman, *Thinking Fast and Slow*, New York: Farrar, Straus and Giroux, 2011; and James Prater, Konstantinos Kirytopoulos, and Tony Ma, 2017, "Optimism Bias Within the Project Management Context: A Systematic Quantitative Literature Review," *International Journal of Managing Projects in Business*, Vol. 10, Issue: 2, pp. 370–385.

[3] Perhaps because they tend to focus on government-sponsored projects, those who believe optimism and misrepresentation drive project results do not appreciate that effective project system governance will neutralize the effects of the optimism bias and make misrepresentation very hard to sustain. I guess it is ironic that governments often run poorly governed project systems, but that is not an inherent feature of government project organizations.

because megaprojects are necessarily tightly woven projects and are therefore more susceptible to cascade failures.

Project performance degrades incrementally with size until projects approach about $300 million. Then degradation of project outcomes begins to accelerate. By the time project size approaches $1 billion, the average project performance is significantly worse for cost effectiveness, cost overruns, slip in the execution schedule, and operability. This degradation causes large losses of project value for owners and their shareholders.

Contracting strategy intersects with size and complexity in a number of ways. Understanding the difficulty that size and complexity cause for contracting makes it possible to side-step the worst effects. First, as size increases, it becomes more likely that the project is contracted as a one-off event. The only contracting strategy that is not one-off that can accommodate megaprojects is repeat supply chain. However, RSC contracting tends to be limited to a particular region and a particular type of project. Partnering alliances could in principle be used for large complex projects but seldom were used even in the heyday of that strategy in the 1990s. A megaproject would exceed the capability of most partnering alliance contractors and would be disruptive to the workflow of all other projects within the partnering alliance purview. As discussed in several places already, a one-off engagement contract is not self-enforcing.

When contracts are not self-enforcing, the principal-agent problem at the heart of the contracting problem comes to the fore. The principal-agent problem is exacerbated by the lack of transparency in the contractor's behavior on large and complex projects. Small projects provide line-of-sight management possibilities that are not available in large complex projects. This places much more burden on the contract to define the rules of engagement.

As project size increases, some elements of owner practices tend to improve such as clarity of objectives, assignment of roles and responsibilities, and owner control. Others, however, tend to degrade, and that degradation affects the effectiveness of some contracting strategies. The most important practice that degrades with project scale is front-end loading. Poorer front-end loading degrades the cost performance of all of the main EPC contract forms and Re/Re at about the same rate. However, Re/LS is only marginally affected by poorer FEL. The Re/LS form forces enough separation between engineering and construction that the effects of poorer FEL can be mitigated. All of this mitigation disappears, and the effects of FEL return when the Re/LS form is used on a schedule-driven project. Schedule acceleration occurs, but it is traded for cost performance.

Finally, as size increases, the number of organizations involved in a project increases. It becomes necessary to assemble the scopes into multiple packages so that the size of any one contract does not become too large for a contractor to handle. The larger the contract size, the thinner the market that is in play. Contractors are limited in contract size by their bondability and balance sheets. In principle, contractors could form joint ventures to improve the size of contract they can handle. Although that route is sometimes taken, it is known to be quite risky for owners because it is very dependent on the ability of the joint venturers to work together. Therefore, multiple packages with multiple prime contractors is the usual solution. Multiple prime contractors, however, mean more interfaces for the owner to manage and more opportunities for contractors to interfere with each other, which creates the basis for claims.

Packaging Scopes

Packaging scopes is an art form. The following elements have to be weighed and balanced:

- The number of prequalified and truly interested contractors that are capable of executing one or more of the scope packages. Good and early prequalification is a must.
- How much work the interested contractors can take on.

- How many contenders there will be for each package. Each package must have at least three and preferably four willing bidders.
- The state of the market.
- The strength of the owner personnel to manage interfaces.
- Local content constraints.
- If the desire is to bid the packages EPC-LS but one or more of the packages does not lend itself to EPC-LS, how will the mixing of contract approaches at the single site affect the work?
- Project logistics—do the defined packages enable the contractor personnel to access the site close to their work area, or do they cross another contractor's area? Is it possible to organize the packages so that each package and contractor will have its own laydown area? Can fences be constructed to separate the contractors' work areas? If some of the packages are to be fabricated as large modules, how does the delivery and installation schedule interfere with other contractors' work?

The potential for interference is perhaps the biggest concern. In a multiprime arrangement, interference risk generally belongs to the owner with the contractors only required to be cooperative to the extent reasonable.

When contracting with multiple primes, the contracting strategy must center around a single contracting approach, especially with respect to compensation scheme of the constructors. Mixing lump-sum and reimbursable construction risks labor migration from the lump-sum contractors to the reimbursable contractors in the event of labor shortage, not an unusual situation for large projects. If the nature of the work requires some mixing of constructor compensation schemes, the contract terms and conditions must provide very clear rules about hiring labor away from other contractors onsite. The enforcement of those rules requires a functioning access control process at the gates.

TABLE 11.1   **How Contracting Strategies Respond to Increasing Scale**

Contract Strategy	Scale Effects		
	Cost	Overruns	Slip
EPC-LS	Moderate increase	No effect	No effect
EPC-R	Sharp increase	Sharp increase	No effect
EPCM	Sharp increase	Sharp increase	No effect
Re/LS	No effect	No effect	Tendency to *decline*
Re/Re	No effect	Small increase	Tendency to *decline*
Functional Specification	Small increase	Small increase	Moderate increase
Design Competitions	No effect	No effect	No effect
Guaranteed Max	Small increase	No effect	No effect
Convert-to-LS	Uniformly high	Sharp increase	Moderate increase
Integrated Project Delivery	Sharp increase	Sharp increase	Moderate increase
Repeat Supply Chain	No effect	No effect	No effect

Given all of the complexities of large projects, many owners are tempted to hire a project managing contractor (PMC) either to assist or to take over primary responsibility for managing the project. However, as we have discussed elsewhere,[4] hiring a PMC often creates more problems than it solves. If the owner is hoping to follow an EPC-LS strategy for most of the work, the hiring of a PMC will dissuade many contractors from bidding, particularly if the PMC will also be allowed to bid and execute any part of the scope. Today, very few contractors want to serve in the PMC role without access to an execution role. Increasingly we are seeing PMC contractors simply hire the PMC staff "from the street" and charge premium prices for doing so. Owners on large

[4]See Merrow, *Industrial Megaprojects*, 2011 op. cit., pp. 299–300.

projects are better served hiring the same people as individual contractors and foregoing paying the large markup.

Referring to Table 11.1, of the 10 contracting strategies we have quantitatively evaluated in this analysis, only 4 show no tendency for performance to degrade their cost performance with increasing project size—Re/LS, Re/Re, design competitions, and repeat supply chain. For the most part, cost growth (cost overruns) follows the same pattern as cost effectiveness. The split strategies, Re/LS and Re/Re, remove the incentive of the contractor to start field or fabrication too early by changing contractors. The split form then allows the owner to effectively fix problems and re-sequence work as needed between engineering and construction or fabrication.

Design competitions and repeat supply chain projects also display no performance degradation with larger size, despite being EPC-LS contract forms. Design competitions tend to be extraordinarily well-defined projects, and well-defined projects tend to have no cost growth and limited schedule slip because all of the optimism that accompanies early estimates and schedules has been squeezed out by the good definition. Repeat supply chain projects tend to benefit from a learning curve for cost. The benefits of that learning curve accrue to the contractors rather than the owner, but given the cost effectiveness of the projects, the owner has no reason to be concerned about that.

Again referring to Table 11.1, three contracting strategies degrade cost performance very seriously as projects pass through about $400 million and are often disastrous megaprojects: EPC-R, EPCM, and IPD. EPC-R projects are often the most intrinsically risky. They are more likely to be remote, new technology, or very large brownfield projects. EPC-R is also the form that owners usually end up with when their attempts to secure a traditional EPC-LS falter due to lack of contractor interest. The surprise member of this sad group is EPCM, but the case narratives for these projects point straight to construction management problems. Very large EPCMs often end up with too many constructors for the EPCM to manage effectively. Inevitably when there are a large number of constructors, a few of them will not be very good and the EPCM will need to step in. Too often, they are not up to the challenge.

Convert-to-LS and IPD falter at large scale for different reasons. Convert to LS is a bad contracting form at all sizes, but scale makes it even worse. The moral hazards that it poses become more extreme as size increases. The "off-ramps" might be workable at small and intermediate size but are altogether impossible at large size. IPD/alliancing is a very complex contractual structure. As the number of players involved increases (as it will with size), the chances of getting the multiple agreements needed in place in a timely way decline and the opportunities for opportunism by one or more of the contractors increase. In IPD, owners often believe that they do not have to actively control the project because the contractors are incentivized to manage the interfaces. This is a failure to economize on the need for trust.

Referring to the final column in Table 11.1, when we look at slip in execution schedule, the effects of scale are greatly muted, and two strategies, Re/LS and Re/Re, tend to improve slip as scale increases. I have controlled for the completeness of FEED in all cases. I believe the small response of slip to increasing scale is because slip is ubiquitous in *all* project sizes. Schedule slip is responsive to cost growth for all projects taken together ($Pr.|t| < .0001$), with slip increasing one-third of 1 percent for every 1 percent increase in real cost. However, when I separate the data by contracting strategy, the effects of scale are small on schedule extension.

CHAPTER 12

Toward Fair, Balanced, and Smart

Contracting is very likely the single most difficult element of project management. It requires a broad range of skills—strategy, understanding of legal concepts, good relationship skills, negotiation skills, understanding of the projects market, and the ability to put oneself in the other person's shoes. In my experience, it causes owner project managers more stress than any other part of their job. Because contracting is stressful, there is an understandable temptation to look for a magic fix for the problem—an approach that will solve all problems. Alas, the magic fix will not be forthcoming here (or anywhere else).

The relationship between owners and contractors is often characterized as fraught with conflict. Some conflict does exist at the organizational level; it is real and unavoidable because of the principal-agent problem, moral hazards, and the reality of human fallibility—what my clergyman brother would call "original sin in action." The only misalignment of goals that is *necessarily* present is the owner's desire for lower cost versus the contractor's interest in being more profitable. There is no point in pretending that misalignment does not exist. If that were the only misalignment problem, however, contracting wouldn't be so difficult.

The serious problems arise when the risk profile of the project does not turn out as expected. Sometimes this is due to bad luck (e.g., the market heated up and escalation became an issue, or bad weather complicated execution, and so forth). Murphy is still the patron saint of projects. Sometimes, the contractor was not competent to do the work or could not find the people he assumed would be available. However, much more often there is something amiss with the project fundamentals: the business objectives changed or were never very clear, a previously missing owner function showed up at an inopportune time, or the front-end loading contained holes and errors that threw execution into chaos.

Contracting cannot fix fundamental problems with projects, but good contracts can help limit the damage. Contracts that are clear and honestly assign risk are the best that can be done to control conflict at the organizational level between owners and contractors and between primes and subs. The intractable project-damaging conflicts between contractors and owners at the organizational level are usually caused by surprises about who was carrying which risk. The more complete and transparent the risk assignment, the less likely those surprises are to occur. The complete elimination of conflict at the organizational level is a futile and therefore irrelevant goal.

The existence of inherent and irreducible conflict at the organizational level does not need to exist and for the most part does not exist at the level where it most counts—the workface. Some believe that any organizational tension must bleed into the workface and therefore should be eliminated. But that just plain isn't true. If conflicts exist at the workface, they are not generated by the organizations but by the same forces that can create conflict in any human interactions: lack of mutual respect and willingness to cooperate.

I have worked with many project teams in FEED and execution over the course of my career. Many times on good projects, I cannot distinguish who is owner from who is contractor, *and the contractual form offers no clue.* Lump-sum or reimbursable, EPC or split, the working relationships between owners and contractors are controlled by the quality of project leadership on both sides far more than any other factor *when the project fundamentals are sound*. When the project fundamentals are poor, even extraordinary leadership will struggle to avoid the blame game.

What Contracts Should Do

A contract should lay out the scope of work in as much detail as reasonably possible. In defining the scope, the contract should be especially clear at the "edges" of the work where it must interface with the work or systems of others. It should define the rights and duties of both parties, lay out the payment scheme, describe the change process, and provide the usual contractual requirements—breach provisions, dispute resolutions, force majeure, etc. But above all else, contacts should assign risks and discuss why particular risks were assigned the way they were in the contract to facilitate conflict resolution during execution if the need arises. A good contract should leave both parties feeling secure that if they do their roles well, they will be successful. Far too often the end of contract negotiations has at least one party ready to go on the defensive for the duration of the project.

What Contracts Should Not Attempt to Do

Contracts should not be expected to manage the project. That is the task of project leadership on both sides. The contract should not attempt to dictate behavior through penalties or bribes—whoops, excuse me—incentives. The contract should not seek to "foster collaboration." Contracts should do what they are supposed to do and leave project management to the participants. Almost all nasty disputes are picking through the detritus of bad projects. And those were almost always bad projects from the outset. Owners must remember it was usually their shortcomings that started the project in the wrong direction. Rather than spending hours giving depositions and bending the truth into a pretzel in arbitration or court, the parties should be in deep conversation about what went wrong and why.

Very few owners or contractors go into a project intending to exploit the other side. Unfortunately, there are exceptions. I once asked an owner business sponsor why he was suing a contractor (for more than its net worth) over a project that the owner screwed up. His answer: "For the money, of course, this is just one of 23 suits I have going." And to balance that, I know of a major contractor who carefully inflates the bulk materials in hard-to-find places on every reimbursable ·project they do in order to increase their take. So yes, there are predators on both sides. But most contractors and most owners simply want a good project that makes both parties successful. Neither wants the contract to unfairly disadvantage the other party.

It is not, however, enough for the contract to be "fair and balanced." The contracting strategy must be selected to fit the project's goals, the project's characteristics, the owner capabilities, and the skills of the contractors available to execute the project. And the project must be set up to succeed by the owner on the front end. "Fair and balanced" is good. "Fair, balanced, and smart" is far better.

The Primacy of the Owner Role

All contractors are aware—perhaps painfully so—that they are dependent on the owners for their livelihood. Just as with any other professional services relationship, clients are everything. The owner hires the contractors; the owner sets the contractual basis for the project, although contractors may seek to influence the strategy. This dependency of contractors on owners sets up some of the pathology that often seeps into the relationship—such as "You're the boss," while figuratively rolling your eyes and thinking, this guy doesn't know what's he talking about.

However, there is an even deeper dependency that owners and contractors often miss: the dependence of every project's health (and therefore riskiness) on the performance of the owner, often before the contractor is engaged. The data tell a compelling story: if the business case is not sound, if the owner team is not strong, and if the front-end loading is not completed before execution begins, the project, the contractor, and the owner team are set up to fail.

The contractual strategy modulates how the failure plays out. In some forms failure is exacerbated by the contracting strategy, and in other cases it is mitigated.

- Poorly prepared EPC-LS projects bog down in the mud of endless change orders. If the change order process does not work extraordinarily well, claims result. When the claims resolution process fails, arbitration or litigation completes the project cycle.
- Failing EPC-R and EPCM projects crank what seem to be endlessly inefficient hours in both engineering and construction and ultimately end in mutual disgust between owner and contractor at the end. These forms, however, rarely result in arbitration or litigation because the owner has taken on essentially all risk and cannot shed it.
- Alliance/IPD projects fall into an orgy of acrimonious finger-pointing in execution and feelings of betrayal all around or become exercises in unseemly denial.
- Failure in the split form projects is characterized by less acrimony because the form provides an opportunity to recover and refocus between engineering and construction that is not afforded by the EPC forms. Engineering may have been a debacle, but construction tends to be at least mediocre.

In principle, it is possible for a contractor to take a well-prepared and thought-out project and utterly destroy it. Certainly, owners have accused many a contractor of doing so. However, in practice it is rare to the vanishing point to actually see such projects. The contractor that would take a good project and destroy it could not survive in the market because if the contractor would destroy a good project, they would never succeed on *any* project and would be quickly driven out of business.

Returning to a Normal Relationship

A number of years ago, Ted Kennedy, the executive chairman of EPC firm BE&K, gave the keynote speech at a large conference of the owners and contractors of the process industries in the United States. Ted was the consummate gentleman and friend to all of us fortunate enough to have known him. His speech started this way: "To my contractor colleagues here today, I have only one thing to say: we are a bunch of whores. [Stunned silence] And to my friends on the owner side, you are the pimps." (His head of business development later told me that he wanted to slip quietly under the table.) Ted's point was a profound one: the relationships between owners and contractors had come to resemble a series of "one-night stands" rather than a healthy business relationship.

There is an old expression in contracting that "the owners make the market." That is true, of course, in the simple sense that buyers—customers—make any market, not sellers. In contracting, that old expression has a much deeper meaning—owners make the *relationship*. As we have already discussed in several places in this book, the business relationship between owners and contractors is not a normal relationship between a provider and user of professional services. For most industrial projects larger than the site or business unit–managed projects, the contractual relationship is a one-off transaction.

This situation has developed and steadily deteriorated over the last 30 years. Most attempts to change the dynamic have been to embrace collaborative contracting approaches such as integrated project delivery. As we have discussed, those approaches have been largely unsuccessful in industrial projects. They have been unsuccessful in my view because they do not address the central problem.

Owners have created the transactional approach to contracting by failing to honor the fundamental implicit agreement in professional services relationships: good work leads directly and *predictably* to more work. In other words, when a contractor performs well on a project, that performance will *substantially* increase the chances of getting the next project from the owner that requires similar expertise. Almost no industrial owners honor that principle today.

The rise in transactional contracting was the logical concomitant of the weakening of owner engineering and project organizations. Strong owner project organizations were able to carefully measure and track contractor performance and had the freedom to reward good work. As procurement organizations came to have more influence over contracting, transactional contracting become the rule rather than the exception. The only contracting strategy that has a clear nontransactional methodology among the 10 strategies we have reviewed is repeat supply chain, and note that RSC does this without altering the contracts themselves.[1] IPD/alliancing talks about collaboration but is nonetheless a one-off arrangement; relationships are not the goal.

With the exception of traditional[2] EPC lump-sum, any contracting strategy could be used in a relational self-enforcing

---

[1] The other contracting form that is formally relational is partnering alliances. We did not quantitatively evaluate partnering alliances here because of lack of observations in the 21st century. They are discussed in Chapter 6.

[2] Recall that the traditional form calls for a formal bidding round after the conclusion of FEED and the issuance of an ITB. Usually when this form is used, giving preferences for past good work is not allowed and would probably create real problems in developing an adequate pool of bidders.

manner. But if we are going to return to a more orderly and normal professional services relationship between owners and contractors, the owners will have to lead the way.

Suggestions for Owners

The following are suggestions for owners:

- If the projects organization does not currently control contracting decisions, the first task is to gain that control. The projects organization should lead the contracting process from contract strategy formation in early FEL-2 through prequalification to actual selection of contractors in late FEL-2 and FEL-3. Contracting strategy is an integral part of project management. It is not a purchasing process, and it is not a transaction. Smart contracting decisions depend on deep project management understanding and expertise. No other organization within any owner has the depth of expertise needed. This does not mean that other functions do not have important roles; they definitely do. It means that decision control must be with the projects organization.

- Some owners try to make every project and every situation fit a single contracting strategy. Others go with whatever strategy strikes the project team as best and end up completely eclectic and scattered. Neither approach is sensible. Select a few contracting strategies that fit with the business drivers for most (not all) of your projects.

  - If predictability in schedule and cost have real business value for the company, consider GMP plus one cost-driven strategy, such as Re/LS and another such as incentivized Re/Re for schedule-driven projects.

- If your businesses produce commodities, then capital cost effectiveness is normally the most important attribute of the project system. Consider design competitions for large projects and Re/LS for others. Look to develop repeat supply chains wherever it appears feasible. If the market is low, consider EPC-LS, but do not make it your staple because markets do not stay down forever.

- If your businesses produce high margin specialties, consider Re/Re and learn how to use the construction contracting market well. If unit rates are widely available, that is a good Re/Re alternative. If you need speed, learn how to incentivize the engineering firm, but keep it simple.

- If your businesses are required to commit to projects during FEL-2, which is common for industrial gases companies, pipelines, and renewables projects subject to reverse auction bidding, consider partnering alliance FEED and engineering contractors. It is probably best not to include construction and construction management services in such partnering alliances because of the local nature of construction activities.

- Don't be cheap. Contractor fees are a miniscule element of total capital cost. Yet many owners seem far more concerned that a contractor is making too much fee than in generating a strong project result. When owners try to squeeze contractor fees, the contractor must look for other ways to make a profit. (Remember, contractors have shareholders too!) Non-fee approaches to making profits harm owners, so don't make it necessary.

- When a contractor performs well, honor the implicit bargain that is essential to a healthy relationship: ensure that contractor is advantaged in getting the next similar project. Nurture relationships with those contractors. Make other contractors envious of that relationship.

Suggestions for Contractors

The following are suggestions for contractors:

- Push back forthrightly on risks you cannot manage or cannot carry. Nobody wants to snatch defeat from the jaws of victory during negotiation of terms and conditions, but sometimes that has to be risked. Many of those negotiating on the owner side do not understand that pushing a risk the owner controls onto the contractor actually costs the *owner* money. It creates losses for contractors too, but that is unlikely to change minds. Try to force clarity in risk assignment.

- When promoting your services for a job, be careful about your choice of words. I am not suggesting that you should advertise your weaknesses, but sometimes contractor promises about what they can do sound like repealing the law of gravity. I was recently involved in a situation in which the contractor had described the owner's manifestly shoddy work on the front end as "FEED quality." It wasn't pig feed quality. But those words eviscerated the contractor's defense when the results of the owner's poor work resulted in a terrible project and the resulting lawsuit.

- If you find an owner who honors the implicit bargain of more work for good work, you need to honor it as well. Owners who behave in that way should become customers for life.

Appendix: Description of Independent Project Analysis, Inc.

The Source of Project Data

Independent Project Analysis, Inc. (IPA) was founded in 1987 to provide a unique benchmarking and research capability for capital projects. Our mission is to conduct and apply empirical research to help industrial companies deliver capital assets more effectively. IPA is the preeminent advisory firm for capital project systems, translating our knowledge into competitive advantage for our clients. IPA focuses solely on capital projects and capital project systems. We support projects and projects systems everywhere in the world.

IPA's Project Evaluation System® consists of a comprehensive rigorous methodology to assess a project at various points in its evolution from business case to scope to preparation for authorization. Projects are assessed again after the end of startup and finally after 12 to 18 months of beneficial operation. The data collection process uses a consistent data collection instrument and requires both collection of documents and a series of interviews with members of the owner project team, the business sponsor, and frequently the primary contractors executing the project.

Over the course of IPA's history, more than 20,000 capital projects with a capital value in excess of $6 trillion USD have been collected in the manner described and added to the organization's databases.

Industrial sectors included are

- Commodity and specialty chemicals
- Mining minerals and metals
- Pharmaceuticals
- Oil and gas production projects
- Petroleum refining
- Consumer products
- Electric power production projects of all kinds
- Full range of renewables and carbon capture

A distinguishing feature of the IPA databases are their depth, granularity, and accuracy. The databases are managed by a group of data scientists and applications developers. The data feed a group of more than 40 professionals who conduct research that explores the relationships between practices and outcomes of capital projects. The Project Research Division of IPA has groups supporting the benchmarking and analysis of the following:

- Cost and schedule tools
- Organizations and teams
- New technology commercialization
- Carbon management
- Renewables
- Site and sustaining capital projects and systems
- Client-funded research

New and better tools to evaluate projects and project systems are developed regularly and deployed by IPA's project analysts.

The IPA Institute is the educational arm of the company and provides a range of beginner and advanced courses on key topic areas in project management. IPA Capital Solutions supports the implementation of new project system work processes and practice improvements for our clients.

While supporting benchmarking and knowledge sharing within the global projects community, IPA maintains strict confidentiality of all confidential and proprietary information and enforces full adherence to the Benchmarking Code of Conduct.

Glossary

CAD   Computer-aided design.

CM   Construction management or construction manager.

Compliance project   A project the primary purpose of which is to align facilities with regulatory or legislative mandates, which are most often environmental, health, or operational safety requirements.

Convert to EPC LS   This contractual form starts out reimbursable in FEED and carries the contractor into execution on a reimbursable basis until about 60 percent detailed design complete at which point the contractor offers a lump-sum amount to complete engineering and construction. Also called *convertibles*.

Cost index   Measures the competitiveness of a project's capital cost by comparing it to projects of similar scopes built by others across the industry. A value of 1.0 is industry average with numbers above being more expensive and numbers below being less expensive.

Cost predictability   Measures the ratio of actual end-of-project capital cost to the estimate made at final investment decision. Estimated and actual costs are fully normalized by excluding scope changes, differences caused by location, and the effects of currency fluctuations. Also called *cost growth* or *cost deviation*.

Cycle time index   Measures the competitiveness of a project's elapsed time between the start of scope development and the end of startup. End of startup is when the facilities are in steady-state operation, which is not necessarily operating at intended capacity.

DART rate   This is a U.S. government Occupational Health and Safety Administration term for workplace injuries, accidents, or illnesses that result in days away from work, restricted work activity, or forced job transfer. The rate is measure as incidents per 200,000 construction hours worked.

Design competition   A contractual approach that entails hiring two or more FEED contractors that will work side by side to complete FEED on a reimbursable basis and will then provide an EPC lump-sum bid to execute the project.

E&I   Electrical and instrumentation. A type of work on a process facility. Also a engineering discipline and a construction discipline.

EP   Engineering and procurement (of equipment and engineered materials).

EPC   Engineer, procure, construct is an approach to contracting in which a single firm (or possibly consortium or joint venture) will be assigned responsibility for all main execution activities, including detailed engineering, purchase of equipment, and engineered materials such as structural steel and concrete, and will construct using their own construction labor force. EPC refers only to how much of the work will be assigned to a single contractor for executing a scope of work, not how the contractor will be paid. When the EPC contractor also does front-end engineering (FEED), we dub this form F-EPC.

EPC contractors   Contractors capable of performing engineering, procurement, and construction.

EPC-LS   This refers to an EPC contract in which the contractor is compensated on a lump-sum (fixed price) basis. EPC-LS refers to what we call "traditional EPC-LS," which is front-end engineering that results in preparation of an issuance of an invitation to bid and then receipt of lump-sum bids by a number of EPC firms. This contractual form is also called Design Build.

EPC-LSTK   This refers to an EPC-LS contract in which the contractor conveys a facility that is ready to operate, hence "turnkey."

EPCM   This is an EPC contract form in which a single contractor will execute detailed engineering, procure, and construction management but will not execute construction with their own forces but rather use construction firms to construct facilities.

EPC-R   An EPC contract form in which a single contractor will execute detailed engineering, procure and construct using their own construction labor force and will be paid on a reimbursable basis. Generally, the contractor will be paid a fixed fee rather than a percentage fee. This form is sometimes called cost-plus-fixed-fee (CPFF).

EVC   Engineering value center—a contractor office located in an area where engineering work can be acquired for significantly lower hourly rates than the contractor's home office.

FEED   Front-end engineering design. This is engineering work in the final stage of front-end loading (FEL) to prepare engineering for execution. It involves completing the facilities layout and plot plans and all piping and instrumentation diagrams (P&IDs) to the point they are issue for design (IFD). For a typical process facility, the engineering would be about 25 percent complete.

FEL   Front-end loading. FEL consists of the work process and work to prepare capital projects for execution. It is generally laid out in three phases or stages: business case development (FEL-1), development of the project scope (FEL-2), and preparation for execution (FEL-3).

FID   Final investment decision is the owner's authorization of the project for execution. It is also sometimes called *authorization for expenditure* (AFE) or sanction.

FPSO   Floating production, storage, and off-loading (an oil and gas production facility offshore).

Force majeure   A contract clause listing unexpected events that will excuse contactor and/or owner from some of their obligations under the contract. Examples of a force majeure event are floods and other extreme weather events, wars, pandemics, etc.

Functional spec   Functional specification (aka duty spec or performance spec) is a contracting approach that entails the owner creating a document detailing the functionality they require from a facility and then allowing contractors to bid (usually lump-sum) to provide a facility that achieves the desired result. Functional spec involves least owner work and most contractor discretion.

GC General contractor is a construction firm capable of providing construction management and construction services for facilities. Some GCs can provide the full range of construction, while others perform a particular form of construction (often mechanical) while performing construction management for disciplinary subcontractors.

GHG Greenhouse gases such as carbon dioxide and methane.

GMP Guaranteed maximum price. A reimbursable EPC contractual form that establishes a ceiling amount for the contracted work. Costs over the ceiling amount will be borne by the contractor.

HAZOP Hazardous operations analysis. Systemic analysis of process performance in startup, shutdown, and emergency conditions performed using the P&IDs and other engineering documents. Performed by a cross-functional team.

Home office The major office from which a contractor's work will be done, especially referring to engineering work.

IFD Issued for design means that the piping and instrumentation diagrams have been reviewed and approved and are ready for detailed design to proceed.

Incentives Payments to contractor that are contingent on some performance criterion. We generally use the term *supplemental incentives* because all contracts already include incentives in their payment scheme. Supplemental incentives may be for a specified cost outcome, schedule performance, production performance, and even behavioral items such as cooperativeness and collegiality.

IPA Independent Project Analysis, Inc., is a project evaluation, benchmarking, and projects research organization that collected all of the data used in this book and the analytical tools used in examining those data.

IPD and IPD/Alliance Integrated project delivery, which is also called *alliancing*, is an incentivized reimbursable contracting approach that combines all contractors, and sometimes major vendors as well, into a group that will share in any incentive package. IPD includes an all-contractor agreement that is intended to encourage cooperation and collaboration among all participants.

IRR Internal rate of return—a measure of investment profitability.

ITB Invitation to bid. This is a document sent to contractors that contains a scope of work and draft contract terms and conditions and invites the contractors receiving the document to prepare and submit bids to perform the scope of work.

KPI Key performance indicator, a business term for measures of functional performance.

LDs for Delay Liquidated damages are a contractually agreed upon amount that the contractor will reimburse the owner for each day of unexcused delay in completing work, usually on lump-sum work.

Moral hazard Situation in which a party that controls a risk has no incentive to avoid or mitigate the risk because they bear no negative consequences (and may even gain) when a risk materializes.

MTO Estimate Material takeoff estimate. This is a detailed cost estimate that measures the quantities of materials to be installed from the engineering drawings, especially the P&IDs.

NTE Not to exceed. See GMP.

Off-ramp An off-ramp is a method outlined in the contract for an owner to discontinue the work of the contractor without triggering a breach of contract.

P&IDs Piping and instrumentation diagrams are engineering documents that provide information on runs of pipe between pieces of equipment and positions and types of instruments that will be used to control a process. The P&IDs include information on line sizes, position and types of valves to control flows, and other details. The preparation of the P&IDs is usually done as part of front-end engineering design (FEED) prior to authorization of the project. At the end of FEED, the P&IDs should be "issued for design," which means ready to start detailed engineering.

PM   Project manager (can refer to either owner or contractor position).

PMC   Project managing contractor. This is a contractor hired to supervise the work of other contractors. The PMC sometimes augments the owner team and sometimes largely replaces an owner team.

Prequalification   The process of establishing which contracting firms will be eligible to be considered to execute a project. Firms that do not meet the prequalification criteria will be excluded from the project.

Principal-agent problem   The principal-agent problem is the reality that when someone (the agent) is asked to do work on behalf of and for the benefit of someone else (the principal), the interests of the principal and the interests of the agent are never perfectly aligned.

QC   Quality control.

Rand   Rand Corporation, a research organization based in Santa Monica, California.

Recordable rate   Any work-related injury or illness that results in a fatality, DART (defined previously), or medical attention above first-aid. The rate is per 200,000 hours.

RSC   Repeat supply chain contracting is using the same set of contractors and major suppliers for a series of similar capital projects. RSC usually does not involve a multiproject contract but an informal agreement between owner and the suppliers to work together repeatedly.

Schedule-driven   Refers to the owner placing top priority on minimizing execution time and a willingness to spend additional capital to (attempt to) achieve speed.

Schedule index Measures the competitiveness of a project's execution time as measured from start of detailed engineering to mechanical completion (all facilities ready to start operation in principle). Industry average is 1.0 with numbers above being longer and number below being shorter.

Schedule slip Measures the ratio of actual execution time to time promised at project authorization in percent. 0 percent is right on promised time, above 0 percent is the percent delay, and negative numbers are percent early. The actual schedule is corrected for extraordinary events outside the control of the project system.

Split-form contracting This form, which is also sometimes called Design-Bid-Build, contractually separates detailed engineering and procurement from construction management and construction. In also all cases, the contractor who performs detailed engineering and procurement also performed the front-end engineering (FEED). We dub this F-EP or FEP. There are four possible forms of split-form contracting, the first two of which are commonly used:

> **Re/LS**, which is reimbursable FEP followed by lump-sum construction

> **Re/Re**, which is reimbursable FEP followed by reimbursable construction

> **LS/LS**, which is lump-sum FEP followed by lump-sum construction

> **LS/Re**, which is lump-sum FEP followed by reimbursable construction

Stage-gated process An owner project work process in which phases (stages) of work are defined that culminate in decision points (gates) for governing project development and execution. There are usually a minimum of three stages and gates prior to authorization of a project.

Standard deviation Also called standard error. A statistical term describing the variation around a mean (average) value.

The standard deviation is the square root of the sum of the squared absolute errors from the mean. A single standard deviation on both sides of a mean value accounts for about 68 percent of the variation. Two standard errors account for 95 percent of the variation.

TIC Total installed cost—the full capital cost of a completed facility.

T&M Time and materials, a method of payment usually for construction contractors that reimburses contractor for hours and materials and a markup (profit).

WOM World open market.

Unit rate A reimbursement approach, usually for construction, that reimburses contractor by units of installed materials, e.g., per foot of pipe.

Index